Activists and t

Activists and the Surveillance State

Learning from Repression

Edited by Aziz Choudry

and

Between the Lines

First published 2019 by Pluto Press
345 Archway Road, London N6 5AA

www.plutobooks.com

British Library Cataloguing in Publication Data
A catalogue record for this book is available from the British Library

ISBN 978 0 7453 3781 4 Hardback
ISBN 978 0 7453 3780 7 Paperback
ISBN 978 1 7868 0372 6 PDF eBook
ISBN 978 1 7868 0374 0 Kindle eBook
ISBN 978 1 7868 0373 3 EPUB eBook

Published in Canada 2019 by Between the Lines
401 Richmond Street West, Studio 281, Toronto, Ontario, M5V 3A8

www.btlbooks.com

Cataloguing in Publication information available from Library and Archives Canada

ISBN 978 1 77113 435 4 Paperback
ISBN 978 1 77113 437 8 PDF eBook
ISBN 978 1 77113 436 1 EPUB eBook

This book is printed on paper suitable for recycling and made from fully managed and sustained forest sources. Logging, pulping and manufacturing processes are expected to conform to the environmental standards of the country of origin.

Typeset by Swales & Willis

Simultaneously printed in the United Kingdom and United States of America

Contents

Acknowledgements

Drawing from the knowledge of activists and critically engaged academics, this book asks what people did, didn't, could and should learn about the power of states and capital from activists/movements viewed as threats to national security and targeted by state (and state-corporate) security operations, harassment, surveillance, infiltration and disruption, highlighting lessons learned and missed opportunities. The idea for a book of this kind has been percolating for many years – in countless conversations, discussions and debates with a wide range of people, stretched across cities, countries and continents as well as in reflections on my own and others' experiences. I am blessed with a great network of friends and comrades with whom to think and act.

I deeply appreciate the contributions of all of the chapter authors. This is not an easy topic to write about, not least for those whose lives have been, or are directly impacted by state surveillance, harassment, infiltration and worse. But this book is also a testament to the historical and ongoing resistance of ordinary people to the national security state.

Many thanks to David Shulman at Pluto Press for his interest in, and enthusiasm for this book project, and to the rest of the Pluto team for their production and design work. My heartfelt gratitude also goes to Désirée Rochat whose careful preparation of the manuscript for publication embodied editorial assistance par excellence. Sincere thanks to Jeanne Brady for her careful and efficient copy-editing, and Adam Bell at Swales and Willis for his help in the production of this book. I also acknowledge support from my Canada Research Chair in Social Movement Learning and Knowledge Production.

While working on this book, my friend, colleague and comrade Abby Lippman passed away. We had had many conversations, over several years, over cups of tea at her kitchen table, and on marches and demonstrations on the streets of Montreal, about the issues, struggles, politics and histories in this book. Having shared the proposal with her, I had imagined that she would read the final product, hopefully with interest, with her usual sharp eye and mind, dry sense of humour and generosity of spirit. This book is dedicated to Abby.

All royalties for this book will be donated to The Right2Know Campaign (South Africa). Website: https://www.r2k.org.za

PART I

1

Lessons learnt, lessons lost

Pedagogies of repression, thoughtcrime, and the sharp edge of state power

Aziz Choudry

The use of secret police and state security intelligence agencies to disrupt, undermine, divide and rule political opposition to the prevailing social political and economic order has a long history. This is true in liberal democratic states, as elsewhere. People have also always resisted these and other forms of repression. As Radha D'Souza argues in Chapter 2, to effectively struggle against the surveillance state requires a deeper understanding of the architecture of power within which state surveillance operates as well as its transnational dimensions. Many of today's covert (and overt) policing and state security policies, practices and concepts have their roots in counter-insurgency techniques tested against earlier anti-colonial/independence struggles, in policing Black life under slavery and Indigenous Peoples' resistance. The term 'pedagogies of repression' captures two kinds of lessons 'taught' by state security agencies, practices and laws. Knowing or suspecting that one is being spied upon by the state can have serious impacts on those who have suspicion cast on them and those around them. This is arguably an intended pedagogical effect of state security practices that seeks to discipline and isolate those targeted, spread fear and deter others from dissenting or organising to challenge the status quo. We are taught to comply and follow dominant economic and political orthodoxies. But other forms of learning also arise, including learning to resist and to ask why this keeps happening in states which claim to be democracies. While there has been important documentation of state repression against a number of historical and ongoing social struggles, the question of lessons learnt (and missed) by activists from such experiences has been far less explored. The chapters in this book critically share and engage with activist understandings of, and resistance to state security practices, including critiques of the state which are informed by reflection upon, and confrontation with these forms of repression and surveillance.

Over time, different forms of political dissent in liberal capitalist democracies have been constructed as subversion, extremism, terrorism and radicalism. No factual basis is required to label an individual or a group as subversive, extremist, or terrorist. For example, the term 'subversion' has notoriously flexible parameters, especially when employed within an operational culture which frequently equates challenges to prevailing political and economic orthodoxies with criminality. The 'enemy of the state' may change, but the concept of 'national security' remains elastic enough to be applied as needed to protect the interests of the ruling elites of the day and thereby complement other coercive state practices (Kinsman, Buse & Steedman, 2000; Kinsman & Gentile, 2010). This ruling perspective routinely constructs political dissent, ideas and ideologies that challenge the prevailing social, economic and political order as criminal activity, a threat to national security and/or violent extremism. Meanwhile governments and businesses (and often in collaboration) continue to expend massive public and private sector resources for surveillance, infiltration and other forms of covert operations, targeting activists and social movements, in the interests of protecting capital and state power (Smith & Chamberlain, 2015; Lubbers, 2012; Seigel, 2018). Theirs is an acronym and codename-filled world of agency names, programmes and initiatives, from COINTELPRO to PROFUNC, to ECHELON.[1]

State or corporate spying, infiltration, the use of informants and agents provocateurs, profiling and intimidation do not necessarily succeed at producing compliant subjects. Nor, for many people, are national security regimes and state security agencies detached from their everyday lives. For those who are surprised at the role of military/defence intelligence in multi-agency state security teams, committees, programmes and taskforces, or in surveillance of activists and social movements, we might recall the long history of the police and military working together inside and outside of US borders since the eighteenth century (Seigel, 2018). This is also the case in Australia, Aotearoa/New Zealand, Canada and the United Kingdom (UK), where ministries and departments of defence and military intelligence as well as civil agencies collaborate closely, now often under the rubric of integrated threat assessment initiatives and multi-agency fusion centres. Besides the more obvious state security agencies and bodies, and their networks of agents and informants, a broad range of other government departments, as well as other organisations, including private sector agencies, may be requested to assist in covert surveillance and other intelligence operations.[2] This routinely includes immigration authorities, but also security services within state corporations and private companies, port and airport authorities, university staff, municipal authorities, and state bureaucracies concerned with Indigenous Peoples. In some cases, as in Britain under the Prevent duty, health and education workers are expected to report on those to whom they provide service (See Ahmed, Chapter 8).

Serge's (2005) account of Okhrana (Tsarist police) surveillance and state repression in early twentieth-century Russia reminds us that the criminalisation of dissent and state surveillance, including techniques familiar to many activists, pre-date the Cold War and 9/11, which are often seen as key dates marking the start or expansion of the security state. For example, I was politicised during the Cold War, and grew increasingly aware of state spying on, and infiltration and disruption of, anti-nuclear, anti-apartheid, Irish solidarity and Indigenous activism, at least in the UK, Australian and Aotearoa/New Zealand contexts. I also became conscious of apartheid South Africa's state security dirty tricks worldwide, institutional racism within the police and concerns about collusion between British security forces and loyalist paramilitary organisations in Ireland (see also McGovern, 2015), while on the other side of the world, French state security agents[3] bombed Greenpeace's *Rainbow Warrior* in Auckland harbour in July 1985, killing an activist. Elsewhere (Choudry, 2015), I have discussed learning and knowledge production relating to my political organising, a bungled and illegal New Zealand Security Intelligence Service break-in at my home in July 1996, a subsequent legal case that I took against the New Zealand government,[4] and experiences of New Zealand Police political spying and infiltration. I agree with George Smith (2006) about the potential for activists to explore the social organisation of power as it is revealed through moments of political confrontation, in order to change it. This can happen when the state's repressive structures are laid bare when we come up against them. Material experience forms our learning and consciousness. Experiences of state repression can help direct analysis of state power and the interests of capital from the standpoint of those targeted. But a combination of experiential learning with other forms of critical knowledge and political analysis is needed to better understand what lies beneath state surveillance, build a broader politics of resistance, and learn from history.

While this book centres knowledge produced through confrontations with state security practices, as well as critical reflection on past experiences, such critical learning is not guaranteed. Concerning intergenerational learning, for example, how is it that histories of resistance to the security state from earlier periods do, or do not get passed on, and how is it that many of the stories of the repression and surveillance faced in previous decades are forgotten?[5] This book seeks to address the social amnesia, forgetting, or denial that sometimes exists within progressive political milieus and broader publics about continuity and change in histories of 'national security' and political policing, infiltration and disruption, questioning these practices in and across several 'liberal democracies'. Further, it highlights the relationship between these security practices and the nature and power of states and capital.

Security agencies, surveillance and infiltration are just part of wider state power mobilised against dissent and often rely on collaboration from within the groups, movements and communities being spied on. Surveillance of activists, and the use of informants and agents provocateurs, can have a chilling effect on dissent and can destroy lives. Using informers in political policing, Hewitt (2010) asserts, allows governments to 'direct, disrupt and even destroy individuals, groups and movements it does not like or finds threatening' (p. 159). He argues that the use of informers 'can be managed more unobtrusively in "open" societies where it is not anticipated, as opposed to closed societies where the hand is expected to be heavier'. Hewitt also observes that '[t]he presence of informers, either real or imagined, sows division and paranoia and can have a direct impact on operations' (p. 133). Accounts of intimidation, threats and promises made by state security agencies and their private counterparts to try and recruit informants abound across many communities and activist networks.

The extent of mass surveillance and the broad reach of the technologies employed can seem overwhelming. But this book challenges understandings about security practices which sometimes produce an overdetermined sense of state repression's chilling impact and totalising power to discipline and punish dissent. As Maira (2016, and in Chapter 4) notes, one reaction among targeted communities is to normalise surveillance in their everyday lives rather than to bear a burden of private shame. Moreover, what do experiences of state surveillance, political policing, and the criminalisation of dissent tell us about the nature of democracy and freedom in liberal democracies – and the nation-state itself? One starting point is a critique of the idea that state security and the construction of some people and ideas as being 'enemies of the state' is a form of exceptionalism, in contexts where state surveillance of people holding certain political ideas, coming from certain movements and communities has long been routine. Some discussions of security/intelligence practices fetishise technology at the expense of politics and deeper historical perspectives, in ways that can contribute to decontextualised and ahistorical understandings about the security state. It is a challenge for progressive activism to organise around a politics that goes beyond making demands that the spying stop and agencies become more 'accountable' when yet another covert security operation against activists comes to light. Rather, these operations are fundamental to maintaining capitalist relations, organised at the highest levels of the state, and not merely unfortunate excesses or abuses of power.

State security regimes in liberal social democracies have engaged in containing, suppressing and criminalising late nineteenth- and early twentieth-century militant labour organising, and anti-colonial/anti-imperialist resistance movements. From the foundation of Scotland Yard's Special Branch in 1883 to fight what the British authorities viewed as Irish 'Fenian terrorism', to Cold War obsessions with monitoring leftwing political parties (Burgmann, 2014; Leonard & Gallagher, 2014), political spying operations also extended to searching for supposed domestic and foreign communist influences on Indigenous, Black, anti-apartheid, women's, queer, anti-war and Third World liberation struggles, and on trade unionists and student activists, among others in North America, Australia, Aotearoa/New Zealand and the UK (Austin, 2013; Burgmann, 2014; Marx, 1989; Donner, 1990; Hewitt & Sethna, 2012;

Kinsman & Gentile, 2010; Murch, 2012; Smith & Chamberlain, 2015; Milne, 2014; Sethna & Hewitt, 2018).[6]

In recent years, there have been many activist and media exposés of long-standing covert spying, infiltration and disruption operations and practices by police, intelligence, other state security agencies, and private security working for corporations. These include experiences with agents provocateurs, smear campaigns and entrapment. Many accounts focus on the normalising of mass surveillance, and the vastly expanded data collection and analysis capabilities of agencies such as the US's National Security Agency (NSA) and the UK's Government Communications Headquarters (GCHQ) which have been highlighted, for example, by Edward Snowden and Chelsea Manning's whistleblowing and Wikileaks. These have further confirmed or revealed the extent of surveillance and the collaborations between intelligence agencies internationally as well as cooperation with companies such as Google, Apple, Microsoft and Facebook.

The Federal Bureau of Investigation (FBI) and other police and security agencies' infiltration, harassment and surveillance of Muslim communities in the US, the UK, Canada and elsewhere has mushroomed and contributed to a climate of racism and suspicion (Kundnani, 2014; Maira, 2016; see Ahmed, Chapter 8 in this book). Some scholars and activists have drawn parallels between earlier (COINTELPRO) programmes of surveillance, infiltration and disruption of Black activism in the US with contemporary surveillance and criminalization of organizing against state violence against Black communities, such as Black Lives Matter and the FBI's construction of so-called 'Black Identity Extremism' (see Austin, Chapter 6). In the UK, police officers from covert units such as the Special Demonstration Squad of London's Metropolitan Police have used the identities of dead children to infiltrate activist groups and undermine their political campaigns. In some cases, undercover police officers fathered children with activists unaware of their 'partner's' true identity. They infiltrated and spied on the family and friends of Stephen Lawrence, a young Black man murdered by racists, as well as other family justice groups, as part of an attempted smear campaign to discredit calls for further police investigation into Lawrence's killing (Evans & Lewis, 2013). This has led to legal suits, the Undercover Policing Inquiry and a range of activist responses in Britain (see Apple & Lubbers, Chapters 9 and 11).

Attention has also been called to the nexus between private and public security operations, long-standing and newer tactics concerning state security forces and private security companies in relation to intelligence gathering, collaboration and infiltration against communities, movements, workers and activists (Smith & Chamberlain, 2015; Lubbers, 2012). Noting the abundance of mixed or hybrid public-private forms of policing, Seigel recalls:

> the public police's long labour in the service of capital. Public police as a matter of course breach the public-private divide, keeping the 'dangerous classes' in place, protecting financial interests, preserving social order ... The formally private police must also be approached with a clear vision of their complex intertwinings with public police. That is, not only have public police long laboured in the service of capital, but private police do the work of the state.
>
> (Seigel, 2018, p. 21)

Recalling that private police supported colonial ventures by European corporations like the East India Company, and that private police pre-dated the 1830s public police, she observes that 'the two have co-existed ever since, drawing water for both market and state' (p. 22). The forms and details might change, but this process, and these relations continue today. Crosby and Monaghan (2018, p. 17), documenting surveillance of recent Indigenous activism in Canada, note that '[p]rioritizing protest movements as national security threats under the umbrella of critical infrastructure is a product of integrating corporations into the expanding arena of the security state.' They contend that police-corporate collaborations afford extractive corporations the ability to supply intelligence to other partners of the security state, and enhance their capacity to influence the perception and labelling of certain threats. Security and surveillance is a highly lucrative business, and the generation and maintenance of fear – including a never-ending global 'War on Terror' – is in the interests of increasing funding and new opportunities for state and private spying.

As many observe (Kundnani, 2014; Kinsman & Gentile, 2010; Duncan, 2014; Maira, 2016), the 'War on Terror' provides a convenient frame, lens and set of justifications through which states can view a range of dissenting ideas and activities as well as target the latest 'suspect' communities (see also Maira, Kinsman, and Ahmed – Chapters 4, 7, and 8 – in this volume). In this context, Kundnani (2014) notes that political subversion is now often described as radicalisation, and young Muslims are viewed as a convenient testing ground for counter-subversion in its new forms. Meanwhile, he writes that 'the spectacle of the Muslim extremist renders invisible the violence of the US empire. Opposition to such violence from within the imperium has fallen silent, as the universal duty of countering extremism precludes any wider discussion of foreign policy' (p. 14). Kapoor (2018) makes similar observations through a historical lens, contending that '[a]s Fenians[7] came to be synonymized as terrorists and political actions associated with Fenianism referred to as "terrorism", the violence of British occupation, with all the resource extraction that this entailed, was framed as part of the rightful order of empire and civilization' (p. 43). Security state practices seek to deflect attention away from state violence, which is to be viewed as normal, necessary and rational. Kienscherf (2014) argues that liberal social control is best understood as uneven processes of pacification targeting specific individuals, groups and populations through a combination of coercion and consent. Kundnani (2014), writing about forms of 'liberal democratic totalitarianism' expressed through current state surveillance and security practices, suggests that when the 'tools of totalitarian rule are applied only to racialised groups, rather than the population as a whole, the trappings of democracy can be maintained for the majority' (p. 283). Thus, to build broader resistance to national security injustices, there are important lessons about the risks of thinking that it will never happen to you from critically engaging with the imperial and colonial histories of developing surveillance techniques – an idea that the contemporary criminalization of certain movements, activists and communities should reinforce.

THOUGHTCRIME

Many activists and organisers recognise the power of ideas and sharing them with others – so too do economic and political elites. McKnight's (2014) evaluation of the Australian Security Intelligence Organization (ASIO)'s outlook on political dissent during the Cold War could be extended to other contexts. They 'assumed radical ideas were a contagion that infected anyone who worked with communists. Some historians speak of the "disease model" used by internal security agencies like ASIO'

(p. 25).[8] Thus, once tainted by contact with communists or subversives, anyone could become a legitimate target for ongoing surveillance. Pseudo-psychological approaches influence state security programmes, surveillance and the profiling of targets. Such psychological profiling tends to avoid political/social analysis of activists and dissenting ideas, and attempts to identify and categorise individual or group psychological factors, removed from social and political circumstances and seen through a pathologising lens. Who associates with whom, which individuals and organisations, working relationships locally and internationally, internal tensions and divisions – all aspects of political and personal lives of targets can be subject to monitoring and surveillance operations against activists, online and offline. How can progressive activists formulate self-defence against agents provocateurs, infiltration and entrapment and build broader support against tactics which seek to divide people (and their political views) into 'good' and 'bad', 'moderate' and 'radical', and 'constructive' and 'disruptive' camps for broader publics? Especially with increased preventive and predictive approaches to policing, guilt is presumed and authorities do not need proof of an actual material crime, but rather predictions of what people might do.

The 9/11 attacks were opportunistically seized upon by supporters of global capitalism. Institutions like the International Monetary Fund, the World Bank and the World Trade Organization (WTO) had been under sustained siege from social movements. On 24 September 2001, the then US Trade Representative Robert Zoellick expanded the post-9/11 McCarthyism to include global justice activists: 'Terrorists hate the ideas America has championed around the world. It is inevitable that people will wonder if there are intellectual connections with others who have turned to violence to attack international finance, globalization and the United States' (Zoellick, 2001). In a 2000 report on the 'anti-globalisation' movement after the Seattle WTO mobilisations, the Canadian Security Intelligence Service (CSIS) warned against the 'tyranny of small groups, minorities, or even majorities, to prevent the exercise of such rights by trying to shut down meetings as unacceptable in a democracy' (CSIS, 2000). The report stated that protesters were deemed to be a security threat since they were organised and could 'identify and publicize targets, solicit and encourage support, establish dates, recruit, raise funds, share experiences, accept responsibilities, arrange logistics, and promote goals', and because they

> share a mutual antipathy for multinational corporate power. Large corporations with international undertakings stand accused of social injustice and unfair labour practices, as well as a lack of concern for the environment, management of natural resources and ecological damage … underlying the anti-globalization theme is criticism of the capitalist philosophy, a stance promoted again by left-of-centre activists and militant anarchists.
>
> (CSIS, 2000)

For Potter (2011), the labelling of US environmentalists and animal rights activists as terrorists reflects both the protection of corporate profits and a clash-of-civilisations mindset of industry groups, think tanks and politicians. He tracks how since 9/11, the term 'eco-terrorist' has been inserted more into national security dialogue by public relations (PR) firms working for industry, while private crisis management firms produce reports and threat analyses. Potter cites a 2008 Department of Homeland Security report, 'Eco-terrorism: Environmental and Animal Rights Militants in the United States', as typifying how environmental activists are seen as a threat to the US capitalist way of life, individual freedoms and cultural traditions. The report states that these movements directly challenge civilisation, modernity and capitalism (DHS, 2008). Meanwhile, a Royal Canadian Mounted Police (RCMP) internal document entitled 'Criminal threats to the Canadian petroleum industry', dated 24 January 2014, dubbed the 'anti-petroleum' movement a growing threat to Canada's national security. Journalists and a range of organisations noted that the report's highly charged and pro-industry language reflected government hostility toward 'foreign-funded' environmentalists and Indigenous activists (McCarthy, 2015). But that is nothing new.

SOLDIERS OF EMPIRE … AGENTS OF IMPERIALISM?

Imperialism and colonialism have long been at the heart of present-day security states and their security apparatus – in many cases, often overlapping lineages of overseas experiences of counter-insurgency against anti-colonial movements and closer at hand, the policing of Indigenous Peoples and Black communities. Colonial networks of surveillance have typically been embedded throughout every part of the liberal state bureaucracy. They have long had a transnational dimension, well before the contemporary period of growth and consolidation of international intelligence/security alliances, networks and alliances among governments, North and South. There is a lengthy history of agents, soldiers, police, strategies and techniques circulating around the British Empire, for instance.[9]

In Canada, the US, Australia and Aotearoa/New Zealand, security agencies also seemed so preoccupied with finding communist influence or other foreign or external hands that they denied the capacity of Indigenous Peoples to think for themselves. Discussing his declassified ASIO files from the 1970s and 1980s, Gumbaynggirr scholar and activist Gary Foley (2014) notes an 'obsessive preoccupation with possible communist infiltration or manipulation of the Aboriginal rights movement from 1951 till the end of the Cold War' (p. 94). As Foley observes, according to the Australian government and its security agencies: 'All Aboriginal protest was interpreted in the context of the international struggle against communism, which as it happened was a convenient way to ignore the legitimate claims of the Aboriginal peoples themselves' (p. 96). This preoccupation went further than domestic security agencies. For example, a 1988 CIA memo from the Office of East Asian Analysis, partly declassified and released in 2017, recorded Maori activist Syd Jackson's visit to Libya (CIA, 1988).

There are also older histories of intense surveillance, disciplining and policing of Indigenous Peoples that pre-date the Cold War. In Canada, Smith (2009) notes that colonisation and the imposition of liberalism was facilitated, fashioned and justified through extensive disciplinary surveillance of Indigenous Peoples. Late nineteenth- and early twentieth-century surveillance infrastructure included government officials, police officers, church representatives, teachers, medical personnel, ordinary settlers and others, working to instil as normal and natural Anglo-Canadian liberal capitalist values, structures and interests, and colonial power relations, as well as to monitor possible dissent and neutralise resistance.

Pender (2000) documents how, during RCMP monitoring of groups deemed vulnerable to Communist Party influence, its Security Service decided that a Native Studies Program started at Laurentian University in the 1975–76 school year was a '"hotbed" of radicalism, tangible proof of "extremism", and a site for the "Brainwashing of young minds" vulnerable to infiltration by other "subversive" organizations' (p. 111). Declassified documents show how surveillance would be extended into Indigenous communities, and there was concern about the presence of the American Indian Movement (AIM). Canada's security intelligence agencies were using the phrase 'Native Extremism' by the mid-1970s, collaborating with US agencies in continent-wide operations against AIM.

More recently, Secwepemc activist and leader Arthur Manuel (2017) wrote:

> RCMP and national security officers are committed to the old colonial model of decision making in Canada. They follow the precedent set out by decisions that saw colonial rule as sacred and Indigenous peoples as excess baggage. I also know that the RCMP and national security officers have infiltrated our organizations and will use these infiltrators for information to convict us and, very often, as agents provocateurs who try to incite violence, which they can then use to isolate us and give the green light to the RCMP, provincial police or army to violently oppress us.
>
> (Manuel, 2017, pp. 233–34)

Crosby and Monaghan (2018) contend that as Indigenous and environmental movements 'increasingly challenge the Canadian state's ambition to become an "energy superpower" by working with the tar sands, shale gas, and extractivist industries', Indigenous resistance is 'targeted and labelled as "violent Aboriginal extremists" and "environmental criminal extremists"' (p. 179).

Since the Cold War, states and their security forces have worked to justify their existence, and increase their budgets, as they have claimed to respond to calls to become more transparent and accountable, and to project an image of themselves to indicate that they are not the same agencies as they were decades earlier. Yet these moves, which will perhaps involve a commission of inquiry now and then, or an announcement about some new intelligence agency head, often seem little more than cynical public relations exercises which serve to legitimate the further expansion of their power and impunity to act. Churchill and Vander Wall (1990) note that security agencies have a habit of periodically stating 'Don't worry. Everything is OK now' (p.10), and that, unfortunately, many people believe them. They remind us of how COINTELPRO-style operations continued well into the 1970s and 1980s – and are perhaps the rule rather than the exception, with similar operations mounted against AIM, the Committee in Solidarity with the People of El Salvador (CISPES) and a range of groups opposed to US policy in Central America, all dubbed 'terrorist organisations'.

As well as the secrecy that surrounds state security files, notwithstanding some limited releases of information under access to information requests (and questions that must be asked about what gets released, when, why and in whose interests), there are other ways in which the nature and conduct of the security states are hidden from view. For example, Cobain (2016) discusses the routine destruction or removal of official secrets. He argues that these purposely hide histories that would give us a better understanding of the nature and conduct of the (British) state. Destruction or removal of colonial-era files from former colonies on the eve of independence through to a suspicious fire during investigations into the involvement of covert military, police and other security agencies in murders and violent attacks in the North of Ireland serve to allow the British 'to nurture a memory of Empire that was deeply deceptive – a collective confabulation of an imperial mission that had brought nothing but progress and good order to a previously savage world – unlike the French, Italians, Belgians, Germans and Portuguese – those inferior colonial powers whose adventures had been essentially brutal, cynical and exploitative' (p. 132). When it comes to covering up sensitive state security operations, one doubts that destroying or concealing evidence is a uniquely British practice.

Yet resistance to state spying has included organising that draws from the painstaking work accessing and sifting through official documents where they are available, pooling investigative skills and resources, and developing relationships with other progressive activist researchers and investigative journalists. For example, British investigative journalist Phil Chamberlain and blacklisted construction worker and union activist Dave Smith worked together to expose the decades-long collusion between police, security services, a private agency and construction companies, with the complicity of some union officials. They also showed how blacklisting impacts people's lives and livelihoods and the real-life consequences of denying work to trade unionists or workers who raised health and safety concerns, or participated in other political activities (Smith & Chamberlain, 2015).

In this book, Eveline Lubbers' and Emily Apple's chapters discuss ways in which activists in the UK research, educate and mobilise around undercover policing and infiltration. Gary Kinsman and David Austin, in different ways, share examples of using radical history as a tool to understand and confront the security state in Canadian/North

American contexts.[10] Bob Boughton digs into ASIO monitoring of East Timor solidarity networks in Australia and its FRETILIN allies to raise questions about how contemporary activists might deal with state surveillance. Historical work also has the potential to help us more deeply understand the past and the present, to recognise patterns, techniques, strategies, tactics and justifications used to surveill, infiltrate, entrap and cover up.

CONCLUSION: ON THE NEED TO GET RADICAL

Today, the deradicalisation-industrial complex has become a feature of many community, academic and societal landscapes. Now that 'counter-extremism' is de rigueur, observes Liz Fekete, it has spawned

> a new professional class of experts attached to think tanks and university departments who vie for funding and influence. Suffice to say that the type of policy-orientated research engendered by these sorts of institutions proves very useful to all those who want to see the expansion of police powers and the intelligence services, as well as the criminalization of resistance (to austerity measures or fascism, for instance).
>
> (Fekete, 2018, p. 45)

Whether advanced by conservatives or liberals, deradicalisation and countering violent extremism frameworks have arguably contributed to racism, xenophobia, which 'accompanied by security-inspired citizenship reforms and integration policies, have nourished an official nativism' (Fekete, 2018, p. 102), while state violence at home and abroad rages on.

Indeed, the terms 'radical' and 'radicalisation' need to be reclaimed from state-sanctioned deradicalisation frameworks. Kundnani (2014) argues that radicalisation 'in the true sense of the word – is the solution, not the problem'. This entails '[o]pening up genuinely radical political alternatives and reviving the political freedoms that have been lost in recent years' (p. 15). History shows us that in earlier difficult and dangerous times, activists and communities have stood up to domestic covert action, often 'through a combination of militant public protest and careful internal education and preparation within progressive movements' (Glick, in Churchill and Vander Wall, 1990, p. xvi). This book's chapters illustrate some of the rich learning and knowledge production that arise when people come together, collaborate, document and organise against state surveillance. But they also raise challenges for mobilising political resistance and movement-building. Referring to Canada (and this arguably applies to Australia, Aotearoa/New Zealand and the US), Crosby and Monaghan contend that 'the machinations of the security state illustrate the fragility of settler society' (2018, p. 194). In the 1990s, some of my political comrades and I made similar claims about state security operations and political policing in Aotearoa/New Zealand targeting Maori struggles for self-determination and resistance against free market capitalism. Some people dismissed such ideas as too 'radical'. Being truly radical – getting at the roots of the problem – means that today's struggles against the surveillance and criminalisation of dissent must confront the state and capitalist power relations which organize these practices – and dig in for the long haul.

ORGANIZATION OF THIS BOOK

This book is organised into three parts. Part I comprises three chapters: this chapter, and Chapter 2 by Radha D'Souza contextualise the security state and the post-Second World War deepening and broadening of what might be called the 'deep state', and introduce the themes of learning, knowledge production and resistance in relation to state security/intelligence operations. In Chapter 3, Jane Duncan discusses dataveillance through comparing popular/activist responses in three countries – South Africa, the UK and Mauritius. The seven chapters that make up Part II address contemporary and historical examples of state surveillance of activists and communities, and learning and knowledge produced in resisting. Several chapters touch upon colonial dimensions of past and present state security practices, in particular: Sunaina Maira on the targeting of Palestine solidarity organising in the US (Chapter 4); Bob Boughton on Australian state surveillance of East Timor solidarity activism and FRETILIN (Chapter 5); David Austin's interview chapter, on Black experiences of surveillance, repression and resistance in Canada and the US (Chapter 6); Gary Kinsman on pedagogies of resistance to state surveillance and lessons from history in the Canadian context (Chapter 7); Nafeez Ahmed on Prevent and the radicalisation of the British state (Chapter 8), and Valerie Morse on political spying in Aotearoa/New Zealand (Chapter 9). In Chapter 10, Emily Apple documents personal and political impacts of political policing and surveillance in the UK and initiatives that activists have taken to uncover and challenge these activities. Part II comprises a final chapter by Eveline Lubbers which outlines ways in which specific activist experiences of surveillance have given rise to sustained research, education and mobilisation work.

NOTES

1 COINTELPRO: The US Federal Bureau of Investigation (FBI)'s COunterINTELligence PROgram, formally conducted between 1956 and 1971 comprised covert, and often illegal activities to surveill, infiltrate, disrupt, and discredit a broad range of domestic political dissident organisations and movements. PROFUNC: Formally in operation 1950–1983, PROFUNC (PROminent FUNCtionaries of the Communist Party) was a top secret Canadian government project run by the Royal Canadian Mounted Police (RCMP) Special Branch. It identified, listed and spied on suspected Canadian communists and 'subversives', its goal being to facilitate swift detention of thousands of citizens in the event of a national emergency during the Cold War. ECHELON: Also known as the 'Five Eyes', ECHELON is a mass surveillance programme, created in the 1960s, and operated by the US with the four other signatory governments to the United Kingdom – United States of America Agreement (UKUSA), i.e. Australia, Canada, New Zealand and the UK, to monitor and analyse military, diplomatic, private and commercial communications (Churchill & Vander Wall, 1990; CBC News, 2014; Privacy International, 2013).

2 Such cooperation is typically mandated in legislation governing state security and intelligence agencies. For example, see relevant provisions of Australian Security Intelligence Organisation Act, 1979 Intelligence and Security Act, 2017 [New Zealand]; Canadian Security Intelligence Service Act, 1985, and respective laws in other jurisdictions. According to its website (MI5, n.d.), '[a]t any time, several hundred staff may work in MI5 on secondment or attachment from other government departments and agencies.'

3 DGSE, la direction générale de la Sécurité extérieure: French external state intelligence agency.

4 *Choudry v Attorney General (1998)* 16 CRNZ 278 (CA).

5 Political music plays an educative role here, from Christy Moore's popularising of Jack Warshaw's 'If They Come in the Morning (No Time for Love)', to Public Enemy's 'Louder Than a Bomb', to Buffy Sainte Marie's 'Bury My Heart at Wounded Knee'.

6 See also Hoogers (2000) and Mitrovica (2002) on state surveillance of Canadian Union of Postal Workers members.
7 Fenians were nineteenth-century Irish republican nationalists.
8 This is clearly a contagious concept among state security agencies. In December 2012, in an internal document, a Royal Canadian Mounted Police (RCMP) Aboriginal liaison officer likened the Idle No More movement to bacteria: 'it has grown a life of its own all across this nation' (cited in Crosby & Monaghan, 2018).
9 See Pedersen and Woorunmurra (1995) on North-West Mounted Police/ Western Australian Police Force officer Overand Drewry and his role in combating Indigenous resistance in Canada and Australia in the late nineteenth century, and Popplewell (1995) and Sohi (2014) on William C. Hopkinson, former Inspector in the Indian Police Force in Calcutta, who became the leading British and Canadian spy in North America monitoring Indian migrants and reporting any seditious or suspicious behaviour to British and Canadian authorities in the early twentieth century, until he was assassinated in October 1914.
10 Another example is the People's Commission Network, based in Montreal, monitoring and opposing the 'national security agenda' in Canada. See http://www.peoplescommission.org/en/

REFERENCES

Austin, D. (2013). *Fear of a Black Nation: Race, sex, and security in Sixties Montreal.* Toronto: Between the Lines Press.

Australian Security Intelligence Organisation Act, 1979.

Burgmann, M. (ed.) (2014). *Dirty Secrets: Our ASIO files.* Sydney: New South Publishing.

Canadian Security Intelligence Service Act, 1985.

CBC News (2014, 14 October). 'Secret Cold War Plan Included Mass Detentions'. Acessed from www.cbc.ca/news/canada/montreal/secret-cold-war-plan-included-mass-detentions-1.962421 (accessed 11 September 2018)

Choudry, A. (2015). *Learning Activism: The intellectual life of contemporary social movements.* Toronto: University of Toronto Press.

—— & Vally, S. (2018). 'History's Schools: Past struggles and present realities'. In Choudry, A., and Vally, S. (eds), *Reflections on Knowledge, Learning and Social Movements: History's schools* (pp. 1–17). Abingdon and New York: Routledge.

Churchill, W., & Vander Wall, J. (1990). *Agents of Repression: The FBI's secret wars against the Black Panther Party and the American Indian Movement.* Boston, MA: South End Press.

CIA (Central Intelligence Agency) (1988, 25 October). 'Racial Tension: A growing factor in New Zealand politics'. Office of East Asian Analysis memo.

Cobain, I. (2016). *The History Thieves: Secrets, lies and the shaping of a modern nation*. London: Portobello.

Crosby, A., & Monaghan, J. (2018). *Policing Indigenous Movements, Dissent and the Security State*. Halifax/Winnipeg: Fernwood Publishing.

CSIS (Canadian Security Intelligence Service) (2000, 12 August). 'Anti-globalization. A spreading phenomenon'. Report # 2000/08.

DHS (Department of Homeland Security) (2008). 'Eco-terrorism: Environmental and animal rights militants in the United States'. Accessed from http://humanewatch.org/images/uploads/2008_DHS_ecoterrorism_threat_assessment.pdf (accessed 17 August 2018).

Donner, F. J. (1990). *Protectors of Privilege: Red squads and police repression in urban America*. Berkeley, CA: University of California Press.

Duncan, J. (2014). *The Rise of the Securocrats: The case of South Africa*. Johannesburg: Jacana.

Evans, R., & Lewis P. (2013). *Undercover: The true story of Britain's secret police*. London: Guardian Books.

Fekete, L. (2018). *Europe's Fault Lines: Racism and the rise of the right*. London: Verso.

Foley, G. (2014). 'ASIO, the Aboriginal Movement and Me'. In Burgmann, M. (ed.), *Dirty Secrets: Our ASIO files* (pp. 91–111). Sydney: New South Publishing.

Hewitt, S. (2010). *Snitch: A history of the modern intelligence informer*. New York: Continuum.

Hewitt, S. & Sethna, C. (2012). 'Sex Spying: The RCMP framing of English-Canadian women's liberation groups during the Cold War'. In D. Clement, L. Campbell & G. Kealey (eds), *Debating Dissent: Canada and the 1960s* (pp. 134–151). Toronto: University of Toronto Press.

Hoogers, E. (2000). 'In Whose Public Interest? The Canadian Union of Postal Workers and national security'. In G. Kinsman, D. K. Buse & M. Steedman (eds), *Whose National Security? Canadian state surveillance and the creation of enemies* (pp. 246–255). Toronto: Between The Lines Press.

Intelligence and Security Act, 2017 [New Zealand].

Kapoor, N. (2018). *Deport, Deprive, Extradite: 21st century state extremism*. London and New York: Verso.

Kienscherf, M. (2014). 'Beyond Militarization and Repression: Liberal social control as pacification', *Critical Sociology*. 1–16. Accessed from doi:10.1177/0896920514565485

Kinsman, G., & Gentile, P. (2010). *The Canadian War on Queers: National security as sexual regulation*. Vancouver: UBC Press.

——, Buse, D. K., & Steedman, M. (eds) (2000). *Whose National Security? Canadian state surveillance and the creation of enemies*. Toronto: Between The Lines Press.

Kundnani, A. (2014). *The Muslims Are Coming! Islamophobia, extremism, and the domestic war on terror*. London and New York: Verso.

Leonard, A. J., & Gallagher, C. A. (2014). *Heavy Radicals: The FBI's secret war on America's Maoists*. Winchester and Washington, DC: Zero Books.

Lubbers, E. (2012). *Secret Manoeuvres in the Dark: Corporate and police spying on activists.* London: Pluto.

Maira, S. (2016). *The 9/11 Generation: Youth, rights, and solidarity in the war on terror.* New York: NYU Press.

Manuel, A. (2017) *The Reconciliation Manifesto: Recovering the land, rebuilding the economy.* Toronto: Lorimer.

Marx, G. T. (1989). *Undercover: Police surveillance in America.* Berkeley, CA: University of California Press.

McCarthy, S. (2015, 17 February). '"Anti-Petroleum" Movement a Growing Threat to Canada, RCMP Say'. *Globe and Mail.* Accessed from www.theglobeandmail.com/news/politics/anti-petroleum-movement-a-growing-security-threat-to-canada-rcmp-say/article23019252/

McGovern, M. (2015). 'State Violence and the Colonial Roots of Collusion in Northern Ireland'. *Race and Class*, 57(2): 3–23.

McKnight, D. (2014). 'How To Read Your ASIO File'. In Burgmann, M. (ed.), *Dirty Secrets: Our ASIO files* (pp. 21–45). Sydney: New South Publishing.

MI5 (n.d.). 'Who We Are: People and organisation'. Accessed from www.mi5.gov.uk/people-and-organisation (accessed 11 September 2018).

Milne, S. (2014). *The Enemy Within: The secret war against the miners*, 4th edition. London and New York: Verso.

Mitrovica, A. (2002) *Covert Entry: Spies, lies and crimes inside Canada's secret service.* Toronto: Random House.

Murch, D. (2012). 'Countering Subversion: Black Panther scholarship, popular history, and the Richard Aoki controversy', American Historical Association, *Perspectives on History*, October 2012.

Pedersen, H., and Woorunmurra, B. (1995). *Jandamarra and the Bunuba Resistance.* Broome: Magabala Books.

Pender, T. (2000). 'The Gaze on Clubs, Native Studies, and Teachers at Laurentian University, 1960s–70s'. In G. Kinsman, D. K. Buse & M. Steedman (eds), *Whose National Security? Canadian state surveillance and the creation of enemies* (pp. 110–120). Toronto: Between The Lines Press.

Popplewell, R. (1995). *Intelligence and Imperial Defence: British intelligence and the defence of the Indian Empire, 1904–1924.* London: Frank Cass.

Potter, W. (2011). *Green is the New Red: An insider's account of a social movement under siege.* San Francisco, CA: City Lights.

Privacy International (26 November 2013). 'The Five Eyes Factsheet'. Accessed from https://privacyinternational.org/blog/1204/five-eyes-fact-sheet (accessed 11 September 2018).

RCMP (Royal Canadian Mounted Police) (2014). 'Criminal Threats to the Canadian Petroleum Industry', 24 January. Accessed from www.statewatch.org/news/2015/feb/can-2014-01-24-rcmp-anti-petroleum-activists-report.pdf

Seigel, M. (2018) 'Violence Work: Policing and power', *Race and Class* 59(4): 15–33.

Serge, V. (2005). *What Every Radical Should Know About State Repression: A guide for activists.* Melbourne: Ocean Press.

Sethna, C., & Hewitt, S. (2018). *Just Watch Us: RCMP Surveillance of the Women's Liberation Movement in Cold War Canada*. Montreal: McGill-Queen's Press.

Smith, D, & Chamberlain, P. (2015). *Blacklisted: The secret war between big business and union activists*. Oxford: New Internationalist.

Smith, G. (2006). 'Political activist as ethnographer'. In C. Frampton, G. Kinsman, A. K. Thompson & K. Tilleczek (eds), *Sociology for Changing the World: Social movements/Social research* (pp. 44–70). Black Point, Nova Scotia: Fernwood.

Smith, K. (2009). *Liberalism, Surveillance, Resistance: Indigenous communities in Western Canada, 1877–1927*. Edmonton: AU Press.

Sohi, S. (2014). 'Sites of "Sedition", Sites of Liberation: Gurdwaras, the Ghadar Party, and anticolonial mobilization', *Sikh Formations*, 10(1): 5–22.

Zoellick, R. (2001, 24 September). 'American Trade Leadership: What is at stake?' Speech to the Institute for International Economics, Washington DC. Accessed from http://ustraderep.gov/assets/Document_Library/USTR_Speeches/2001/asset_upload_file522_4267.pdf

2

The surveillance state
A composition in four movements
Radha D'Souza

This book considers 'what we did/didn't, should/could learn from activist/movement experiences of security operations, surveillance, infiltration' and such activities.

I

As I write, Facebook founder Mark Zuckerberg is being interrogated by the US Congress for selling personal information for private profit. I try to map the intricate multi-layered web of stand-alone 'facts' that the inquiry throws up. Facebook users volunteered information about themselves which Facebook then sold to Cambridge Analytica, a UK company that provided 'electoral management services', including data mining, data brokerage and data analytics, and specialising in US 'election markets' where it provided services to 44 candidates in various mid-term elections. The company worked on Donald Trump's presidential campaign. All this is on the surface.

I peel back the surface. Cambridge Analytica's CEO was also CEO of nine similar companies that were affiliates of the parent British group, SCL (Strategic Communication Laboratories) Group, a behavioural research and strategic communication services company founded in 1993 by Nigel Oakes. Oakes was a TV producer and advertiser and founder of the Behavioural Dynamics Institute (BDI), a research facility for strategic communication founded in 1990, focusing on the study of mass behaviour and interventions to change it using interdisciplinary approaches, notably psychology. SCL Group provides data-analytic services to defence and civilian organisations including NATO, the UK Ministry of Defence, and the US Sandia National Laboratories. The data is used for combat training institutes such as NATO StratCom Centre of Excellence. Sandia National Laboratories' origins go back to the Manhattan Project which built the atomic bomb. Sandia still operates as a federally funded national security agency for nuclear weapons.

I peel back another layer of the data trade. Sandia became a wholly owned subsidiary of Martin Marietta (later Lockheed Martin Corporation) in 1993. Since 2017, Sandia has been managed by National Technology and Engineering Solutions of Sandia, LLC, a wholly owned subsidiary of Honeywell International Inc. BDI became the not-for-profit affiliate of SCL, where SCL Elections was another member of the SCL Group. SCL Elections provided 'electoral services' to a hundred elections in thirty countries in five continents, including the Hindutva fundamentalist Bharatiya Janata Party (BJP) in India and Uhuru Kenyatta in Kenya. SCL Elections emerged as the 'market leader' in the 'election markets'. 'Election markets' emerged after the National Endowment for Democracy (NED) was established as a non-partisan 'NGO' funded by US Congress in 1983 to promote 'democracy' and 'freedom' around the world.

I peel back yet another layer of the data industry. SCL Group's affiliate, the UK-based Cambridge Analytica, is partly owned by US hedge-fund tycoon Robert Mercer. The Trump campaign bought, and Cambridge Analytica sold, 'electoral management services', a perfectly legal transaction. Cambridge Analytica, as part of its business operations, subcontracted Canadian company Aggregate IQ to provide 'strategic communication services' to the 'Leave' campaign in the UK's Brexit referendum. Cambridge Analytica, SCL Elections, and many other similar data-analytic companies buy their 'scientific' 'electoral management' technologies from Renaissance Technologies, a hedge fund established by the head of Stony Brook University's Mathematics Department who developed the technology for quantitative trading. Robert Mercer, the innovator of 'the science of electoral management', joined Renaissance Technologies as co-CEO after working for the US Air Force Weapons Laboratory and IBM's Thomas J Watson Research

Centre. Mercer's 'science' builds on US military PSYOPS (Psychological Operations), initiated during the World War years. PSYOPS was part of publicly funded science produced in universities and military research institutes and harnessed by Mercer's private companies. Mercer generously 'donated' data to Nigel Farage who led the 'Leave.EU' campaign during UK's Brexit referendum. Being a 'donation', the costs of the data did not count in the spending caps set by the Electoral Commission for the referendum. Mercer also donated millions of dollars to the election funds of numerous conservative candidates, and also to Breitbart and similar 'hard-right' news outlets.

To keep abreast of US 'business and innovation' initiatives, the UK government invests millions annually in research on Big Data and Artificial Intelligence (AI). The money is passed on to public research funding organisations such as the Economic and Social Research Council (ESRC), which uses it to provide periodic rounds of large grants to prestigious British universities for Big Data research. So far, there have been three rounds of funding between 2013 and 2019. Research funding organisations in turn invite universities to enter into public-private partnerships. One such project was run by Dr Aleksandr Kogan, a lecturer in Cambridge University's Department of Psychology who developed the app *thisisyourdigitallife*, inviting millions of users to take a personality test. In the spirit of public-private partnerships promoted by public funding bodies and the UK government's 'business innovation' strategies, Kogan established Global Science Research, a private firm which conducted surveys and supplied the data collected to Cambridge Analytica.

Firms like Henley & Partners complement Cambridge Analytica's 'electoral management services' around the world. Henley is a Jersey-based company founded by the company chairman, the 'passport-king' Dr Christian Kälin whose 'government advisory' services provides post-election services to Cambridge Analytica's clients after a successful election by offering 'citizenship-by-investment' services to cash-strapped Third World states. Being public-funded research, Big Data research and projects benefit other private companies besides the SCL Group and their networks such as data analytic companies like C2i and Inkerman Group, which sell their services to corporations like British Airways, the Royal Bank of Scotland, Porsche, energy giant RWE and others, to spy on activists. For example, Caterpillar hired C2i and Inkerman Group to monitor the parents of peace activist Rachel Corrie who in 2003 was crushed under a Caterpillar bulldozer used by the Israeli Defense Forces against protesters in Palestine.

I could go on and on, peeling away layer after layer after layer.

II

There are so many more countries, companies and activist stories to map. The proliferation of 'trade in surveillance' by data-mining companies has brought forth their own 'Top' lists: Top 10, Top 50 companies and so forth, and the data industry has branched off into its own specialisations – data analytics, data mining, data computing, apps development, platform development and much more. These companies in turn have resulted in 'resistance' in counter-movements like StopDataMining.Me which, one should expect, is mined by other 'regular' data-mining and analytics companies. I have not even touched upon spy agencies like the CIA, MI6 and the SVR (formerly the KGB), as well as the revolving doors between corporate, civil and military bureaucracies, between NGOs like Human Rights Watch, International Crisis Group and other 'civil society' groups and states, or the dazzling new phenomenon of spooks standing – at least 57 of them, we are told – in the mid-term elections to the US Congress on Democratic Party tickets. I have yet to add inquiries like the Undercover Policing Inquiry (UK), or activism opposing the 'snooper's charter' (the Investigatory Powers Act 2016), against which a petition has been signed by 212,743 people thus far; I have not yet discussed Julian Assange, Chelsea Manning and Edward Snowden.

There are the Frank, Pike and Roosevelt inquiries, the 9/11 Commission, the Watergate and Iran-Contra affairs, and all this only in one country – the United States. There are insider accounts of rogue spooks during the pre-social media and Internet era – bestsellers such as Philip Agee's *Inside the Company* on the CIA, Prince Norodom Sihanouk's *My War with the CIA*, accounts by journalists Seymour Hersh, Jack Anderson and ex-CIA officer Victor Marchetti, and stories like the mysterious disappearance of Gary Webb who wrote investigative reports on the Iran-Contra spy network. Each year, as archives are declassified under 30- or 60-year rules and as new facts emerge about old histories of everything from President John F. Kennedy's murder, to CIA covert actions causing mayhem in Stalin's USSR, to regime changes around the world as with the business of Allende, Che, Mossadeq, Sukarno and many others, to the older anti-colonial movements like Ghadar in South Asia and the Mau Mau rebellion in Kenya – all these histories need rewriting each time records are declassified. Perhaps it is best to leave out the Third World altogether. Bringing Third World states into surveillance stories requires an ongoing, permanent research project on surveillance comprising multiple volumes of very precise and accurate facts nailing down every fact with concrete evidence extending over how long? Years? Decades? Centuries?

Every activist and radical scholar knows that Big Brother is everywhere. Every citizen knows, has always known, that taxpayer-funded surveillance is a core function of the state. *Why then are activists, invariably, surprised and/or outraged when a new surveillance story comes to light?* This, in my view, is the real question that activists and scholars need to reflect on when considering surveillance, security operations, infiltration and such activities.

A hundred years ago, Lenin reflected on similar questions about the Russian state in a small pamphlet titled *The State and Revolution.* This pamphlet may be seen as exemplifying social movements learning from the ground up. Lenin grants his readers, mainly organisers and working people, the credit for knowing about their experiences learnt from concrete practices of struggles. Organisers at least know that the state watches everyone. Lenin builds on the knowledge already gained in their struggles and maps the architecture of power that activists are up against in their political organising. In doing so, he discusses what *he* learnt from *his* gurus, Marx and Engels, and the struggles against capitalism that went before him in Europe, in order to draw out key lessons that must inform the Bolshevik programme during a critical moment in Russian history. Lenin's 'social movement learning from the ground up' changed the future of Russia and the world order. Without doubt, social movements must learn from the ground up if they wish to change the world. The question is: what should they learn and how?

Over the past century, the rise of new disciplines – sociology, statistics, econometrics, quantitative methods, computing, communication sciences, management sciences, behavioural psychology, social psychology, media studies, futures studies, game theories, system theories, autopoesis, network theories, and yes, even surveillance studies – have produced dominant knowledge primarily for the purposes of governance. The pivot upon which this new knowledge turns is this thing called a 'fact' – a singular aspect of reality extricated from its social context. This type of knowledge assumes information alone is 'true' knowledge. Good scholarship must therefore seek more 'facts' to test the veracity of facts with 'counter-facts', using better and improved methodologies to uncover reality. How many exposés, case studies and examples, how much more information do we need before we ask: 'what is the nature of this beast that we call the state and why is it always hunting activists?'

The interlocking 'facts' presented in Part I of this chapter suggest connections between hedge funds, consulting firms, major corporations, scientific research, academic scholarship, the military, the media, imperialist states led by the US and UK, protest movements, democratic practices, and management of democracies in the Third World. What are those connections? What methodological moves are necessary for social movements to go beyond narrating activist experiences of surveillance, security operations and infiltration? Information is not experience. Nevertheless, experience can be transformed into information through certain methodological moves that modern knowledge makes within the diverse disciplinary sites of knowledge production. Stories about our experiences are essential first steps to knowledge. But it is just that: the *first* step. The second, third and fourth steps in knowledge production must become sites of resistance to the methodological moves that transform 'our' experiences into information for 'those' experts, if we are to learn from our struggles. So what should/could we learn from activist/movement experiences of security operations, surveillance, infiltration?

III

Where there is state, there is secrecy and surveillance

A state is a juridical entity, a creature of a constitution that establishes public power. A dominant social group with the capacity to organise must come together to establish a state. Public power is the capacity to command and control diverse social classes and groups with conflicting interests and claims. The task of command-control is carried out through two main organs of the state: the armed forces (military and police) and the civil administration. As maintaining the armed forces and administration requires money, the capacity to collect taxes and borrow money is essential for the continued existence of public power. Conflicting classes and groups destabilise the state. State secrets conceal the rivalries and conflicts that underpin the state and give it the appearance of being non-partisan and above conflicts. Surveillance helps to secure the regime and nip dissent in the bud as far as possible.

The modern state is a surveillance state

Whereas we find a wide variety of feudal states depending on landownership and tenure systems, the modern state is quintessentially European in origin and character, and serves as the institutional umbrella for European capitalism. It has touched societies around the world in a variety of ways and transformed them. Whereas land was the pivot for the feudal social order, in the modern capitalist state, commodity production is the organising pivot. The modern state is qualitatively different from pre-modern ones in the way it organises the command-control apparatus and marks a historical transition from the pre-modern states and with it, a transition in the management of state secrets and surveillance.

Unlike feudal states, modern states do not demand allegiance to the person of the monarch or an aristocrat. Modern states demand allegiance to the state as an abstract constitutional entity – abstracted from social attributes of race, class, gender, nationality, religion, etc. – even when all these attributes and related conflicts exist within society. Abstracted from the characteristics of its people, the modern state is a depersonalised sovereign of a symbolic nation – hence the hyphenated 'nation-state'.

Power in pre-modern societies was dispersed. In contrast, centralisation of authority is a characteristic feature of modern states. To function as a depersonalised entity over a large territorial area that is organised around commodity production – an ever-moving, always circulating form of property – the modern nation-state must establish a professional armed force and civil service. Professional armed forces and civil services act as the state's muscle and spine. Being unaffiliated to land or private property owners, the armed forces and civil services must be centralised with command-control structures inscribed in the constitutional settlement of the state.

Armed forces and civil services in modern nation-states depend entirely on the state's capacities to collect taxes and raise loans. To maintain the professionalised, centralised armed forces and civil service, the modern nation-state must collect enough taxes from *all* classes and groups in society (in contrast to pre-capitalist societies). In conflict-ridden societies, states must appear to be above the interests of social classes and groups with conflicting interests. Yet, to collect taxes and borrow money, states must, at the least, not antagonise those with more money, property and resources. The nation-state's strength or weakness depends on how much tax it can collect to keep its spine, sinews and muscles combat-fit. Those who lend money must have enough confidence that the state will repay them with interest. Inability to raise loans weakens the state. Consequently, social conflicts are exacerbated many times over in capitalist societies because all taxpayers/citizens, having contributed to the exchequer, expect to have a say in how their taxes are spent.

'No taxation without representation' became the first principle of democratic governance. However, democratic governance does not do away with social conflicts. Therefore, democratic governance does not do away with the need for secrets and surveillance. Instead, state secrets and surveillance become professionalised, centralised, legalised and impersonal, an activity of the bureaucracies: military and civilian. *National Security* is the organising pivot for the professionalised and legalised procedures and practices of surveillance and state secrecy in capitalist societies. National Security is the flip side of 'taxation without representation' – the other face of democratic governance. All modern nation-states are 'surveillance states' where military, security and surveillance are organised around principles of national security.

The Leviathan is the creation story of the modern nation-state

The seventeenth-century philosopher Thomas Hobbes told the first creation story about the modern state. It is a Leviathan, a towering powerful artificial giant. On the cover of his book *Leviathan*, the torso of the artificial giant comprises hundreds of thousands of miniscule men and the lower body is a vast expanse of a depopulated realm with unoccupied fields, homes, churches, forests, etc. Its head is that of the sovereign with an impressive crown. The *Leviathan* as the modern nation-state is an artificial person, a body-politic analogous to the human body. People and nature are distinct and exist in a hierarchical order where nature is at the bottom of the body-politic. Just as the brain controls the voluntary and involuntary functions of the body, the sovereign must control subjects and nature, and their relationships for the body-politic to function as a single juridical person. As with the natural body, malfunctions and dysfunctions occur within the body-politic. These must be corrected, and in extreme cases the limbs amputated for the survival of the body-politic. Command-control, discipline-punishment continue behind the façade of a unified body-politic, and require state secrecy and surveillance, for national security, i.e. the survival of the nation-state.

According to Hobbes's creation myth, the Leviathan was created by us, the ordinary folks, the working people. Hobbes says people entered into a social contract with each other to create the Leviathan. People agreed that they would voluntarily give up their capacities for self-rule, self-defence and self-preservation to the Leviathan in return for protection. In other words, people agreed that the Leviathan state would have a monopoly over violence, and in return provide the entire nation with security. Why would ordinary folks voluntarily give up their powers for self-defence to a new monster, especially when they did not have a clue about how it would use those powers? When Hobbes wrote *Leviathan*, the English Civil Wars raged – a series of wars taking place in 1642–51 between the Parliamentarians (the 'Roundheads') and the Royalists (the 'Cavaliers'). The Parliamentarians were backed by merchants, the City of London, and the port-cities of south-east England that held a share of the lucrative slave trade and the promises of riches and limitless new possibilities in the New World untrammelled by the traditional authority of the king, the Church and God. The Royalists, in the tradition of feudal monarchies, believed territorial conquests could consolidate their reign and enrich their kingdom. Whereas earlier civil wars were fought between feudal aristocracies over annexation of land, these wars were fought over the establishment of a new type of state – the Surveillance State.

The Parliamentarians formed a new type of army called the 'New Model Army', a professional army with centralised command and control, funded by the Parliamentarians' riches from overseas trade, conquests and landholdings. If we include the civil wars in Scotland and Ireland and the wars between Scotland and England, and Ireland and England, from the mid-1630s onwards, the Civil Wars lasted over two decades, during which time the old order crumbled and a new one had not yet emerged. The *Leviathan* proposed a model nation-state where people could end the Civil Wars by relinquishing their powers for self-defence to a new and improved sovereign that did away with the past inequalities of the feudal era and established a new order as a social contract between the warring parties on fair terms. Hobbes's Leviathan state was inspired by the New Model Army. Hobbes was a Royalist who recognised the need for a new type of state without displacing the old sovereign. Hobbes thus laid the basis for constitutional monarchy, that was neither a republic nor ruled by a divine king, as a possible way forward from the Civil Wars.

Of course, there is no Leviathan and no social contract. It is a creation story. Like all creation stories, it established a new type of social order. The point to note for secrets and surveillance is this. The modern European nation-state is organised in the course of wars everywhere. Wars reorganise the national security apparatus in the surveillance states in new ways.

The panopticon established the governance model for the Leviathan state

In the late eighteenth century, Jeremy Bentham designed the panopticon, ostensibly as a model prison. The panopticon's power as a metaphor for the surveillance state remains with us to this day. At the centre of the model prison is a watchtower with 360° vision surrounded by hundreds of cells. The prisoners cannot see the surveillants in the watchtower as it is screened by wooden slats. Conversely, surveillance personnel can watch every person and come and go as they deem necessary without being seen.

Bentham's inspiration was a factory in Russia designed so that the managers could watch workers more closely with fewer supervisors. Bentham adapted the industrial design to manage workers as a model for governance of state institutions such as prisons, hospitals, asylums and workhouses that were necessary for the smooth functioning of the body-politic. With very few surveillance personnel, it becomes possible for the Leviathan to manage large numbers of prisoners/citizens more efficiently.

When workers/prisoners/citizens know generally that they are being watched, but do not know when, how, or for what purpose, nor the position of the surveillants or angles from which they will be observed, the prisoners will be resigned to surveillance, modify their behaviour, and keep the body-politic working without disruptions. Panopticons impose self-discipline. Since the prisoner will be self-disciplined, the Leviathan will not have to resort to force. In turn, minimal use of force will sustain the mythology of the social contract.

Bentham's panopticon is a command-control model for managing large organisations. It embodies a theory of management and governance for the artificial person mediated by technology. It proposed a new epistemology of surveillance where cost-benefit calculations, industrial design, behavioural psychology, management techniques for large organisations and a philosophy of human ethics all fuse to make prison management the model of governance for the Leviathan.

Why would millions of men and women occupying the Leviathan's body-politic want to keep the monster alive by slaving away for him? Bentham argued it was human nature to seek pleasure and avoid pain. Having surrendered their capacities for self-preservation and self-defence, the miniscule men and women that form the Leviathan's torso will make themselves comfortable in the positions they occupy in the body-politic and avoid discomfort, as far as possible, in their own interest. The panopticon transforms the miniscule men and women occupying the torso of the Leviathan into modern man. The modern man is one who maximises pleasure and minimises pain. The only way people can maximise pleasure and minimise pain is by voluntarily submitting to the discipline of the Leviathan. The idea that maximising pleasure and minimising pain is the driving force that propels human actions as a theory of human agency is now presupposed in all types of governance, public and private.

What if some men and women say that their pain is caused by the Leviathan? If too many miniscule men and women felt that way, it could potentially unravel the body-politic. Precisely for that reason, Bentham argued, the Leviathan must maintain the power to punish in the interest of national security.

The Golem is a robotic automaton that shields the Leviathan and transforms the miniscule men and women in the body politic into miniscule gadgets

Continuous technological improvements of the panopticon enabled surveillants to hand over more of their roles to mechanical surveillance. As technology took over, the surveillants became increasingly less responsible for the governance of the prisons and polities. Notwithstanding these technological improvements, the panopticon caused more dysfunction in the body-politic. Two world wars, colonial uprisings, economic depression and unemployment enlarged the scale of governance. Despite many improvements, the panopticon was too small and inadequate for the task of governance on a global scale, and eventually collapsed under its own weight. As the scope of surveillance expanded to meet war and economic needs, it tore through the Leviathan's body-politic. The renewal of national security became an urgent question for the Leviathan's survival, and that included the surveillants, as well as the millions of miniscule men and women in the body-politic. The Golem emerged from the chaos of two world wars. The Golem is a giant robotic automaton that encases the Leviathan and enhances its powers beyond human imagination.

One hundred and fifty years after Bentham, Norbert Wiener (1894–1964) founded cybernetics, the science of command and control of any system, human and non-human, using communication sciences. Communication, Wiener argued, was the key to command and control of humans by humans, of machines by humans, of machines by machines and of humans by machines. Wiener fathered the Golem. Cybernetics laid the foundations for every type of command-communication-control technologies (3C technologies). Innovated initially for aerial bombings during the First World War (WW1), 3C technologies permeate every aspect of life, and move and shake every sphere of life since the Second World War (WW2). Algorithms exist for every facet of life: from economy, warfare, social relationships, management of nature, society, institutions, laws, biological phenomenon, health, well-being – just about everything. Algorithms crunch all living and non-living matter into number sets. Cybernetics introduces life and dynamism into the algorithms by studying and applying the processes of learning, cognition, adaptation, emergence, convergence, networks, connections and much else to humans, natures and machines. Thus where there is communication, there is cybernetics and where there is cybernetics, there is some form of surveillance. There is some machine and/or human being that is observing and monitoring humans and/or other machines. Cybernetics has the capacity to turn machines into men and men into machines.

The Golem gave two debut performances during the world wars: the Holocaust and Hiroshima–Nagasaki. In the Holocaust, the Golem demonstrated how men could become perfect machines and conduits for 3C operations. In Hiroshima–Nagasaki, the Golem overawed the spectators – surveillants and surveilled alike – with its spectacular mushroom clouds accompanied by thunder, fury and devastation. After the Golem's debut performances, the world wars ended quickly and abruptly. The Golem took the Leviathan into protection by becoming its protective shield. The millions of men and women who occupied the body-politic kow-towed to the Golem, and over time became miniscule gadgets in the resurrected body-politic.

Having created the Golem to defeat the evil forces of fascism during the world wars, Wiener and his colleagues became frightened by what they had created. When they created the Golem, they believed, after the crisis of the surveillance state had passed, fascism defeated, the world wars ended, the Golem would be put to sleep forever. They believed the old and familiar Leviathan would be revived, and everything would be back to the old ways. However, Wiener realised rather late that his inventions had turned the surveillants into what he called 'gadget-worshippers'. The gadget-worshippers had, through their incantations, breathed life into the Golem. 'If I had known they would do this I would have become a shoemaker', Albert Einstein lamented after Hiroshima–Nagasaki. Wiener, the man who fathered and delivered the Age of Information, pleaded with the surveillants not to turn into 'gadget-worshippers' and instead take responsibility for the new technologies of surveillance and the body-politic – to no avail. The surveillants who had turned into devoted gadget-worshippers could no longer exist without the Golem.

Even as US Congressmen interrogate Zuckerberg, Alexander Taylor of the now-defunct Cambridge Analytica has resumed operations as CEO (together with his team) under the new name of Emerdata. People continue to voluntarily provide personal information to Facebook.

Wiener's faithful followers, the anti-surveillance activists, follow in his footsteps, going from pillar to post pleading with surveillants to be more responsible and stop being 'gadget-worshippers'.

IV

The Golem in the epoch of imperialism

The Golem is a warfare state, a gigantic war machine with extraordinary destructive capacities, nurtured by capitalist states during the world wars for 'Total War'. The principle of Total War became a pivotal instrument for reorganising the state apparatus initially to conduct WW2. The warfare state was never dismantled after WW2, but expanded and consolidated during the Cold War and reorganised after '9/11'. A warfare state is a technologically driven apparatus for conducting wars on an industrial scale. To do that, a warfare state must organise the entire social order in warlike ways. A warfare state is designed to mobilise industrial, fiscal, political, scientific, technological, educational, artistic, cultural, ideological, journalistic, humanitarian, civic and every other type of resource and actors in society for war. In the vocabulary of warfare states, this is called 'war preparedness' for 'national security'. Total War integrates institutions of the economy (industrial and fiscal), state (military and civilian), educational (scientific and cultural) and civil society (humanitarian and political), and brings them under a unified system of command-communication-control managed by a hi-tech security apparatus that threads all aspects of governance in the very heart of the state. Social institutions become intertwined and interdependent such that the dualisms that erected boundaries in early modern states such as public/private, civilian/military, economy/politics, wartime/peacetime, national/international, nature/culture, science/ideology become blurred. Wars are no longer an exceptional or temporary occurrence, an intensification and/or extension of political conflicts, but instead a means of extended reproduction of the Golem.

Extended reproduction of warfare states occurs through surveillance. Warfare states establish societies founded on *in*security which becomes the justification for national security in economy, politics and culture. In the economy, insurance becomes a mode of governance for all society by commodifying and financialising insecurity. The insurance industry, also a product of the world wars, requires intrusive surveillance. Political surveillance is no longer the exclusive remit of the armed forces. Surveillance becomes a core seat of governance beyond army and police in the heart of the warfare state. Surveillance is the organising tool not only for the military, not only a tool for monitoring internal and external 'enemies', whoever they may be, but also a means of ordering all aspects of society including economic, political, intellectual, humanitarian, educational, scholarly, journalistic and artistic actors. Surveillance aims to change the behaviour of different actors by using information about them in strategic ways. Sciences like social and behavioural psychology and PSYOPS, i.e. the less visible sciences, work in tandem with more visible technologies like CCTV, biometric data, GPS, or satellite imaging. Surveillance is used to establish a mindset where society accepts that national *in*security is permanent, that war as means of survival is inevitable. Gadget-worshippers in warfare states concede the power to organise the economy, polity and society to the Golem and limit their own agency to mitigating the worst effects of surveillance excesses on individuals. In the cultural spheres, warfare states produce dystopian images of human futures.

The most important difference between the warfare state and earlier modern surveillance states is that whereas the panopticon focused on surveillance of citizens by the state, the warfare state is international in scope, where technologically mediated surveillance is the means to command and control other states. Surveillance is the means for political and economic warfare against other states. The Leviathan state was established in the Epoch of Mercantile Capitalism when the feudal order was dismantled, and a new social order based on commodity production was established. We saw how it laid the foundations for a surveillance state by establishing a centralised state founded on professional armed forces and bureaucracy and established a new social order by reorganising people displaced from the land for commodity production. The Epoch of Industrial Capitalism introduced the panopticon as the dominant model of governance for expanded commodity production. We saw how during the Industrial Epoch, technology mediated governance and enhanced the efficiencies of industries as well as militaries and bureaucracies. The emergence of Transnational Monopoly Finance (TMF) capitalism at the turn of the twentieth century, or the Epoch of

Imperialism, ended the old industrial capitalism and brought down the apparatus of governance, the panopticon state.

From the ruins of the old state, the world wars established a new type of state that found its fullest expression in the United States, where it developed as a complete constitutional apparatus of internal/national and external/international governance. The US warfare state bears the imprint of the Epoch of Imperialism – global in scope and outreach and with the capacities to command and control other states. Not all states have the capacities to command and control other states internationally, or engage in political and economic warfare. Therefore not all states are warfare states. In the Epoch of Imperialism, the juridical state becomes a universal form of political organisation for all societies. Behind the legal frontage of formal statehood, different states have greater or lesser capacities for 'Total Wars' and capacities for surveillance of other states. The world wars established two classes of states: one with capacities for command-control of other states, and those with limited capacities for command-control of other states. TMF capitalism links states in an *imperial chain*, and warfare states produce the military and civilian governance frameworks for the global chains of states. As one link in an imperial chain, each state's position is different, as each state has a different internal structure, history and capacities for resisting external pressures. Surveillance in the Epoch of Imperialism has internal (class, capital, conflicts) and external (positionality in the imperial chain, capacities for 'Total War', the reach of the surveillance apparatus) dimensions. However, the formal equality of states in international law and international relations, and the disciplinary silos in scholarship that reduce states to a legal entity as the point of departure for analysis, has limited our understanding of warfare states and the place of surveillance within it. Security and surveillance are always concrete historical questions. It becomes necessary to locate questions of surveillance and security in the general characteristics of the epoch, as well as the specific place that each state occupies as a link in the imperial chain.

US exceptionalism

The US provides the archetypal model of a warfare state. Its innovations in statecraft during the world wars established it as a world leader of TMF capitalism. The rest of this chapter focuses on the archetypal state in the US, more commonly known as the 'exceptional state'. The imperatives of Total War in the Epoch of Imperialism led all capitalist states to trial and experiment with, to a greater or lesser degree, new models for a state that integrated military, civil bureaucracies, banks, industries, research, education, media and civil society organisations into a single unified warfare state. Fascism and corporatism were the other competing models in Europe, but failed to establish the legal and institutional conditions for the Epoch of Imperialism for reasons that need not be analysed here. The US briefly flirted with fascism and corporatism, but abandoned both. The reasons for the US model's success as a warfare state is beyond the scope of this chapter, except to say that there *are* historical and sociological reasons why the warfare state there emerged in its most complete form.

In the US, the expanding transnational corporations, financiers and bankers led the way in establishing the warfare state. A weak federal state inducted Wall Street (stock-exchange/banks/financial sectors) and America Inc. (transnational monopolistic corporations) into the very heart of the federal apparatus of power as an additional limb of the state, alongside the traditional armed forces and civil services. Wall Street and America Inc. do something much more than pay taxes, lend money and influence the state in policy making, as businesses did in the previous epochs of capitalism. They establish new methods of governance for the entire society, and indeed for the world in the interstate system after WW2.

On the eve of WW1, a war in which the US remained neutral for the first two-and-a-half years, Wall Street and America Inc. organised themselves as collective associations within different industrial sectors and pushed the idea that industrial warfare required 'Total War' and perpetual 'war preparedness'. WW1 established institutions like the War Industries Board (WIB), under the president's executive authority, comprising representatives of numerous industries from iron, steel and automobile manufacturers to canned food and packaging industries. The regulatory model for the new relationship forged between Wall Street, America Inc. and the federal state was self-regulation, self-planning and self-organisation. The 'dollar-a-year' appointments of industry personnel for government services for 'war preparedness' made WW1 the most profitable business of the day. Today's 'revolving doors' between Wall Street, America Inc. and the federal state – well oiled by lobby firms, election financing, PR firms, think-tanks and a network of 'self-organised' non-governmental organisations – were established during the interwar period. WW2 consolidated the integration of armed forces, civilian bureaucracies, Wall Street and America Inc., and laid the institutional foundations for the post-WW2 military-industrial complex.

The same is true of the security-surveillance complex that emerged during WW2. With the exception of historians of security and surveillance, it is forgotten that until WW1, the US did not have a specialist security and intelligence service. The army and navy gathered intelligence for purposes of war and peace and the Sheriff's office had a greater role in policing than the federal police. When WW1 broke out in Europe, America Inc. and Wall Street used US neutrality to initiate forays into security and surveillance in Europe. For example, William Donovan, the 'father' of US intelligence, was sent to Europe during WW1 by the Rockefeller Foundation. En route, he received training in security and surveillance from British secret intelligence services in London. Under cover of US neutrality, Donovan gathered intelligence for Britain and America Inc. The point here is that Donovan's was not a US federal mission but rather a Rockefeller Foundation one. Donovan was a 'silk-stocking' lawyer who represented corporations in Buffalo, New York. He raised and headed a private militia for the Sheriff and led it, first to put down striking workers in Buffalo and later to suppress the Pancho Villa insurgency by Mexican revolutionaries. The one-man security and surveillance apparatus in the person of 'Wild' Bill Donovan, funded by corporate clients and the Rockefeller Foundation, expanded to become a fully-fledged intelligence outfit, the Office of Strategic Services (OSS) by 1942 under the president's executive authority.

Similar stories may be told of the Dulles brothers, John Foster and Allen, both 'silk-stocking' lawyers with the most important corporations of the time, US and German, on their client list. Allen Dulles worked for OSS in Europe, while his law firm managed German reparation money and investments of German corporations. Their mission was to promote foreign policies favourable to their clients. The OSS was legalised and institutionalised by the National Security Act of 1947 to become the CIA. The real story of how the relationships between America Inc., Wall Street and the US security and surveillance apparatus were forged is found in biographies of key individuals who were architects of the warfare state, such as Anthony Cave Brown's *The Last Hero: Wild Bill Donovan – The biography and political experience of Major General William J Donovan, founder of the OSS and "father" of the CIA, from his personal and secret papers and the diaries of Ruth Donovan*, or David Talbot's *The Devil's Chessboard: Allen Dulles, the CIA and the rise of America's secret government*.

Biographical, autobiographical and whistleblower accounts of the security and surveillance apparatus show that the same strategies of governance used for industrial production and fiscal planning during the world wars were used for intelligence, security and surveillance. 'Silk-stocking' law firms crafted the institutional relationships and organisations that would sit within state institutions alongside the armed forces and civil services. If America Inc. 'self-organised' and formed industry associations to represent them in government through the WIB, they 'self-organised' in foreign affairs by establishing organisations like the Council for Foreign Affairs (CFA) to direct their nominees in the government on foreign policy and economic and political warfare overseas. Established in 1922, the CFA is perhaps the oldest organisation of its kind and remains influential today. Allen Dulles played a leading role in shaping the CFA as a platform for leaders of America Inc. and Wall Street to develop a consensual foreign policy that they could take to their nominees within government.

The CIA could act as the foreign policy arm of Wall Street and America Inc. because of its autonomous legal status within the federal state. The US's security and surveillance apparatus is a complex of 17 organisations. The CIA, however, is the only organisation that is an autonomous statutory body not under the direct authority of the executive or the legislature – that is, it is a 'self-governing' body. Wall Street, America Inc. and the 'silk-stocking' law firms headed by men like Donovan and Dulles were instrumental in crafting the CIA's autonomous legal status. For the CIA, a form of state that gave civilian bureaucracies more clout was 'left-wing' and socialist. The CIA's hatred for anything it considered left-wing or socialist becomes understandable when we see its roots in the 'silk-stocking' law firms, Wall Street and America Inc.

Unlike fascist and corporatist models, Wall Street and America Inc. never surrendered their authority to the armed forces or civilian bureaucracies when they joined the government ostensibly to defend their country. Instead, they organised themselves within the government as well as outside through an array of specialist think-tanks, research institutes, associations, and law firms that later branched into specialist legal, lobbying and public relations services. During the Cold War, organisations like the Trilateral Commission, the Bilderberg Society, the Carter Foundation, the Heritage Society and many other private foundations extended the domestic governance model to interstate relations. While organising themselves as special interest associations, their members also occupied public offices within international organisations. The 'dollar-a-year' appointments that industries made to government departments during the world wars paved the way for the blurred state boundaries between public/private, civilian/military, national/international.

The coming together of Wall Street, America Inc., the armed forces and the civil service during the world wars made 'Big Science' possible – that is, scientific research conducted on an industrial scale. Big Science mobilised academics, scientists, universities, educational institutions, think-tanks and government bureaucracies for continued scientific and technological innovations to feed the warfare state. Scientists, scholars and intellectuals became cogs in the wheels of gigantic knowledge industries as wage-workers. If the aeroplane was an invention of Big Science during WW1, the atom bomb continues to exemplify Big Science that produces military-industrial-scientific-civilian-social-ideological infrastructures for society forged by the warfare state. As noted earlier, cybernetics, the most important innovation of Big Science coming out of the world wars, has transformed societies in dramatic ways.

The particular architecture of power in the US allows America Inc. and Wall Street to work within governments to develop legal frameworks for dual-use technologies. Dual-use policies allow public-funded Big Science and technological innovations including surveillance to be adapted for industrial, commercial and trading purposes. For example, aeroplanes were invented for aerial warfare but later used for commercial flights. APRANET was innovated for military uses and adapted as the Internet for commercial uses. Most technological developments of any significance since the world wars were developed by Big Science in the warfare state and passed on to America Inc. and Wall Street for commercial uses. Big Science created and shared scientific and technological infrastructures between America Inc., Wall Street, the armed forces and the civil services. The homogenisation of technological infrastructures enables the warfare state to act as a unified institution vis-à-vis other states in the Epoch of Imperialism.

In the field of ideology and culture, the world wars also established comparable models of governance. Edward Bernays (1891–1995), the 'father of public relations', established the field of scientific propaganda, psychological warfare, advertising, ideological warfare and public relations. Like others of his times, Bernays provided services for America Inc. as PR consultant as well as for the federal government's war mobilisation. He headed the Committee for Public Information in 1917 to promote wartime propaganda. Although the Committee was wound up after WW1, it was reborn as the Writers War Board and the United States Office of War Information under the influence of the OSS's Communications Department during WW2. After the CIA was established as a legal entity, the Office of Policy Coordination unit was created in 1948 as a covert operation within the government to continue the work of ideological and psychological warfare begun during the world wars. Here too, corporate media tycoons operated within the dual-power structures of 'self-regulation' and used the 'dollar-a-year' models of free work for the CIA.

Deborah Davis, in her biography of Katherine Graham, owner of the *Washington Post* (*Katherine the Great: Katherine Graham and her Washington Post empire*), illuminated the blurred boundaries between public and private power in relation to media corporations, the federal state, foreign relations and the security and intelligence apparatus. Initially published in 1979, the CIA, the *Washington Post* board, 'silk-stocking' law firms and America Inc. connived to suppress the book, including persuading the publisher to renege on the book contract and shred 20,000 copies. Started as a wartime measure, in 1950, the CIA's Operation Mockingbird regularised the practice of 'owning' members of the media. In 1977, *Rolling Stone* journalist Carl Bernstein exposed how CIA director Allen Dulles oversaw a media network of 25 newspapers and wire agencies. In the media, wartime arrangements were consolidated and expanded after WW2 ended.

The OSS and early CIA operatives invested much time and effort on Western Europe – in particular, France, Germany, Italy and Greece – including propaganda and media manipulation on a war footing. Like Lenin, the US power elite understood that Western Europe was on the threshold of socialist revolutions. Whereas Lenin established the Communist International to support socialist revolutions and hoped they would follow in the Bolsheviks' footsteps, the OSS and CIA engaged in covert and overt warfare to defeat communist revolutions in Western Europe. This history is important for activists today.

That election financing by corporations remains a major challenge for democratic governance everywhere is generally acknowledged. Beyond financing, the security and intelligence apparatus and their many 'front' outfits, which run jointly with America Inc., Wall Street and corporate media, groom politicians for federal offices by putting them on probation in state legislatures and executives and by engaging them in the complex of think-tanks, institutes and other organisations. *The Devil's Chessboard* details how Richard Nixon was groomed for office by the front outfits. Decades later, one reason why the 2016 US presidential election remains so controversial is because both Bernie Sanders and Donald Trump were outsiders, meaning they were either disqualified by America Inc. and Wall Street (Sanders) or not groomed, tried and tested by them in the states prior to the presidential elections (Trump). The surveillance apparatus, most notably the CIA and FBI, remain at the centre of election controversies because of their failure to prevent an untested candidate from winning. The US warfare state is convulsed by the weakening of the capacities of the warfare state for extended reproduction.

Academic scholars, international law and international relations experts use the epithet 'US exceptionalism' to analyse US policies, as if 'exceptionalism' were a doctrinal legal issue or deviant behaviour in international relations. More recently, the term 'deep state' is used to describe the corporate-security nexus in the state. Mike Lofgren in *The Deep State: The fall of the Constitution and the rise of a shadow government* (2016) argues that the 'deep state' is a shadow government that subverts the constitutional government. He suggests that there are rogue elements, cliques and centres within the state whose deviant behaviours are responsible for subverting the US Constitution and American democracy. These approaches do not, in my view, examine the historical evolution of American institutions that make the US an 'exceptional' state in the Epoch of Imperialism. The CIA is by no means an 'extra-constitutional' centre of power. It is a statutory body that is by law outside the authority of the executive or legislature. The very fact that then-President Ronald Reagan issued an executive order (Order 12333) in 1981 to end assassinations of foreign leaders demonstrates that assassinations were not rogue actions. The revolving doors that operate so smoothly between military, industry and finance are not 'deviant', but were established by successive legitimately elected governments initially under wartime executive powers given to them under the Constitution that were later regularised by the legislatures.

Britain is also a warfare state but not an 'exceptional' or archetypal warfare state. Its secret intelligence service, MI6, was established in 1909 as an expansion of the state's regular police powers. The outbreak of anti-colonial movements was the impulse for initially internationalising the British security and surveillance establishment, not the corporations and stock exchanges as in the US. The security and surveillance apparatus to conduct war against national liberation struggles was adapted and expanded for war against European states. But Britain's war against European states was over the colonies. The institutional infrastructures for Big Science, private contracting, insurance and finance, wartime economic and fiscal planning and other aspects of the Golem were state directed in Britain, in contrast to the corporation-driven state 'self-regulation' in the US. Besides, Britain became a subsidiary state of the US, economically and militarily, after WW2. Germany and Japan attempted fascist models, but were defeated and absorbed as stronger links in the imperial chain. Colonial states were established by the empires ostensibly to bring modernisation and 'progress', but never developed strong militaries and bureaucracies and their corporations remain largely foreign and transnational.

Activism against warfare states

From time to time during periods of political unrest, activists have exposed the warfare state's security and surveillance activities. In the post-Vietnam War period, there were many challenges to the security apparatus. For example, in the early 1970s, in a daring raid, the Citizens' Commission to Investigate the FBI, a leftist activist group in the US, broke into the FBI's Pennsylvania office and took over a thousand classified documents. The raids uncovered the federal Counter Intelligence Programme (COINTELPRO), a covert, illegal surveillance project that infiltrated political organisations in order to discredit and disrupt them. Three books – Churchill and Vander Wall's *Agents of Repression: The FBI's secret wars against the Black Panther Party and the American Indian Movement* (1988) and *The COINTELPRO Papers: Documents from the FBI's secret wars against domestic dissent* (1990), and Glick's *War at Home: Covert action against U.S. activists and what we can do about it* (1989) – brought home the truth that the warfare state was not limited to the CIA and foreign affairs somewhere outside of the country. In the context of Wikileaks and other whistleblowers, it is useful to recall that Operation Shamrock and Operation Minaret, both operated by the National Security Agency, intercepted hundreds of thousands of telecommunication and wire messages overseas and at home, including diplomatic missions, since WW2, with the full cooperation of telecommunication companies such as International Telephone and Telegraph (ITT). Given this uninterrupted trajectory of expansion of interceptions, what is new in the cooperation of Facebook and Google, beyond technological innovations using Big Science?

Scandals and inquiries have dogged the US security and surveillance apparatus since their founding years, beginning in 1949. The Watergate and Iran-Contra corruption scandals in the early 1970s and mid-1980s respectively led to a series of investigations into the activities of the vast complex of federal security and surveillance agencies. Between 1947 (when the CIA was established) and 2005, at least 14 major public inquiries into the security and surveillance apparatus have been conducted in the US alone – roughly one every four years. The inquiries have produced various recommendations and reforms, but the vast complex of 17 federated security and surveillance agencies continues to grow. In 2010, the *Washington Post*, in an investigative report by Diana Priest and William M. Arkin, 'Top Secret America: A Hidden World, Growing Beyond Control' (19 July 2010), reported that some 1,271 government organisations and 1,931 private companies work on programmes concerning counter-terrorism, homeland security and intelligence in about 10,000 locations across the US, employing 854,000 employees with top-security clearances.

So far, I have discussed one warfare state, no doubt an archetypal one. The US spends 65 percent of the global expenditure on intelligence services. The others trail behind. Britain's intelligence budget in 2015 was £2.48 billion (US$3.35 billion). Comparing spending is misleading, however. As links in an imperial chain of states, the other warfare states (the Allied and Axis powers – Britain, France, Japan, Germany mainly) are interlinked through numerous intelligence contracting and sharing agreements such as the 'Five Eyes' agreement between the US, Britain,

Australia, Canada and New Zealand, as well as NATO, various treaties establishing military bases and much else. If the US is the leader of TMF capitalism, its warfare state governs the world.

How many more surveillance stories do we need, how much more data and information, before we ask: what do we want to do with the Golem, if anything at all?

The central question that contributors to this volume were asked to address is '*what we did/didn't, should/could learn from activist/movement experiences of security operations, surveillance, infiltration*' and such activities.

Can we locate our individual, group and local experiences of security operations, surveillance and infiltration in relation to all of the above?

A NOTE ON BIBLIOGRAPHY

Form constrains substance. Academic disciplines discipline substantive arguments by imposing certain formats and conventions that I call the 'quote and cite' format. 'Quote and cite' formats either impel scholars to remain within a certain bandwidth of literature, or orient writings towards a particular discipline, or impede the development of holistic arguments within the shorter formats of articles and opt instead for book-length works. These formats become particularly problematic in social movement studies and activist scholarship, where a vast sea of undocumented experiences and insights must be crunched into a format designed primarily for natural sciences. Instead, I have adopted the essay format and provide a selected bibliography that has informed my arguments.

SELECTED BIBLIOGRAPHY

All URLs accessed in August 2018.

Abella, A. (2009). *Soldiers of Reason: The Rand Corporation and the rise of the American empire.* Boston, MA and New York: Mariner Books.

Ackerman, S., & Pilkington, E. (2015, 16 March). 'Obama's War on Whistleblowers Leaves Administration Insiders Unscathed', *Guardian.*

Accessed from www.theguardian.com/us-news/2015/mar/16/whistleblowers-double-standard-obama-david-petraeus-chelsea-manning

Ahmed, N. (2015, 4 October). 'Top 15 Intelligence Agencies with Biggest Budgets in the World', *insidermonkey.com.*

Ambinder, M., & Gardy, D. B. (2013). *Deep State: Inside the government secrecy industry.* Hoboken, NJ: John Wiley & Sons.

Bentham, J., & Beauchamp, P. (1995). *The Panopticon Writings.* London: Verso.

Brown, A. C. (1984). *The Last Hero: Wild Bill Donovan – The biography and political experience of Major General William J. Donovan, founder of the OSS and "Father" of the CIA, from his personal and secret papers and the diaries of Ruth Donovan.* New York: Vintage Books.

Budiansky, S. (2016). *Code Warriors: NSA's codebreakers and the secret intelligence war against the Soviet Union.* Knopf Doubleday Publishing Group.

Cadwalladr, C. (2017, 26 February). 'Robert Mercer: The big data billionaire waging war on mainstream media', *Guardian.* Accessed from www.theguardian.com/politics/2017/feb/26/robert-mercer-breitbart-war-on-media-steve-bannon-donald-trump-nigel-farage

—— (2017, 7 May). 'The Great British Brexit Robbery: How our democracy was hijacked', *Guardian.* Accessed from www.theguardian.com/technology/2017/may/07/the-great-british-brexit-robbery-hijacked-democracy

Care, A. (2018, 20 March). 'Scientist Caught up in Cambridge Analytica Data Scandal "Happy to Testify to the FBI"', *Cambridge News.* Accessed from www.cambridge-news.co.uk/news/cambridge-news/cambridge-analytica-gsr-alexsandr-kogan-14434862

Cecil, R. (1994). 'Five of Six at War: Section V of MI6', *Intelligence and National Security,* 9(2); 345–353.

Churchill, W., & Vander Wall, J. (1988). *Agents of Repression: The FBI's secret wars against the Black Panther Party and the American Indian Movement.* Cambridge, MA: South End Press.

—— (1990). *The Cointelpro Papers: Documents from the FBI's secret wars against domestic dissent.* Boston, MA: South End Press.

Cillers, J., & Mason, P. (eds) (1999). *Peace, Profit or Plunder? The privatisation of security in war-torn African societies.* South Africa: Institute for Security Studies.

Clark, L. (2016, 8 December). 'MI6 Boss Brands the IP Act a Vital Weapon in the Battle against the "Existential Threat" of the Web', *WIRED.* Accessed from www.wired.co.uk/article/mi6-speech-alex-younger-investigatory-powers-bill

Coppes, C. (2016, 11 September). 'Edward Snowden, Surveillance Deep State and Collapsing Order', newsletter. Accessed from www.chuckcoppes.com

Correspondent (2013, 26 June). 'UK Spy Agencies Get $154 Mn Bonus Amid Sweeping Cuts', *Russia Today.* Accessed from www.rt.com/news/uk-intelligence-spy-budget-increase-252/

Crum, W. L., Fennelly, J. F., & Seltzer, L. H. (1942). *Fiscal Planning for Total War.* New York: National Bureau of Economic Research.

D'Souza, R. (2010). 'When Unreason Masquerades as Reason: Can law regulate trade and networked communication ethically?' In G. Cheny, S. May and D.

Munshi (eds), *Handbook of Communication Ethics* (pp. 475–493). New York and Oxford: International Communication Association, Routledge/Lawrence Erlbaum.

—— (2013). 'Review Essay: Justice and Governance in Dystopia', *Journal of Critical Realism*, 12(4): 518–537.

Davies, G. A., & Johns, R. (2012). 'British Public Confidence in MI6 and Government Use of Intelligence: The effect on support for preventive military action', *Intelligence and National Security*, 27(5): 669–688.

Davies, N. (2008). *Flat Earth News: An award-winning reporter exposes falsehood, distortion and propaganda in the global media.* London: Chatto & Windus.

Davis, D. (1979 [1991]). *Katherine the Great: Katherine Graham and her Washington Post empire.* New York: Sheridan Square Press.

Department for Business, Innovation & Skills (2013, 14 January). 'UK "£600 Million Investment in Eight Great Technologies"', government press release. Accessed from www.gov.uk/government/news/600-million-investment-in-the-eight-great-technologies

Dorril, S. (2000). *MI6: Fifty Years of Special Operations.* London: Fourth Estate.

—— (2015). 'Russia Accuses Fleet Street Journalists and MI6 during the Cold War', *International Journal of Press/Politics*, 20(2): 204–227.

Doward, J., & Gibbs, A. (2017, 4 March). 'Did Cambridge Analytica Influence the Brexit Vote and the US Election?', *Guardian.* Accessed from www.theguardian.com/politics/2017/mar/04/nigel-oakes-cambridge-analytica-what-role-brexit-trump

Edgerton, D. (2005). *Warfare State: Britain, 1920–1970.* Cambridge: Cambridge University Press.

ESRC (Economic and Social Research Council). UK's research funding for Big Data projects – Phase 1, Phase 2, Phase 3 and related projects can be accessed from ESRC website using keyword search from https://esrc.ukri.org/search-results/?keywords=big+data&siteid=esrc

Evans, R., & Lewis, P. (2011, 14 February). 'Revealed: How energy firms spy on environmental activists', *Guardian.* Accessed from www.theguardian.com/environment/2011/feb/14/energy-firms-activists-intelligence-gathering

Foster, P., & Evans, M. (2017). 'Exclusive: How a tiny Canadian IT company helped win the Brexit vote for Leave', *Telegraph.* Accessed from www.telegraph.co.uk/news/2017/02/24/exclusive-tiny-canadian-company-helped-swing-brexit-vote-leave/

Gardner, F. (2015, 9 July). 'Budget 2015: What is the new Joint Security Fund?', *BBC News.* Accessed from www.bbc.com/news/uk-33469450

Ghosal, D. (2018). 'Mapped: The breathtaking global reach of Cambridge Analytica's parent company', *Quartz.* Accessed from https://qz.com/1239762/cambridge-analytica-scandal-all-the-countries-where-scl-elections-claims-to-have-worked/

Glick, B. (1989). *War at Home: Covert action against U.S. activists and what we can do about it.* Cambridge, MA: South End Press.

Goldman, Z. K., & Rascoff, S. J. (eds) (2016). *Global Intelligence Oversight: Governing security in the twenty-first century.* Oxford: Oxford University Press.

Gray, F. (2018). 'Revealed: Cambridge Analytica and the Passport King', *Spectator.* Accessed from https://usa.spectator.co.uk/category/columnists/freddy-gray/

Hanley & Partners (n.d.). Accessed from https://www.henleyglobal.com/about-the-firm/

Hobbes, T. (1998). *Leviathan.* J. C. A. Gaskin (ed.) Oxford: Oxford University Press, 1998.

Holden, P. (2016). *Indefensible: Seven myths that sustain the global arms trade.* London: Zed Books.

Issenberg, S. (2012). 'How Obama's Team Used Big Data to Rally Voters', *MIT Technology Review.* Accessed from www.technologyreview.com/s/509026/how-obamas-team-used-big-data-to-rally-voters/

Kiyani, A. (2016). 'Group-Based Differentiation and Local Repression: The custom and curse of selectivity', *Journal of International Criminal Justice,* 14(4): 939–957.

Koistinen, P. A. C. (1980). *The Military-Industrial Complex: A historical perspective.* New York: Praeger Publishers.

Kone, A. M. (2013). 'The Military-Industrial Complex in the United States: Evolution and expansion from World War II to the War on Terror', *Inquiries,* 5(8): 1/1. Accessed from www.inquiriesjournal.com/articles/749/the-military-industrial-complex-in-the-united-states-evolution-and-expansion-from-world-war-ii-to-the-war-on-terror

Lashmar, P. (2013). 'Urinal or Conduit? Institutional information flow between the UK intelligence services and the news media', *Journalism,* 14(8): 1024–1040.

Lehrman, Y. (2010). 'The Weakest Link: The risks associated with social networking websites', *Journal of Strategic Security,* 3(2): 63–72.

Leigh, D., & Harding, L. (2011). *Wikileaks: Inside Julian Assange's secrecy.* London: Guardian Books.

Lenin, V. I. (1993, 1999). *State and Revolution.* Progress Publishers, Lenin Internet Archive. Accessed from marxists.org

Lofgren, M. (2016). *The Deep State: The fall of the Constitution and the rise of a shadow government.* New York: Viking.

Lucas, S., & Morey, A. (2000). 'The Hidden "Alliance": The CIA and MI6 before and after Suez', *Intelligence and National Security,* 15(2): 95–120.

Lyon, D. (2010). 'Liquid Surveillance: The contribution of Zygmunt Bauman to surveillance studies', *International Political Sociology,* 4: 325–338.

Macklin, G. D. (2006). 'Major Hugh Pollard, MI6, and the Spanish Civil War', *The Historical Journal,* 49(1): 277–280.

Martin, P. (2018). 'The CIA Democrats: Part One', *World Socialist Web Site,* published by the International Committee of the Fourth International. Accessed from www.wsws.org/en/articles/2018/03/07/dems-m07.html

—— (2018). 'The CIA Democrats: Part Two', *World Socialist Web Site,* published by the International Committee of the Fourth International. Accessed from www.wsws.org/en/articles/2018/03/08/dems-m08.html

—— (2018). 'The CIA Democrats: Part Three', *World Socialist Web Site*, published by the International Committee of the Fourth International. Accessed from www.wsws.org/en/articles/2018/03/09/dems-m09.html

McLauchlan, G. (1997). 'World War I and the Transformation of the U.S. State: The wartime foundations of U.S. hegemony', *Sociological Inquiry*, 67(1): 1–26.

Morgan, R. (2016). 'Oversight through Five Eyes: Institutional convergence and the structure and oversight of intelligence activities'. In Z. K. Goldman and S. J. Rascoff (eds), *Global Intelligence Oversight: Governing security in the twenty-first century* (pp. 37–70). Oxford: Oxford University Press.

Noyes, K. (2014, 13 June). 'These Big Data Companies Are Ones to Watch', *Fortune Magazine*. Accessed from http://fortune.com/2014/06/13/these-big-data-companies-are-ones-to-watch/

Pinola, M. (2013). 'The Top 50 Companies That Mine and Sell Your Data (and How to Opt Out)', *Lifehacker*. Accessed from https://lifehacker.com/the-top-50-companies-that-mine-and-sell-your-data-and-1482645222

Poulantzas, N. (1970 [1979]). *Fascism and Dictatorship: The Third International and the problem of fascism*. London: Verso.

Price, D. (2007). 'Buying a Piece of Anthropology: The CIA and our tortured past', *Anthropology Today*, 23(5): 17–22.

Priest, D., & Arkin, M. W. (2010, 19 July). 'Top Secret America: A hidden world, growing beyond control', *Washington Post*. Accessed from http://secure.afa.org/edOp/2010/Washington_Post_Intelligence_Series.pdf

Punit, I. S. (2014). 'Cambridge Analytica's Parent Firm Proposed a Massive Political Machine for India's 2014 Elections', *Quartz*. Accessed from https://qz.com/1239561/cambridge-analyticas-parent-firm-proposed-a-massive-political-machine-for-indias-2014-elections/

Ronson, J. (2001). *Them: Adventures with extremists*. London: Picador Classic.

Rosenbach, E., & Peritz, A. J. (2009). *Confrontation or Collaboration? Congress and the intelligence community*. Cambridge, MA: Harvard Kennedy School; Belfer Center for Science and International Affairs.

Rufford, N. (2003, 28 December). 'Revealed: How MI6 sold the Iraq War', *Sunday Times*. Accessed from www.thetimes.co.uk/article/revealed-how-mi6-sold-the-iraq-war-r5xpjg5d99x

Ogundipe, S. (2018, 3 May). 'SCL Elections, Cambridge Analytica Shut Down after Facebook Scandal', *Premium Times*. Accessed from www.premiumtimesng.com/news/headlines/267005-scl-elections-cambridge-analytica-shut-down-after-facebook-scandal.html

Sandia National Laboratories. Accessed from www.sandia.gov/about/history/index.html

Scahill, J. (2007 [2008]). *Blackwater: The rise of the world's most powerful mercenary army*. London: Serpent's Tail.

Shorrock, T. (2013, 16 March). 'Obama's Crackdown on Whistleblowers: The NSA Four reveal how a toxic mix of cronyism and fraud blinded the agency before 9/11', *The Nation*. Accessed from www.thenation.com/article/obamas-crackdown-whistleblowers/

Silverstein, K. (2000). *Private Warriors*. New York and London: Verso.

Stop Data Mining Me (website) (2018). Accessed from www.stopdatamining.me/

Talbot, D. (2015). *The Devil's Chessboard: Allen Dulles, the CIA and the rise of America's secret government*. New York: Harper Collins.

The Real News (2017, 23 December). 'Five Corporations Hire Two Intelligence Firms to Spy on Activists' *The Real News Network*. Accessed from https://therealnews.com/stories/five-corporations-hire-two-intelligence-firms-to-spy-on-activists

Thomas, J. (2018, 18 March). 'How a Cambridge Academic Became Embroiled in a Huge Facebook Data Scandal', *Cambridge News*. Accessed from www.cambridge-news.co.uk/news/cambridge-news/cambridge-analytica-aleksandr-kogan-facebook-14428339

Thompson, I. (2018, 20 March). 'Is Alexander Nix an Evil Genius or an Idiot?', *Vanity Fair*. Accessed from www.vanityfair.com/news/2018/03/alexander-nix-suspended-cambridge-analytica

Waddell, B. (1994). 'Economic Mobilization for World War II and the Transformation of the U.S. State', *Politics & Society*, 22(2): 165–194.

—— (1999). 'Corporate Influence and World War II: Resolving the New Deal political stalemate', *Journal of Policy History*, 11(3): 223–256.

—— (2001) 'Limiting National Interventionism in the United States: The warfare-welfare state as restrictive governance paradigm', *Capital & Class*, 74: 109–139.

—— (2012). 'When the Past Is Not Prologue: The Wagner Act debates and the limits of American political science', *New Political Science*, 34(3): 338–357.

Walpole, J. (2013, 17 December). 'Top 10 Companies That Mine and Sell Your Data: Opt out now', *The American Genius*. Accessed from https://theamericangenius.com/tech-news/top-10-companies-mine-sell-data/

Warner, M., & McDonald, J. K. (2005). *US Intelligence Community Reform Studies since 1947*. Washington, DC: Centre for the Study of Intelligence.

Whitman, J. Q. (1991). 'Of Corporatism, Fascism, and the First New Deal', *American Journal of Comparative Law*, 39(4): 747–778.

Wiener, N. (1964). *God and Golem, Inc.: A comment on certain points where cybernetics impinges on religion*. Cambridge, MA: The MIT Press.

Woodward, R. (2005). 'From Military Geography to Militarism's Geographies: Disciplinary engagements with the geographies of militarism and military activities', *Progress in Human Geography*, 29(6): 718–740.

Younger, A. (2016, 8 December). 'Full Text of Speech by the Head of MI6 "Remarks by the Chief of the Secret Intelligence Service"', *Scribd*. Accessed from www.scribd.com/document/333638719/MI6-Chief-Alex-Younger-full-speech

3

Activist learning and state dataveillance

Lessons from the UK, Mauritius and South Africa

Jane Duncan

In 2013, Edward Snowden leaked documents that revealed that the National Security Agency (NSA) – the United States (US) government agency responsible for signals intelligence – had abused its mass communication surveillance capabilities to spy on millions of people, even if they were not suspected of any crimes. Despite the global outrage at these revelations, and the massive privacy invasions they revealed, privacy and anti-surveillance activists have not achieved many gains in limiting the uses of communication surveillance to that which is reasonably necessary. While the US government has been forced to roll back its bulk collection of telephone records to appease public outrage, other mass surveillance programmes continue unabated. Many other governments are seeking to maintain or even expand their mass surveillance capabilities (Privacy International, 2015). In 2016, the United Kingdom (UK) government passed an extremely invasive surveillance law, the Investigatory Powers Act, despite domestic opposition, and which is likely to set a negative precedent for surveillance laws elsewhere. Furthermore, other data-intensive forms of surveillance, such as biometrically based identification systems and 'smart' CCTV, continue to spread faster than the policies designed to regulate their privacy impacts.

Why has the massive outrage at Snowden's revelations not translated into effective activism that curbs unaccountable, unjustified mass state surveillance? This chapter seeks to answer this question. Using in-depth interviews with key protagonists, it seeks to identify the factors that give rise to effective activism, by drawing comparatively on the learning experiences of anti-surveillance activists in the UK, Mauritius and South Africa. The UK faces serious terrorism threats; consequently, it is a major surveillance power in that its surveillance equipment is exported around the world and it also places other countries under surveillance. Yet, struggles to rein in mass surveillance in the UK have not been very successful, with major global consequences. South Africa is a mid-level power that faces no significant national security threats, and consequently its justifications for engaging in surveillance are weaker than those of the UK. Yet its surveillance powers are extensive, although it offers some interesting examples of activist experiences with reining in state security powers. Mauritius is a tiny island nation with little geo-strategic importance for the major global powers and faces no real national security threats; yet, it too engages in mass surveillance of its citizenry. But it also has a rich history of political activism, and at least one struggle against state surveillance has been relatively successful.

THE PROBLEM

In order to understand why data-driven mass surveillance (or what Roger Clarke has called 'dataveillance' (1988, pp. 498–499), has become so intractable, it is necessary to identify the main factors behind its growth. Smarting from some of the most recent significant intelligence failures of recent history, intelligence agencies have sought ways of improving their intelligence-gathering and analysis capabilities. However, of all these forms of intelligence, and originally of military origins, signals intelligence, drawn from data-intense 'smart' surveillance technologies such as Closed Circuit Television (CCTV), Unmanned Assistance Vehicles (or 'drones'), communication networks and a range of other data-driven devices, have come to play an increasingly important role in intelligence gathering. This form of surveillance has become more possible as there are more datasets than ever before to store and analyse. In fact, state and consumer surveillance programmes have converged to the point where it has become difficult to separate them. The state relies on private security companies to store huge datasets in the 'cloud', while the private sector depends on ever-expanding surveillance programmes for their profits. Mass state surveillance could not function without outsourcing some of the collection and analysis to private companies, as states typically do not have the capacity to maintain such large datasets: PRISM, one of the mass surveillance programmes about which Snowden leaked documents, revealed the extent to which the NSA was reliant on the datasets of private communication providers for its surveillance activities. State intelligence has also been used to advance countries' commercial interests, especially for imperial powers that risk losing their dominance in global affairs (Price, 2014; McCoy, 2014). Thus it has become increasingly commonplace to see economic intelligence being included in the ambit of national security, and consequently for intelligence agencies to gather intelligence on economic threats to domestic companies operating abroad. In any event, intelligence has been linked intimately to the expansion of empire. In the case of South Africa before apartheid, for instance, the British government prevented the South African government of the day from establishing its own separate intelligence agency, to weaken its ability to operate independently from its colonial masters. Only in the 1960s did the apartheid government develop its own intelligence-gathering capabilities, under the watchful eye of the British (O'Brien, 2011, pp. 16–72).

Data-driven forms of intelligence gathering reduce state intelligence agencies' need to rely on costly, risky human intelligence. Automated analysis of data networks using selectors (or keywords used to search communication networks) is also meant to introduce an element of objectivity to intelligence work, as machines select the communications to be examined rather than humans (Ten Human Rights Organisations, 2015, pp. 17–18). Dataveillance, on the other hand, provides governments with a politically low-cost form of social control, as abuses are very difficult to detect, whereas when intelligence agencies engage in physical surveillance, their operations can always be uncovered and exposed (Bellamy Foster & McChesney, 2014). Surveillance can provide governments with a powerful tool of social control. They can use surveillance, or the threat of surveillance, to create fear that organised violence will be used against perceived opponents. Fear of being watched may also force people to self-police their own behaviour, as theorised by Foucault in his appropriation of Bentham's panopticon (Foucault, 1979, pp. 200–216). The 2008 global recession has also increased neoliberal precarity and expanded the number of surplus populations. Yet, at the same time, global resistance to neoliberal austerity has increased. As a result, the system has required more expansive, sophisticated forms of social control, and data-driven surveillance tools have enormous utility in this regard (Cox, 2013; Fernandez, 2010; Cox & Nilsen, 2014; Bellamy Foster & McChesney, 2014).

Biometrics, consisting of the digital impressions of physical characteristics such as fingerprints, irises, or voices for the purposes of identification, is a supposedly secure method of identifying people. Consequently, it is being used in a range of civil or state security functions. Computerisation has allowed state agencies to store and process huge amounts of biometric data, which has seen their uses spreading. Data-driven biometric systems enable state surveillance in very powerful ways, providing the state with some of the most intimate details about a person to monitor them and track their movements (Breckenridge, 2014, p. 12; Donovan, 2015, pp. 815–833). However, the fact that physical characteristics are used for identity management at all trigger privacy concerns, in that some of the most personal features of an individual – namely their body parts – are being collected and stored by the state for identification purposes, which interferes with a person's bodily autonomy as an aspect of privacy. Furthermore, biometrics are not fool-proof when it comes to individual identification, as they suffer from controversially high margins of error and can be replicated (or 'spoofed') to fool biometric readers (Tillmann, 2009).

However, intelligence agencies are not all-powerful and may become embroiled in damaging scandals if they are caught engaging in unwarranted political surveillance. In this regard, intelligence history is replete with examples of domestic counter-intelligence measures being used, under the political direction of government officials, to track the activities of social and political movements that are considered threatening to hegemonic interests, even if they are engaging in legitimate activism that does not involve any discernible threat to national security. These practices have cast a pall on the supposed political neutrality of state surveillance practices and the uses to which they are put (Fernandez, 2010; Duncan, 2014). These cases point to a broader truth about surveillance – namely that it is not being used simply to fight crime and terrorism, but to stabilise social relations more broadly by collecting information on those who may expose or challenge how society is currently organised. What marks the contemporary period out from previous periods, though, is the sheer number of information sources available to the agencies, as communication has become digitised. More services have become linked to the Internet, leading more people to generate vast amounts of data about activities as diverse as their travel habits and electricity usage. Following the September 11, 2001 attacks some countries used the heightened global security measures, as well as the growing number of new data sources held by public and private institutions, to place political activists under surveillance, although the expansion of security powers was under way even before then. For instance, New Zealand's definition of national security was stretched to include the country's economic and international well-being as far back as 1996 (Gill & Phythian, 2012, p. 24; Choudry, 2005). South Africa followed suit in 2003 (Africa, 2012, p. 117).

Activists who resist unaccountable and unjustifiable dataveillance are faced with major challenges. The lack of visible victims of surveillance makes it a much more difficult problem to raise public consciousness about, and consequently to organise around. An additional problem is that the state has sold surveillance as a necessary evil to counter criminal activities, and threats to national security, especially those posed by terrorists. Consequently, there is a very real danger that citizens can fall victim to what Lina Dencik and Jonathan Cable have called 'surveillance realism', where they become resigned to pervasive surveillance as a necessary trade-off in return for greater security (Dencik & Cable, 2017, pp. 763–781).

ANTI-SURVEILLANCE CONCEPTS AND ACTORS

In order not to fall victim to 'surveillance realism', it is important to see the problem in an empowering way. However the conceptualisation of these struggles in liberal democratic terms has individualised the problem as a struggle for privacy and autonomy of the individual. Seeing the problem in this way fails to address the question of why surveillance has become so important to social control, who is likely to be most affected by the problem, and consequently, which social forces are more likely to challenge these practices successfully.

Dominant 'common-sense' conceptions of privacy have been heavily influenced by Samuel D. Warren and Louis Brandeis's understanding of privacy as the right to be left alone (Bennett, 2011, pp. 487–488). Other definitions have emphasised the control that individuals can exercise over their own information and the right to enjoy solitude, intimacy, anonymity and reserve (Westin, 1970, p. 7). The danger of an individualised approach to privacy is that when it comes up against a collective right – such as the right to protect a country's national security from threats – then almost inevitably, the individual right will give way to the collective right. Consequently, individualised conceptions of privacy provide poor protection against state attempts to expand surveillance powers on national security grounds (Cate, 2006, pp. 341–378).

In order to address these deficiencies in how privacy has been understood and protected, some scholars have attempted to develop the social and collective content of the right to privacy. They have argued that not only are privacy protections necessary for guaranteeing individual autonomy, but democracy itself could not function without these protections. People would find it difficult to associate with one another openly, which could hamper their ability to organise and engage in collective action. These arguments are meant to give privacy more gravity, hopefully with a view of making governments and courts think twice about dismissing the right as being unimportant relative to other pressing societal interests (Steeves, 2009, p. 203; Bennett, 2011, pp. 487–488). As valuable as efforts to develop a sociality of privacy are, they do not necessarily address why privacy is under such attack and consequently, they have little to say about how this problem should be addressed. In other words, they lack a political perspective on the problem and are often silent on the social justice aspects of privacy (Lyon, 2015, p. 79). Doing so would require linking privacy to broader issues of social and commercial control (Fuchs, 2011, pp. 220–237; Giroux, 2015, pp. 108–140).

At the same time, the 'datafication' of more areas of life has opened up vast new sources of information for state and private surveillance actors. Vast datasets can be linked together and used to build up a profile of a person's travel and reading habits, interests, activities and networks. While undoubtedly, the ability to profile people is of huge value in organised crime and terrorism investigations, this ability can also be misused to identify, track and crack down on political dissidents (Silitski, 2006, p. 6). The fact that people may participate in their own commodification and even repression through the oversharing of massive amounts of data is a cultural phenomenon that still needs to be understood more fully (Lyon, 2015, p. 16).

If privacy is to remain a touchstone concept for anti-surveillance struggles, then it needs to emphasise those violations that affect the overwhelmingly working-class base of society rather than its more elite members. Furthermore, it needs to do so by re-conceptualising it as the right to resist surveillance by dominant groups, push back against the tendencies of these groups to hide their abuses, and strengthen the abilities of subaltern groups for collective action (Fuchs, 2011, pp. 220–237). Rights-based discourse is also unlikely to address fundamental questions of how power is organised in society, as it tends to focus on individuals claiming their rights, while remaining silent on the conditions that are needed for those rights to be socialised. As a result, privacy activists must defend individuals against invasions of their privacy, while creating the conditions for the most dispossessed in society to enjoy this right, which would mean addressing the highly unequal social relations that allow the few to enjoy privacy at the expense of the many.

What also does not help matters is that much of the theorisation of surveillance – which often uses Bentham's 'panopticon' as a touchstone concept – tends to have a paralysing effect, in that it sees surveillance as being everywhere and nowhere. In order to bring agency back into the picture, it is useful to draw on Cox and Nilsen's (2014) conceptualisation of the state as 'a movement from above', consisting of individuals who can be challenged, rather than a faceless structure that cannot be changed through activist agency. Resistance must address the wider context in which the surveillance state is expanding, which is the growth in the exercise of arbitrary power, particularly after the 2008 global financial crisis when resistance to austerity measures spread across the globe, leading to non-conventional actors taking to the streets, actors of whom states had very little knowledge or understanding of, which prompted an expansion in surveillance capabilities. This growth requires an organised political response that links resistance to surveillance to resistance to capitalism. Resistance actors should also seek to sharpen contradictions between the various actors undertaking surveillance; for instance, between state surveillance agencies and private communication service providers, as the latter have become concerned about losing profits as their users withdraw from electronic communication networks out of fear of surveillance.

Apart from analysing the concepts used by anti-surveillance activists, the actors themselves also need to be analysed. Which social forces are most likely to change how society is organised, including the fact that it is premised increasingly on systematic violations of privacy? However, much of the organised resistance to widespread surveillance has been led by non-governmental organisations (NGOs) that have expertise in how information and communication technologies impact on rights such as privacy and freedom of expression, rather than mass movements, in spite of the fact that historically mass movements have often been subjected to surveillance, even in countries that consider themselves democracies. As important as they are, anti-surveillance struggles led by NGOs risk depoliticising the problem, by reducing it to a rights-based struggle for civil rights, such as the right to privacy. They are also unlikely to command the kind of social power exercised by mass movements, and consequently they are unlikely to enjoy the traction needed to ensure that their arguments and ideas are taken seriously.

ANTI-SURVEILLANCE STRUGGLES IN THE UK

Anti-surveillance activists have, without doubt, won some significant gains. In the UK, from 2004 a single-issue campaign against state control of personal identity, called No2ID, successfully opposed the government's attempt to introduce biometric identity cards and a centralised identity database. They warned against the dangers of what they called the 'database state' (or a state that relies increasingly on the storage and analysis of massive databases of information, or 'big data'), which they claimed operationalised the government's wish to manage society by keeping a constant check on its citizens. The government eventually scrapped the plans in 2010 and repealed its enabling statute the year after (Wills, 2013, pp. 163–179; Electronic Frontier Foundation, n.d). Privacy International's director Gus Hosein was involved in the UK campaign against the ID card, and so could reflect on his learning from that experience. Speaking in his individual capacity, he argued that the government faced a perfect storm of factors in responding to the controversy, and these factors made for a successful campaign. The public and media discourse was cynical about the government's claim that an ID card system would help fight terrorism and other serious crimes, as suspicious individuals could be identified more seriously, and not even the 2005 terrorist attacks on the London underground rail system (the '7/7' attacks) swayed public opinion to accept the measure. According to Hosein:

> The beauty of British political activism is different from the beauty of British civil society. With British political activism, a bunch of people came together and started campaigning, they can organise a million signature campaign on an issue. Even though they may have no media training, they can organise in response to media calls. Before you know it, thousands of people get in touch with their MPs [Members of Parliament] and say, 'but I read about it in the newspaper'. That kind of activism is so dynamic in this country. A professional NGO on the other hand could sit down with an MP and the MP would say 'I have no interest in what you're saying as you have no constituents.' And that NGO cannot get constituents, but that naturally emerging activism, constituents contacting MPs, it's the tabloid media raising the issue, that's how the whole thing starts to fall apart.[1]

However, a mere six years later, the political climate had shifted fundamentally, and the tradition of activism referred to by Hosein had all but disappeared from anti-surveillance work, which became driven by specialist NGOs. Despite the widespread public outrage about the expansiveness of the programmes as exposed by Snowden, and the ongoing controversies about the effectiveness of mass surveillance relative to more traditional intelligence efforts, the UK government responded by not only defending its existing bulk powers, but also seeking new powers through a controversial new Investigatory Powers Bill, which was passed into law in the dying days of 2016. The Act gives the UK's intelligence and police agencies sweeping powers to spy on the communications of its and other countries' citizens on vague grounds, and with inadequate oversight. It has written unprecedented new mass surveillance powers into law, such as bulk hacking. It also required communication service providers to cooperate with the authorities if required to do so, by providing access to their datasets. When the Act was still a Bill, Home Secretary Theresa May boasted that it would set the 'gold standard' for government spying around the world (Don't Spy on Us, 2016). On the other hand, the Scottish National Party's spokesperson Joanna Cherry refuted May's argument, pointing out that the Bill could set a dangerous precedent and a bad example internationally (Mason & Trevis, 2016).

If the Bill was so controversial, then why were anti-surveillance activists so unsuccessful in preventing it from being amended before it was promulgated into law? When they conducted a survey of the level of knowledge in the UK about the Investigatory Powers Act, the UK-based human rights NGO Liberty found that nearly three-quarters of British adults knew nothing about the Act, or had not heard of it. This lack of knowledge about the Act suggested that anti-surveillance campaigners did not take public awareness-raising seriously enough, which was a perhaps unsurprising outcome of the preferred campaign strategy. According to Dencik and Cable, campaigners focused their efforts on specialist NGOs and other 'expert communities' working on privacy and data protection issues. In doing so, they failed to involve social movements that focused on a range of social justice issues, even if they themselves had direct experiences of being spied on (such as the environmental movement). As a result, these movements felt alienated from the campaign and deferred to the expert communities that emphasised individualised rather than social or collective conceptions of privacy (Dencik & Cable, 2017, p. 776). Such conceptions would focus on the right of social and subaltern movements to resist surveillance by dominant groups, as well as their right to prevent these groups from using secrecy to prevent scrutiny of income differentials, or tax evasion, for instance (Fuchs, 2011, pp. 220–237).

Campaigners also faced an uphill battle in convincing the mainstream press to question the Bill, and most of the outrage was confined to the liberal-left newspaper the *Guardian*, that had carried the Snowden revelations in the UK. The Liberal Democratic Party, which usually adopted a libertarian approach to surveillance, was decimated at the polls in 2015, and the Labour Party bought into and reproduced dominant security discourses uncritically. In fact, the failure of Labour to present practical alternative strategies to heightened surveillance was a key reason why the campaign failed; activists failed to engage with their MPs, and convince them of the dangers. This meant that potential allies who could have been convinced to side with anti-surveillance activists, including in Parliament, were not engaged. As a result, mainstream public discourse was largely pro-surveillance and dominated by politicians: a discourse cemented by the wave of terrorist attacks in Europe as the Bill was being considered.[2] So, ironically, in spite of the uptick in anti-surveillance activism in the wake of the Snowden revelations, campaigners failed to win significant gains. Commenting on this anomaly, Hosein said:

> We have to own some of the failure [around the Investigatory Powers Act], which is [that] we made this entirely about intelligence agencies, we made this all about mass surveillance, we didn't articulate a positive framing of the issue, we didn't get into the *Telegraph* or *The Times* or the *Daily Mail* …
>
> It's not easy to frame it [the Bill] positively. There were powers in there that you wouldn't want any government having, apart from your own. For example we can frame the struggle as being one for secure devices, not just that government is trying to stop bad people. [We needed to say,] you are going to be affected by this in the following ways. [In the campaign] we didn't relate to the British lived experience. Privacy advocates and technology rights advocates in the old days were accustomed to not having any friends, so we worked really hard to get the message across. But now tech issues have become cool, we have our own media for crying out loud, we have our circuits, and we intermingle with each other. There isn't the same sense of need to reach out. There's a comfort in our world-view, a liberal NGO club that doesn't attempt to get into the right-wing media.[3]

Given the narrow framing of the issues around the Bill, it was small wonder that the public became resigned to security discourses as an inevitable feature of a landscape where terrorist threats were real and present. As a result, there was no significant mass opposition to the Bill (Hintz & Dencik, 2016). This analysis suggests that anti-surveillance campaigns that are driven by specialists, and that eschew, or do not pay sufficient attention to, building effective mass opposition by relating anti-surveillance work to popular issues and mass struggles, are more likely to fail.

STRUGGLES AGAINST THE BIOMETRIC ID CARD IN MAURITIUS

It could be assumed that the state's security apparatus (especially its national security apparatus) is extremely difficult to challenge, owing to the information asymmetries between this part of the state and citizens. Furthermore, it could be dangerous and even life-threatening to challenge the coercive capacities of the state (including its surveillance capacities) as activists risk being branded as national security threats. However, there are positive examples where activists have learned how to extract accountability for invasive state surveillance practices. For instance, in 2013, the Mauritian government introduced a Mauritius National Identity Scheme 'smart' ID card, similar to the one the UK government envisaged before it abandoned its plans. The biometric information stored on the card was then verified against information contained in a centralised national population register. Every citizen over the age of 18 had a duty to register, and were guilty of a criminal offence if they refused (Ministry of Technology, Communication and Information, 2017, pp. 1–2). The government argued that the cards would be secure, as their fingerprints and other personal details were stored in a contactless microchip that was difficult to tamper with. These advanced security measures, it argued, would help the government stamp out identity fraud and theft (Bignaux, 2013).

While on the surface of things, this initiative sounded laudable, Mauritians rose up and opposed the ID card, claiming that it threatened privacy and even democracy itself. The government's plans were particularly draconian, though, as they required residents to carry their identity cards at all times. What gave the campaign such traction was the history of colonialism, slavery and indentured labour in Mauritius. The island nation was colonised by the British, French and Dutch at different stages in its history. The Dutch introduced slavery to Mauritius, which was subsequently replaced by indentured labour in the nineteenth century, when Indians were sent to work on the sugar plantations as a form of debt bondage (Peerthum, 2012). Indentured labourers were required to carry identity cards at all times, which created widespread resentment against mandatory identification systems. This history meant that many Mauritians' ancestors had lived experiences of population registration being abused for social control purposes, and the smart ID card system therefore reminded them of this hated history, and created the basis for a mass consciousness about its dangers.

The campaign formulated several demands, including one that the government should destroy the biometric database and stop the ID card from being mandatory. A popular campaign slogan, 'It's part of you', made citizens aware of their right to exercise control over their biometrics, as this data was tied intimately to their personhood. Campaigners relied on national radio to spread the message, which proved to be hugely popular as a consciousness-raising tool, and they organised a front with trade unions in the country. Activists who were entirely new to issues relating to biometrics and data protection began to study the issues and they transmitted their learnings through the front. They also produced their own posters and leaflets, organised petitions with other organisations and conducted door-to-door visits and teach-ins. Campaigners used village councils to conduct public education on the dangers of the system, although many of these councils ended up complying. In the campaign, activists made links between workers' rights and the state's surveillance efforts, including through the ID card system.[4] In the process of doing so, they turned what could otherwise have been an issue dominated by the technical part of society into a mass issue that focused on the repressive framework underpinning the system.

In addition to engaging in popular education, the campaign engaged in direct action. In an attempt to frustrate the process of converting their identity cards to the new 'smart' system, campaigners organised 'go-slows' at the ID conversion centres, where citizens were required to convert their old identity documents to the new 'smart' version. Citizens were encouraged to go to the centres and slow down the process deliberately, and workers at the centres were encouraged to do the same. Another form of passive resistance was to go to the conversion centre to obtain their identity document, but refuse to register their fingerprints.[5] These efforts fostered a popular consciousness about the dangers of biometric technologies, which spread beyond the ID card. Workers began to refuse to provide fingerprints for registration purposes at their workplaces, and started criticising cameras on buses as violations of their privacy. However, people continued to register in their numbers, not because of an inherent faith in the technology, but because they feared a prison sentence or a large fine if they did not comply.

In spite of the state's gains in coercing many citizens to enrol, the campaign could not be ignored, especially by those in the parliamentary opposition. Senior members of the opposition were brought over to the side of the campaign, and supported its objectives. Three court cases were brought against the system on constitutional grounds (such as the right to privacy), including by the ex-vice prime minister and the ex-minister of justice. One of these cases resulted in the Supreme Court declaring that while the taking and recording of a citizen's fingerprints was permissible on public order grounds, the storage and retention of this information in a centralised database of citizens' biometrics was unlawful. As a result of this judgment, the government destroyed the database, and converted the biometric system from a one-to-many system, requiring the verification of a person within an entire population, to a one-to-one system, where a person's identity was confirmed through a comparison of their biometric data with previously registered data. However, the government continued with the mandatory enrolment of citizens and the requirement to present proof of identity to the police on demand, which meant that in spite of this limited victory, the campaign continued (Lalit Du Klas, 2017).

One of the key protagonists in the struggle against the ID card system was a socialist organisation called Lalit Du Klas, which was critical of a strategy that relied overwhelmingly on a legalistic approach. Lalit grew out of mass workers' movements in Mauritius. These movements remain central to many struggles in the country, including against the ID card. This has infused the struggle with a mass participants' character, a political understanding of surveillance as a form of social control and a healthy scepticism about rights-based approaches to fighting surveillance, whose endpoint is the defence of a right such as privacy without aspiring to change the character of society. As Lalit Du Klas activist Rajni Lallah has argued:

> Constitutional challenges, without strong political movements behind them, are blunt tools for getting the state to respect peoples' freedom from state control. Naturally, this is so, because the judiciary is part of the state. In fact, because of the shortcoming in legal challenges, in many countries those opposing similar biometric ID cards have chosen to rely on political mobilisation instead of the courts. In the UK, US and Australia, victories were won without recourse to the courts, and in these countries there are still no compulsory ID cards acting like a kind of 'pass law'. And in the case of Australia, those spearheading the struggle used mobilisation to show up the need for better legal protection for privacy from state and private firm surveillance.[6]

The conditions for the generalisation of anti-surveillance demands are likely to continue in Mauritius, and even intensify in the years to come. The country is highly dependent on the sugar industry, and the downturn in the industry is placing pressure on working conditions. As a result, the country's working class remains highly mobilised, which makes it more likely that anti-surveillance campaigns will continue to have a mass character.

ANTI-SURVEILLANCE STRUGGLES IN SOUTH AFRICA

UK activist experiences highlighted the strengths and weaknesses of a single-issue campaign: namely the ability to focus consistently on a technically complex issue. But this strength can also be a weakness, in that wily governments are more able to marginalise these campaigns if they do not enjoy significant social power. The Mauritian experience attests to the strengths of approaching anti-surveillance work by integrating it into the work of existing mass organisations, rather than concentrating campaign efforts on creating new specialist single-issue organisations. One option of drawing on the strengths of single-issue campaigns, while limiting their weaknesses, is to adopt a 'movement-of-movements' approach, where coalitions are formed between mass movements and NGOs on specific issues. For these campaign coalitions to be successful, though, they would need to accept the realities of working-class leadership, and consciously steer away from NGO dominance. Rather, NGOs need to play a support role, providing technical expertise to the campaign without dominating it. Campaigns involving coalitions of movements and NGOs working on issues of mutual interest are fraught with difficulties, but if handled with maturity, they can achieve significant results.

A case in point is the Right 2 Know Campaign (R2K), a coalition of NGOs and movements established in 2011 in South Africa to campaign against a Protection of (State) Information Bill (euphemistically called the 'Secrecy Bill'), that threatened to give the state sweeping powers to classify information, thereby keeping the information out of the public domain. By campaigning systematically against the Bill, R2K and other civil society organisations managed to win significant concessions from Parliament which narrowed the scope of the Bill, but did not mitigate all its problems. Buoyed by these successes, R2K expanded into other areas, including surveillance. The links to the Secrecy Bill were not difficult to understand. Later iterations saw the Bill giving wide-ranging powers to classify information to the country's security services (referring mainly to the South African Police Service, the State Security Agency – the country's civilian intelligence agency – and the South African National Defence Force). At the same time, R2K and other organisations raised concerns about these services becoming central to the power base of the president, Jacob Zuma – a process that led to them popularising the term 'securitisation', and referring to the security services' leadership as 'securocrats' (McKinley, 2013). R2K expressed concern that the Secrecy Bill was an indicator of the increasing power of the securocrats in the everyday functioning of government and the state, leading to increasingly securitised 'solutions' to South Africa's myriad social problems (such as suppressing protests rather than addressing their underlying grievances). Once the Secrecy Bill was framed in this way, it was a short walk for R2K to begin campaigning against unaccountable state surveillance as a means of frustrating citizens' right to know.

Freedom of information could be considered an elitist issue, with little relevance to mass movements. As a result, it is tempting to limit campaigns for this right to niche NGOs. However, by the time the Secrecy Bill emerged, South African social movements and some NGOs had developed a great deal of experiential knowledge about how to 'mainstream' right-based work in mass movements. A case in point was freedom of expression. Up until the early 2000s, freedom of expression was typically the preserve of media freedom NGOs. However, the intensification of neoliberalism in the late 1990s generated a range of new social movements largely outside the control of the ruling alliance led by the African National Congress (ANC). Movements such as the Anti-Privatisation Forum (APF) and the Soweto Electricity Crisis Committee (SECC) emerged to campaign against water and electricity cut-offs and the commodification of basic services more generally (McKinley, 2013; Duncan, 2009, pp. 106–127).

As these movements' activism intensified, so did state surveillance and repression, which laid the basis for them to raise popular demands for freedom of expression. In the process, they re-orientated the right of freedom of expression away from being a media right and towards being a popular right, practised in more direct and unmediated ways, such as through staging protests and demonstrations, picketing and pamphleteering, and holding mass meetings. Progressive NGOs used a 'train the trainer' approach to undertake popular education in these movements and build their capacities to defend their rights themselves, rather than relying on the NGOs (Duncan, 2009, pp. 105–127). This pedagogic approach had a lasting impact on movements, in that while most of the movements that were established at this stage collapsed, activists took these learnings into other movements, including R2K, which made the popularisation of the right to information an easy process. It also meant that activists had a store of knowledge about the strengths and weaknesses of rights-based approaches, in that rights could be extremely useful in defensive struggles, but often had little conceptual traction in offensive struggles, which rather had to be conceptualised as struggles to change how power is organised in society.

In any event, it was not difficult to develop a popular basis for anti-surveillance work in South Africa, given its long and sorry history of abuses of the intelligence capacities of the state. On the government's own admission, the country faced no major terrorist threat. Nevertheless, it has mobilised the concept of 'national security' to criminalise the 'enemy within', namely an increasingly vocal layer of movements and organisations seeking to break politically with the increasingly unpopular ANC-led alliance, those who represent these movements legally, the academics who research movements, and investigative journalists. But activists did not buy these 'national security' scare tactics. South Africa's apartheid history means that older activists have historic memories of surveillance abuses, ideas of how to challenge them, and a healthy suspicion of state claims about the uses to which surveillance is being put (Duncan, 2014, p. 9). In other words, surveillance abuses, and broader abuses of the concept of national security to justify massive repression are still part of their lived experiences. These factors made the onset of 'surveillance realism' less likely in the country, and created the basis for intergenerational learning about state surveillance and its dangers. The older generation has been able to transpose learnings from the analogue environment under apartheid to a new post-apartheid digital environment, so much a part of the lives of the younger generation. In this environment, activists operated with a collective understanding of privacy, seeing its violation as an injury that hampered their ability to organise and engage in society, rather than their ability to withdraw from society:

> I think it's because the government is afraid that people can end up rising against them. So activists are an easy target because most of the protests here are coordinated by us. They want to know our friends, our thoughts and our plans.
>
> (Thembelihle Crisis Committee activist)

> They want to get into our heads. They think we are planning evil against them so they surveil our phones, social networks and emails. They are always building a case against us. Instead of seeing us as concerned citizens who want the best for our people, they think negatively about us. I think that's why we are on the firing line.
>
> (R2K Western Cape activist)[7]

While intelligence gathering focusing on political activists has been a practice dating back to colonialism and apartheid, in the post-apartheid period, it could be traced back to the 2000s, when social movements struggling for land and against the commodification of basic services were established. In 2005, members from the Vaal and Thembelihle affiliates of the APF informed the organisation's leadership that they had been approached by National Intelligence Agency (NIA, a predecessor of the SSA) operatives and offered money to be NIA informants about APF meetings and activities.[8] More recently, in the wake of the mining struggles in the platinum belt of South Africa, evidence emerged of state agencies and private security colluding to gather intelligence on political and trade union activists. These realities mean that surveillance, including new data-driven forms of surveillance, had the potential to become a mass issue, and consequently anti-surveillance demands will be more difficult to marginalise than in the UK.

Knowing that they are vulnerable, South African activists have resorted to individual and collective measures to protect their privacy. More activists are encrypting their communications, favouring face-to-face communications, switching phones off during public meetings (although state agencies can switch mobile phones on again if they have been infected with intrusion software), and prescreening Facebook friends and Twitter followers. Others update their anti-virus software constantly and avoid opening attachments unless they are absolutely sure that they are bona fide. However, these threats have eroded trust inside organisations, and bred a climate of suspicion: as one activist noted, 'the rule is trust no one.' Yet at the same time, activists make extra efforts to use tried and tested methods of mobilisation, rather than relying on social media, which lessens the possibility of them descending into 'slacktivism'. Ironically, the lack of Internet penetration in South Africa's poorer communities has been something of a boon for activists, as it has made their work more difficult to track, which is probably why physical surveillance techniques are still so prevalent. According to one activist:

> We use the word-of-mouth to spread the information in informal settlements. This is much better than using new media, which can be monitored, plus most of our members cannot afford them. We call for community meetings where we plan for demonstrations and marches.
>
> (Thembelihle Crisis Committee)[9]

The anti-surveillance campaign work of R2K and others is still yet to have a discernible impact on national policy, although it has taken up a national campaign against privacy-invading national policies and laws. But already it has turned what could otherwise be considered a fairly arcane issue about privacy into an issue of national concern that links to broader concerns about inequality and repression of the social forces that are fighting this scourge.

CONCLUSION

If anti-surveillance campaigners are going to be successful, they need to take people where they are found and relate the work to their everyday experiences and concerns. They need to use local knowledge to build understanding of the issues, and relate rights such as privacy to popular experiences of this right. Technical knowledge can be built in mass movements, if technically proficient NGOs have the humility to place those social forces that are most likely to change how power is organised in society at the centre of anti-surveillance work.

A political understanding of the problem of dataveillance, that moves beyond a rights-based approach, and recognises the root of the problem – which is the growth in the exercise of arbitrary state power as neoliberalism intensifies (Giroux, 2015, pp. 108–140) – is more likely to be both effective and sustainable. Intensified collaboration between state and private actors have also greatly increased the scope for surveillance practices. What is key, though, is an approach to anti-surveillance work that builds the capacity of mass movements to take on anti-surveillance campaigns themselves, rather than outsourcing the struggle to specialist NGOs. In fact, NGO employees need to make conscious efforts to work their way out of their jobs. Once these learnings are incorporated into anti-surveillance work, then activists may start to enjoy some truly significant victories over these most secretive and intractable enclaves of state and commercial power.

NOTES

1 Author's interview with Gus Hosein, Privacy International Offices, London, 7 April 2017.
2 Author's interview with Gus Hosein, Privacy International Offices, London, 7 April 2017.
3 Author's interview with Gus Hosein, Privacy International Offices, London, 7 April 2017.
4 Author's interview with Rajni Lallah, Lalit Du Klas offices, Rosehill, Mauritius, 23 June 2014.
5 Author's interview with Rajni Lallah, Lalit Du Klas offices, Rosehill, Mauritius, 23 June 2014.
6 Author's interview with Rajni Lallah, Lalit Du Klas offices, Rosehill, Mauritius, 23 June 2014.
7 Admire Mare's interviews with civic activists, conducted at the offices of the Socio Economic Rights Institute, 19–20 October 2015.
8 Email correspondence with Dale McKinley, 24 April 2013.
9 Admire Mare's interviews with civic activists, conducted at the offices of the Socio Economic Rights Institute, 19–20 October 2015.

REFERENCES

Africa, S. (2012). 'The Policy Evolution of the South African Civilian Intelligence Services: 1994 to 2009 and Beyond' (unpublished paper). Accessed from https://repository.up.ac.za/bitstream/handle/2263/20766/Africa_Policy(2012).pdf?sequence=1 (accessed 29 October 2017).

Bellamy Foster, J. & McChesney, R. (2014). 'Surveillance Capitalism: Monopoly-finance capital, the military-industrial complex, and the digital age', *Monthly Review*, (66)3, July–August. Accessed from http://monthlyreview.org/2014/07/01/surveillance-capitalism/ (accessed 4 November 2017).

Bennett, C. (2011). 'In Defence of Privacy', *Surveillance and Society*, 8(4): 487–488.

Bignaux, L. (2013). 'Mauritius New Identity Cards to Cost $40m', *Africa Review*, 12 July. Accessed from www.africareview.com/News/Mauritius-to-issue-new-identity-cards-to-citizens/-/979180/1912750/-/iidn5/-/index.html (accessed 17 November 2017).

Breckenridge, K. (2014). *Biometric State: The global politics of identification and surveillance.* Cambridge: Cambridge University Press.

Cate, F. H. (2006). 'The Failure of Fair Information Practice Principles'. In J. K. Winn (ed.), *Consumer Protection in the Information Economy* (pp. 341–378). Aldershot: Ashgate.

Choudry, A. (2005). 'Crackdown', *New Internationalist*, Issue 376, 1 March. Accessed from https://newint.org/features/2005/03/01/targeting-activists/ (accessed 7 June 2016).

Clarke, R. (1988). 'Information Technology and Dataveillance', *Communications of the ACM*, 35(5): 498–499.

Cox, L. (2013). 'Changing the World Without Getting Shot: How popular power can set limits to state violence'. In Australia Study Centre for Peace and Conflict Resolution (eds), State of Peace Conference. Vienna/ Berlin: LTI-Verlag.

—— & Nilsen, A. (2014). *We Make Our Own History: Marxism and social movements in the twilight of neoliberalism.* London: Pluto.

Dencik, L. & Cable, J. (2017). 'The Advent of Surveillance Realism: Public opinion and activist responses to the Snowden leaks', *International Journal of Communication*, 11(1/2): 9–18.

Donovan, K. P. (2015). 'The Biometric Imaginary: Bureaucratic technopolitics in postapartheid welfare', *Journal of Southern African Studies*, 41(4): 815–833.

Don't Spy on Us (2016). 'DSOU Calls for Complete Rewrite of Investigatory Powers Bill' (blog post), 11 February. Accessed from https://www.dontspyonus.org.uk/blog/2016/02/11/dsou-coalition-calls-for-complete-re-write-of-investigatory-powers-bill/ (accessed 4 November 2016).

Duncan, J. (2009). 'Thabo Mbeki and Dissent'. In Glaser, D. (ed.), *Mbeki and After: Reflections on the legacy of Thabo Mbeki* (pp. 105–127). Johannesburg: Wits University Press.

—— (2014). *The Rise of the Securocrats: The case of South Africa.* Johannesburg: Jacana Media.

Electronic Frontier Foundation (n.d). 'Success Story: Dismantling UK's biometric ID database', undated blog post. Accessed from www.eff.org/pages/success-story-dismantling-uk%E2%80%99s-biometric-id-database (accessed 7 November 2017).

Fernandez, L. (2010). *Policing Dissent: Social control and the anti-globalisation movement.* Toronto: Rutgers University Press.

Foucault, M. (1979). *Discipline and Punish: The birth of the prison.* Middlesex: Penguin Books.

Fuchs, C. (2011). 'Towards an Alternative Concept of Privacy', *Journal of Information, Communication and Ethics in Society*, 9(4): 220–237.

Gill, P. & Phythian, M. (2012). *Intelligence in an Insecure World.* Cambridge: Polity Press.

Giroux, H. A. (2015). 'Totalitarian Paranoia in the Post-Orwellian Surveillance State', *Cultural Studies*, (29)2: 108–140.

Hintz, A & Dencik, L. (2016). 'Expanding State Powers in Times of "Surveillance Realism": How the UK got a "world leading" surveillance law', *OpenDemocracy*. Accessed from www.opendemocracy.net/digitaliberties/arne-hintz-lina-dencik/expanding-state-power-in-times-of-surveillance-realism-how-uk (accessed 10 November 2017).

Lalit Du Klas (2017). 'New Phase in Long Battle Against ID Cards' (blog post), Lalit Du Klas. Accessed from www.lalitmauritius.org/en/newsarticle/1946/new-phase-in-long-battle-against-id-cards/ (accessed 17 November 2017).

Lyon, D. (2015). *Surveillance after Snowden.* London: Polity Press.

Mason, R. & Travis, A. (2016). 'Snoopers Charter Will Set Bad Example to the World, Says SNP', *Guardian*, 14 March. Accessed from www.theguardian.com/world/2016/mar/14/snoopers-charter-labour-threatens-to-hold-up-bill-over-privacy-fears (accessed 25 August 2018).

McCoy, A. W. (2014). 'Surveillance and Scandal: Weapons in an emerging array for US global power', *Monthly Review*, 66(3) July–August. Accessed from http://monthlyreview.org/2014/07/01/the-new-surveillance-normal/ (accessed 27 July 2016).

McKinley, D. (2013). 'The Right 2 Know Campaign (South Africa): Building a national movement for freedom of information and expression'. Johannesburg: Rosa Luxemburg Foundation. Accessed from www.r2k.org.za/wp-content/uploads/R2K-RLF-2013.pdf (accessed 20 November 2017).

Ministry of Technology, Communication and Information, Mauritian Government (2017). 'Press Communique: National Identity Card' (press statement), 20 April. Accessed from http://mnis.govmu.org/English/Documents/Press%20Commununique_200417.pdf (accessed 17 November 2017).

O'Brien, K. (2011). *The South African Intelligence Services: From apartheid to democracy 1948–2005*. London: Routledge.

Peerthum, S. (2012). 'The Long Struggle for Freedom: Slavery and resistance in Dutch Mauritius', *Le Maurician*, 31 January. Accessed from http://www.lemauricien.com/article/%E2%80%9C-long-struggle-freedom%E2%80%9D-slavery-and-resistance-dutch-mauritius-c1638-1710 (accessed on 21 November 2017).

Price, D. H. (2014). 'The New Surveillance Normal: NSA and corporate surveillance in the age of global capitalism', *Monthly Review*, 66(3), July-August. Accessed from http://monthlyreview.org/2014/07/01/the-new-surveillance-normal/ (accessed 27 July 2016).

Privacy International (2015) 'Mass Surveillance' (blog post). Accessed from https://privacyinternational.org/topics/mass-surveillance (accessed 25 August 2018).

Silitski, V. (2006). 'Contagion Deterred: Pre-emptive authoritarianism in the former Soviet Union (the Case of Belarus)', Centre on Democracy, Development and the Rule of Law Working Paper. Accessed from https://cddrl.fsi.stanford.edu/sites/default/files/Silitski_No_66.pdf (accessed 20 November 2017).

Steeves, V. (2009). 'Reclaiming the Social Value of Privacy'. In I. Kerr, C. Lucock and V. Steeves (eds), *Lessons from the Identity Trail: Anonymity, identity and privacy in a networked society* (pp. 191–208). Oxford: Oxford University Press.

Ten Human Rights Organisations (2015). '10 Human Rights Organisations vs. the United Kingdom: Applicants' reply to observations of the Government of the United Kingdom', application number 24960/15. Accessed from www.documentcloud.org/documents/3115985-APPLICANTS-REPLY-to-GOVT-OBSERVATIONS-PDF.html (accessed 27 October 2017).

Tillmann, G. (2009). 'Stolen Fingers: The case against biometric identity theft protection', *Computerworld*, 27 October. Accessed from http://www.computerworld.com/article/2528553/it-management/opinion--stolen-fingers--the-case-against-biometric-identity-theft-protection.html (accessed 7 November 2017).

Westin, A. (1970). *Privacy and Freedom*. New York: Athenaeum.

Wills, J. (2013). 'The United Kingdom Identity Card Scheme: Shifting motivations, static technologies'. In Colin J. Bennett and David Lyon (eds), *Playing the Identity Card: Surveillance, security and identification in global perspective* (pp. 163–179). London: Routledge.

PART II

4

Coming of age under surveillance

South Asian, Arab and Afghan American youth and post-9/11 activism

Sunaina Maira

Technologies of regulating 'radical' Muslim Americans and repressing 'extremist' Muslim and Arab American youth and enemy subjects, within and outside the US, are used by the national and global security apparatus as part of an expanding culture of surveillance and securitisation. Within this national security framework and counter-terrorism regime, Muslim Americans who challenge or resist US policies of global hegemony, especially its wars in West and South West Asia, are demonised as 'anti-American' militants and anti-Western fanatics and defined primarily through the lens of Islam and national security. Imperial technologies of surveillance, repression and regulation produce subjects, and politics, to be monitored and contained even while other forms of political subjecthood and alternative notions of politics bubble up from below. This chapter draws from an ethnographic study in Silicon Valley in northern California, that explores the political subjecthood of young people targeted in the War on Terror in the context of neoliberal multiculturalism and permanent surveillance. It draws on my interviews and fieldwork with college-age Arab, South Asian and Afghan American youth (Muslim as well as non-Muslim) – some of whom, but not all were involved in collective political organising – in the South Bay and Fremont/Hayward between 2007 and 2011 (Maira, 2016).

The larger project focuses on how these youth have turned to rights – especially civil rights and human rights – to respond to Islamophobia, racism and imperial wars, and how they simultaneously grapple with the limits of rights-based activism. Under the PATRIOT Act and with the expanded powers given to law enforcement and intelligence agencies to 'preempt' terrorism, Arab, South Asian (particularly Pakistani), Afghan, Iranian and Muslim Americans in general have been subjected to surveillance as well as detention and deportation. Yet the racial othering and surveillance targeting Muslim and Arab American youth did not begin on September 11, 2001. It is not exceptional, but is situated in the longer, global history of US imperial policies in West and South Asia and in relation to other, domestic processes of criminalisation, surveillance, regulation and elimination of racialised peoples by the US state.

The young people I spoke with struggled with the surveillance, policing and disciplining of their politics as they came of age in the post-9/11 era, particularly of political expression and activism outside of the boundaries of what the state deems 'moderate' Muslim politics. Many grappled with the exceptional censorship and demonisation of the Palestine solidarity movement, both by the state and by Zionist groups. Solidarity with Palestine is often a key marker of presumed radicalisation, as Muslim and Arab American youth who oppose US foreign policy in the Middle East or visit 'radical' Muslim websites that include criticism of Israel are subjected to state surveillance in a climate in which solidarity with Palestine is often conflated with support for terrorism (American-Arab Anti-Discrimination Committee, 2008). This repression in the domestic War on Terror often remains invisible, however, for it is conducted through covert means, such as the use of undercover FBI informants, infiltration and entrapment. Furthermore, Obama's domestic War on Terror at the time drew on counter-radicalisation practices in Britain in a transnational circuit of ideas and policies that focused on 'criminalization of ideological activities,' surveilling and entrapping Muslim American youth, and dividing Muslim communities through the bait and switch of the 'good (moderate)' versus 'bad (radical)' Muslim (Kundnani, 2014, pp. 9, 13).

It is important to note that the template for the War on Terror was manufactured in the 1980s to demonise those resisting US hegemony as well as US allies in the Middle East, particularly Israel, and led to the 'suturing of Israel and the U.S. as defenders of "Western" values against

"Islamic fanaticism" or "Islamofascism"' (Kundnani, 2014, p. 45). There is a long history of surveillance of Arab and Muslim Americans, especially after the 1967 Arab–Israeli War. This has involved cooperation between US and Israeli intelligence, increasing during the Iranian hostage crisis in 1979–81, and the first Gulf War in 1991–92, and which persists to this day (Kumar, 2012). After 9/11, mass surveillance expanded and electronic surveillance was authorised under the PATRIOT Act and in intelligence law – including by Obama – as evident in the controversies over the mass surveillance secretly authorised under the Foreign Intelligence Surveillance Act (FISA). Hence, surveillance is actually constitutive of the imperial state and its secret wars deemed necessary to both protect and project 'democracy', while it represses dissent domestically and globally.

My research focuses on the work of surveillance in shaping the everyday, political culture of the national security state, as it has evolved since the Cold War and in the context of the 'new Cold War', as well as the many 'hot' wars waged by the US, from Iraq to Afghanistan, and proxy wars, such as in Yemen (and now Syria). Surveillance is fundamentally a technology of disciplining and managing racialised populations within neoliberal capitalism, and a racialised mode of governmentality for the imperial state. The culture of surveillance relates to the exceptionalist discourse of US democracy and sovereignty, on the one hand, and to neoliberal governmentality, on the other – both of which are deployed to resolve the tension that emerges between the police state's repression and notions of American 'freedom' in the War on Terror. This tension is negotiated by those who experience the brunt of policing and the contradictions of 'democracy' in their daily lives, through sentiments of fear and anxiety, but also defiance or outrage.

I argue that surveillance is key to the post-9/11 culture wars for the counter-terrorism regime targets, and also produces gendered and racialised bodies as objects fit for surveillance. The central tropes of the contemporary culture wars are those of liberal democracy and freedom, embedded in contestations over Islam, gender and sexuality. These are also *racial* wars and *class* wars, masked by the language of liberal multiculturalism and colour-blind or 'diversity' speech. In the cultural, racial and class wars, now exacerbated under Trump, technologies of surveillance produce a 'state of conscious and permanent visibility' of the objects of the War on Terror. This hyper-scrutiny has shaped the political culture of young people from targeted communities and also produced self-surveillance and self-regulation (Foucault, 1995, p. 201).

This chapter explores how some young people reframe and challenge surveillance through tactics of counter-surveillance, which include individualised, dispersed practices in their daily lives that subvert surveillance through 'quiet encroachments' (Bayat, 2013 [2010], p. 46). Talking to Muslim Americans and Arab, South Asian and Afghan American youth made me realise the ways that strategies of living with, accommodating to, or resisting surveillance have become part of the coming-of-age experiences of the 9/11 generation. This aspect of the cultural and social impact of surveillance needs greater attention, as revelations of new forms of surveillance and old and new covert programs proliferate. What does it mean for young people to live in the *everyday of surveillance*?

SURVEILLANCE EFFECTS

Nearly all the young people I spoke with talked about the climate of hyper-surveillance and the chilling effect it had on dissent and understandings of what it meant to be 'political' and 'social' in their everyday lives. Arab, South Asian and Afghan American youth have grown up in a climate in which they have to self-consciously regulate, or re-narrate, their social and political lives as targets of permanent surveillance (Sirin & Fine, 2008). They live in a moment where the state engages in warrantless wiretapping, monitors private emails and Facebook, and infiltrates mosques and activist groups with undercover informants (MacArthur, 2006–07; Maira, 2007). So it is not just those who are involved with formal political organisations who have reason to be fearful, or self-conscious, about the production of selfhood and sociality. For example, Azma, a Pakistani American woman, said that her mother would talk to her on the way to school about critiques of the official narrative about 9/11:

> My mom – actually when it [attacks of 9/11] first happened, she started researching online conspiracy theories ... And my dad got really angry at her because he told her that the FBI could be tracking your computer, so don't do that. And so she said that if you don't want me to do it at home, I'll do it at the library but he's, like, 'No, that's even worse!'

The fear of surveillance becomes internalised so that it produces a regulatory apparatus through auto-censorship, without the need for direct state repression. The objects of surveillance have to confront the fact that they live in a 'military-spy state', where freedom of expression is racially distributed (Mendieta, 2011, p. 2).

The social and cultural registers through which surveillance becomes a part of daily life are what I describe as *surveillance effects*: processes through which surveillance becomes normalised, even as it is resisted. For Foucault (1995, p. 201), 'surveillance is permanent in its effects.' Surveillance effects shape political culture and ideas of selfhood, producing objects of surveillance and subjects of surveillance as well as of self-surveillance. Foucault's (1995) model of the panopticon describes a system of surveillance which targets people in plain sight, producing the 'principles of [their] own subjection' to technologies of management and regulation of population without the need for coercion; this then produces a blurring of the line between 'who is watching and who is being watched' and the 'affective resonance' of surveillance – fear, paranoia, anxiety, vigilance, frustration, outrage, or bravado (Puar, 2007, p. 129). Surveillance effects bridge the psychic and political ripples generated by the War on Terror for those living in the neoliberal military-spy state.

I argue that 'surveillance stories' help do the regulatory work of surveillance by deepening anxieties and producing self-regulation among those who are the objects of surveillance, by virtue of their race, religion, nationality, citizenship status, or political activities. For example, Laila was a Pakistani American who had attended an Islamic school in Fremont which received threats after 9/11, and where the teachers were mostly Arabs and Afghans. She recalled that when students were discussing the war in Iraq, 'the teacher yelled at us and said, "Don't discuss it! Especially in school because it's not safe" – Like, they really prevented us from discussing it. I don't know if this is true but we've made jokes that it's because our mosque was taped.'

In 2012, the stunning investigation by Associated Press of the New York City Police Department's (NYPD's) surveillance programme revealed that 'mosque crawlers' and undercover informants, called 'rakers' (generally Muslim or Arab themselves), had been deployed to ferret out suspicious Muslim and Arab Americans, including students and youth, 'monitoring daily life in bookstores, bars, cafes, and nightclubs' in 'suspect neighborhoods'. This was part of a 'human mapping program' in cooperation with the CIA and drawing on Israeli surveillance techniques, and extending beyond New York State (Associated Press, 2012, p. 5).[1] But this was really just the 'tip of the iceberg', as communities systematically targeted by the surveillance state were well aware (Kumar, 2012, p. 144). The NYPD also infiltrated Occupy Wall Street and Palestine solidarity rallies during the Israeli war on Gaza in 2009 (Kundnani, 2014, pp. 136–138). Some young people on campuses that had been surveilled by the NYPD used social media, including Twitter, to challenge this secret program with subversive humour. The Yale Muslim Student Association created a Facebook page, 'Call the NYPD', with photos of Muslim college students holding signs declaring, 'I am a … Blonde, Call the NYPD' (Khabeer & Alhassen, 2013, p. 308). The revelation of this infamous 'demographics unit' triggered (some) outrage in the general public and sparked the first mainstream discussion of surveillance since 9/11, which expanded with the revelations by WikiLeaks and Edward Snowden's exposé in 2013 of mass surveillance by the secret PRISM and XkeyScore programs of the NSA and CIA. The responses by young people, including on social media – the very medium of their surveillance – illustrate creative forms of countering surveillance by publicising it on the terrain of popular culture.

The counter-radicalisation regime has constructed a socio-psychological model of how youth, in particular, adopt 'extremist' or jihadist politics, with the help of the counter-terrorism industry – including think-tanks, terrorism studies experts and law enforcement – which has been influenced by Israeli approaches as well as CIA practices during the Cold War in Afghanistan and Pakistan (Kundnani, 2014, pp. 83, 127). Law enforcement agencies, such as the NYPD and others, have used behavioural models of 'radicalization' based on four stages: 'pre-radicalization, self-identification, indoctrination, and jihadization' (American-Arab Anti-Discrimination Committee, 2008, p. 39). These deeply racialised models target particular youth subcultures and popular culture affiliations. Markers of the 'self-identification' stage include 'urban hip-hop gangster clothes' as well as 'traditional Islamic clothing, growing a beard' and involvement in 'social activism and community issues' (Kundnani, 2014, p. 134). This stage-based model that presumes to chart the psychosocial, theological and political trajectory of 'jihadization' has been the basis of FBI surveillance and entrapment operations targeting Muslim American youth. While not all counter-radicalisation experts follow this model, the conflation of 'disaffection, youth alienation, radical dissent, religious fundamentalism' is pervasive as is the assumption that certain youth subcultures (associated with Black youth) lend themselves to the making of terrorists and must be monitored (Kundnani, 2014, p. 120). Of course, this ignores the radicalisation of alienated white Christian youth recruited by militant, white supremacist organisations which has gained greater attention since Trump's election.

The surveillance regime has inevitably transformed what forms of religious, political and even cultural 'self-identification' Muslim American youth perform or narrate. With the consolidation of the image of the 'homegrown' terrorist, supplementing the threatening spectre of foreign terrorists, the security apparatus is increasingly involved in defining Muslim American identities and routes of 'proper' and improper socialisation and politicisation. In the US, the Community Partnership programme was established by the federal government in 2011 to 'identify "credible" voices within the American Muslim community and build an "Alliance of Youth Movements" as a bulwark against extremism' (Aidi, 2014, p. 214). The distinction between 'moderate' and 'radical 'Muslim subjecthood is thus co-constituted with the surveillance regime which has created racial and gendered objects of surveillance, overlapping with the profiling of Black and Latino youth as deviant 'brown' threats to the nation (Silva, 2016).

Racialised and gendered profiling and FBI undercover operations are part of a strategy of 'preventative' or 'anticipatory prosecution', as the state relies on infiltration and an aggressive pursuit of sting operations (Sherman, 2009). A 2014 study found that 'the vast majority of arrests in the war on terror' (between 2001 and 2010) were cases of pre-emptive prosecution based on 'suspicion of the defendant's ideology and not on his/her criminal activity' or incidents where the government manipulated non-terrorist criminal activities; these included cases involving arrests for 'material support of terrorism' which criminalise 'charitable giving and management, free speech, free association, peacemaking, and social hospitality' (Downs and Manley, 2014, pp. 1–2). Due to this pattern of predatory prosecution, or lawfare, South Asian, Arab and Afghan Americans live in what Mimi Nguyen (2012, p. 167) calls a 'preemptive present' of permanent surveillance.

THE SURVEILLED COUNTER-SURVEILLANCE

In the face of increasing state scrutiny of Muslim Americans, and surveillance of Afghans, Arabs, Pakistanis, Yemenis and others in northern California, various public campaigns have been launched to challenge racialised panopticism and its chilling, regulatory effects on surveillable subjects. For example, a coalition of San Francisco civil rights groups discovered that the San Francisco Police Department (SFPD) had signed a secret agreement with the FBI in 2007 that assigned local police to work directly with the Joint Terrorism Training Task Force (JTTF) without civilian oversight (Dubal, 2012, pp. 47–49). The Coalition for a Safe San Francisco – including immigrant rights, Muslim American and Palestine solidarity activists – challenged the SFPD and held hearings in 2010 on racial and ethnic profiling and surveillance by the FBI, which included testimonials from local community members and ultimately overturned the secret SFPD-JTTF agreement. In San Jose, civil rights organisations spoke out in public forums in 2011 against collaboration between the San Jose police and the Department of Homeland Security. In 2014, the San Jose Peace and Justice Center organised a campaign against the SJPD's purchase of a drone for aerial surveillance, which if deployed would have made San Jose the first Bay Area city to have a drone flying overhead.[2] These campaigns, generally framed in the language of civil liberties and anti-racism, reveal an archive of 'surveillance stories' that has steadily accumulated and highlight strategies of counter-surveillance that are both organised and public as well as private and part of the everyday activities of surveillance.[3]

Strategies of counter-surveillance have been used by civil rights campaigns and by young people to make surveillance itself the object through exposing and protesting state surveillance. For example, in Irvine, California, members of the local mosque informed the FBI of an informant who made provocative statements about jihad.[4] Students on college campuses who are involved in Palestinian rights activism have been subjected to surveillance and harassment by Zionist groups and blacklist campaigns as well as disciplinary measures and censorship by university administrators. This was dramatized in the 'Irvine 11' case in 2009 that criminalised Palestine solidarity activists at the University of California at Irvine, due to pressure from Israel lobby organisations, as well as in numerous other incidents of anti-Palestinian repression on campuses since then (Abunimah, 2014; Barrows-Friedman, 2014). In the wake of the prosecution of the Irvine 11 activists (who were Arab and Muslim American), students began doing silent protests nationwide at events featuring Israeli soldiers and have walked out with their mouths taped. There is a quick education in the methods of the surveillance state that produces new repertoires of creative tactics by youth. This strategic political performance highlights the repression of critiques of US-backed Israeli state terror and dramatizes the gap in the discourse of 'free speech' and US democracy.[5]

There is also an awareness among the youth I spoke to that the surveillance state and counter-terrorism regimes are globalised. Palestinian and Muslim American youth and Palestine solidarity activists who are involved in political movements in the US are subject to interrogation and detention at Israeli borders and sometimes even deported, based on intelligence sharing and Israel's regime of hyper-surveillance of Muslims, Arabs and political activists. The US and its allies are part of a transnational apparatus of surveillance, policing and repression that is resisted by global solidarity movements and networks of young people, from Santa Clara to Cairo and from Ferguson, Missouri to Gaza, Palestine.[6]

There is a gendered politics at stake in post-9/11 surveillance, given the state's investment in policing and profiling Muslim and Arab males. The focus on the radicalisation of young Muslim and Middle Eastern men as threats to 'homeland security' means that expressions of bravado, anxiety, courage or subversive humour are indeed filtered through an often heightened self-consciousness by young men about what it means to embody the terror threat in the US today. The gendered profile of Muslim and Arab terrorism is not watertight, as the surveillance state targets young women as well, if less frequently, and there is increased scrutiny of Muslim American women since incidents such as that involving a Pakistani American couple in San Bernadino in 2015.[7]

One way that youth who are in the bull's eye of the surveillance state respond to the perceived stigma of profiling or surveillance as suspect bodies is to turn their experience of surveillance into an achievement – a badge of honour. For example, Jamil, an Indian Muslim American who was born in San Jose, and whose mother is Indian-South African, had grown up going to the Muslim Community Association (MCA) in Santa Clara with his friends, which he described as a 'home base.' Jamil recalled:

> Especially at MCA, when I drove down ... on the right pole there was a huge beige box with three or four antennas, and they used to be listening into MCA through that box. My brother used to do rounds at security and he was like, 'What is that box?' and they were like, 'It must be the FBI.' And apparently there was FBI listening across the street.

Jamil shared a surveillance story that further highlighted the normalisation of surveillance:

> It's definitely crazy at times, like okay, one crazy story – after 9/11, our house was bugged and there was a van outside of our house forever. They rigged the phone lines. Because my dad was involved with CAIR [Council on American Islamic Relations] and the family was tied with CAIR, because he's a Muslim leader. And I know a couple of other kids I hung out with, their parents were also really active and they were, like, 'Yeah, we also heard it too.' So how we noticed it was ... there's this weird van sitting in front of our house and ... we could hear this weird clicking noise in the phone, like, we knew they were listening.

Surveillance effects involve attempts to make meaning of and narrate surveillance through sedimented knowledge that has circulated since the McCarthy era, as well as immigrant experiences of surveillance in other countries. Even if electronic wiretapping no longer always produces proverbial 'clicks' on the phone line, reports have revealed that FBI agents have indeed been stationed in neighbourhoods with concentrations of Muslim Americans and targeted community leaders. It is crucial to read this not simply as an empirical account of knowledge of surveillance technologies but rather as knowledge of the *intimacy* of the state's intrusions into everyday life.

Jamil's story also illustrates awareness of the markers of surveillability, since Muslim American community leaders such as his father, who were publicly engaged in Muslim civil rights organisations such as CAIR, were likely to be surveilled. Surveillability becomes an index of the political significance of the object of surveillance, demonstrating the implications of surveillance effects for post-9/11 political subjecthood. This inversion of the stigma of surveillance is perhaps also an affective or psychic strategy to deal with the anxiety of acknowledging oneself as an object of surveillance, by reclaiming the political agency of surveillance and reasserting the need to continue to engage in dissenting politics despite, and in some cases *because* of, the climate of repression. Jamil and other youth renarrated their surveillability as 'radical' political subjects, asserting the need for public politics and challenging the racialised surveillance regime, but at the same time, potentially normalising the everyday of surveillance. These are the paradoxes of surveillance effects for the 9/11 generation living in the military-spy state.

RESISTANCE AND COALITIONS: 'STOP THE FBI'

Proliferating reports of surveillance of Muslim American, anti-war, Palestine solidarity, Black Lives Matter and Standing Rock activists have established the ongoing link between state surveillance and political repression and produced coalitions protesting surveillance. One well-known case of surveillance that involved anti-war activists from Silicon Valley and generated outrage but also anxiety in progressive movements across the nation, including among young activists, was the FBI raids and grand jury subpoenas of labour and anti-war activists from Minneapolis, Chicago, and San Jose in 2010.[8] Twenty-three anti-war, labour and solidarity activists who had been involved with organising related to human rights in Colombia and Palestine were issued subpoenas to appear before a grand jury. The activists, all seasoned left organisers, launched a highly successful national campaign, the Committee to Stop FBI Repression, that held meetings and protests across the country, galvanising public opposition to FBI raids and surveillance.[9] The campaign also organised a national conference in November 2011 and created a coalition linking anti-war, labour, civil rights, and Palestine and Colombia solidarity movements. These cross-movement alliances were apparent to me at a regional conference of the Committee to Stop FBI Repression I attended in Oakland in 2011, that drew young Arab, South Asian and Muslim American activists, as well as other progressive-left activists who helped spark a national movement against surveillance.

In January 2011, I attended a Stop the FBI rally in San Jose organised by the South Bay Committee Against Political Repression. Held outside San Jose State University, a small but ethnically diverse crowd of various ages chanted slogans as cars driving by occasionally honked in support. The Raging Grannies, three older women, sang satirical ditties about

FBI repression such as 'The FBI is Coming to Town' to the tune of 'Jingle Bells'. The speakers included an older white labour activist, who connected the FBI raids and the Palmer raids targeting socialists in the 1920s.[10] A progressive Japanese American activist, Masao Suzuki, situated the campaign in the history of profiling and incarceration of Japanese Americans during the Second World War and the ongoing surveillance of Muslim Americans. Sharat Lin, an Asian American community activist and director of the San Jose Peace and Justice Center, spoke about the US wars on Afghanistan and Iraq, the detention of up to 5,000 Muslims in the US after 9/11, and the need for 'real democracy' in the US. The protesters eloquently traced connections between the domestic and global fronts of the US War on Terror and also of historical regimes of repression and surveillance.

This public protest was one of many organised by the Committee to Stop FBI Repression in the Bay Area and across the US, some in front of FBI and federal offices, highlighting the alliances forged by activists in opposition to the surveillance state. However, this movement also highlighted the difficulties of mobilising those systematically targeted for surveillance and outside of organised political movements. It was striking that one of the most well-organised national campaigns against the FBI until that moment was launched by labour and anti-war activists who were largely white Americans, as well as solidarity activists who had been targeted in the Midwest (including Arab American activist Hatem Abudayyah and Vietnamese American Anh Pham). This was not surprising, for these veteran activists used their organising skills and resources to unleash a highly effective, national campaign. But I noticed there were few South Asian, Arab, or Afghan Americans at the San Jose rally, including young people, which was probably due to the anxiety about public protest. It is also important to acknowledge that dissent is manifested not only in the street, and 'politics' must be considered more broadly, especially for youth and in a military-spy state. As Bayat (2010, pp. 28–29) argues, 'non-movements' based on 'widespread collective (if fragmented) practices' can be effective in escaping detection in a climate of political repression and hyper-surveillance, as in Egypt or Iran. In the US, too, everyday tactics and affective strategies developed by youth are important to consider as acts of counter-surveillance.

Young Arab, South Asian and Afghan American activists I spoke to were, of course, aware of the impact of surveillance on their own political organising. For example, Aisha, a young Palestinian American woman who grew up in Fremont, recalled the campus surveillance of student-labour organising in which she had been involved: 'Campus police were out with cameras when we were holding rallies and sit-ins. You wondered how much of it was going back to the administration? SOC (Students Organizing for Change) provided a space to assert ourselves politically but it also revealed repression. Was it going back to the FBI?' Aisha astutely observed that knowledge of surveillance and repression is a key element in politicisation. Oppositional movements, such as the Stop the FBI campaign, reveal the repressiveness of the state which then helps expose the repressiveness of liberal democracy, so surveillance is an important site of resistance. As Alain Badiou argues:

> whenever there is a genuinely political event, the State reveals itself. It reveals its excess of power, its repressive dimension ... For it is essential to the normal functioning of the State that its power remains measureless, errant, unassignable. The political event puts an end to all this by assigning a visible measure to the excessive power of the State.
>
> (Badiou, 2005, p. 145)

While Badiou's argument is important in thinking about the role of counter-surveillance, both public and private, in challenging illusions of freedom in liberal democracy and exposing the power of the police state, the excesses of the surveillance state produce real fear and anxieties among young people. Aisha wondered about the implications of intelligence gathering by campus as well as state agents:

> Was it going back to the FBI? We were getting arrested, would it limit our prospects for getting a job? I know petitions are part of the information age, which means you put signatures, and also photos on the Web. We were part of the radical left but we were also trying to be part of the system, we wanted jobs for our economic livelihood. So we had to be strategic about how to assert our political views, we started signing petitions as organisations rather than as individuals. We were worried about going to graduate school.

Aisha's comments speak to the implications of surveillance for financial security as well as organising strategies, concerns not to be taken lightly given the profusion of blacklists of faculty and students involved in Palestine solidarity and BDS (Boycott, Divestment, Sanctions) campaigns. Awareness of surveillance has shaped the political culture of student organising in the post-9/11 era and there is a cautiousness in this generation about the possibilities social media offers for both effective virtual organising and electronic surveillance.[11] In fact, technology and social media have become sites of danger, of *excessive* knowledge production of surveillance by and about those who are targets in the War on Terror. One young Palestinian American woman, a youth activist in the Bay Area, said she decided not to use a cell phone or Facebook for six months, because she strongly suspected that she was being surveilled and wanted to get off the grid as much as possible. Some Muslim, South Asian and Arab American activists have resorted to face-to-face conversations to discuss sensitive issues – old-school methods from the COINTELPRO era. Campaigns such as Stop the FBI and the work of the Defending Dissent Foundation have produced challenges to surveillance embedded in a defence of progressive-left movements. A Defending Dissent Foundation comic book about FBI entrapment states that the aim is to connect groups targeted by surveillance to build a 'culture of solidarity against repression across political boundaries and issue silos by highlighting the shared experience of repression and resistance'.[12]

CONCLUSION

Surveillance effects are complex, and there is more work to be done on the ways in which they are reshaping political subjectivity in racial, gendered, sexual and classed terms in the current moment and permeating social life in the 9/11 generation. Surveillance is key to the project of producing and regulating subjects fit for neoliberal democracy. The long war against terrorism has been accompanied by racial and cultural wars that involve a battle over the meaning of democracy as well as of civil and human rights. I argue that surveillance produces the language of democracy just as neoliberal democracy produces and requires surveillance. That is, domestic surveillance and repression and US overseas interventions in the War on Terror are justified through the discourse of saving others for neoliberal democracy. These others, who must be rescued, regulated and re-engineered to enter Western modernity and enjoy its material as well as gendered and sexual freedoms, are *racial* others, and it is a racialised logic of surveillance and containment that fundamentally defines the culture wars. 'Uncivil' protests, such as those by Palestinian and Muslim American students opposing imperial violence and US-backed occupation, are policed and criminalised by a surveillance apparatus that includes state agents and also anti-Palestinian and Islamophobic organisations. These experiences have propelled many youth to challenge the exceptionalisation of US democracy and to critique the colonialist and racial logics underlying the professing of 'benevolent imperialism' in rescuing oppressed Arabs and Muslims, from Iraq to Afghanistan.

While some young people and activists resist surveillance by calling for a rehabilitation of US democracy and reform of state policies, others offer a radical critique of the imperial state and have built alliances between different communities and movements under surveillance. Immigrant rights and sanctuary-city activists are part of the movement that has grown in the Trump era to resist federal agents and intelligence gathering. Rapid response networks and 'Migra [immigration enforcement] Watch' groups have formed in solidarity with undocumented and vulnerable communities to oppose the state's racist surveillance, deportation and detention policies. These forms of counter-surveillance or 'sousveillance' also help rethink political organising, strategies and frameworks, beyond the parameters prescribed by liberal democracy and civil rights, and aim to create a progressive culture of de-securitisation in resistance to the military-spy state. This organising has built on the experiences of post-9/11 activism to reframe 'security' by challenging the culture of policing and surveillance and to engage in a defence of communities and movements under attack by the imperial state.

NOTES

1 See reports at 'AP's Probe into NYPD Intelligence Operations'. Accessed from http://www.ap.org/Index/AP-In-The-News/NYPD (accessed 8 July 8 2012).

2 The San Jose Police Department (SJPD), civil rights advocates and community activists later discovered, already had at least one JTTF officer assigned to the FBI under a secret memorandum of understanding, who followed federal, not local, guidelines (personal communication with Veena Dubal, 25 August 2013).

3 The SJPD announced in 2011 that it would include Immigration and Customs Enforcement (ICE) officers through a DHS program, Community Shield, and consider participating in the SAR initiative. This came on the heels of a campaign by the Coalition for Justice and Accountability against racial profiling and use of force by the SJPD, that resulted in a city taskforce and changes to urban policing policies in 2010. Raj Jayadev, 'Advocates Balk as San Jose Police Consider Fed Surveillance Program', *New America Media*, 27 July 2011. http://newamericamedia.org/2011/07/rights-advocates-balk-as-san-jose-police-consider-federal-surveillance-program.php (accessed 9 July 2012).

4 Jerry Markon, 'Tension Grows between Calif. Muslims, FBI after Informant Infiltrates Mosque', *Washington Post*, 5 December 2010. http://www.washingtonpost.com/wpdyn/content/article/2010/12/04/AR2010120403710.html (accessed 9 July 2012).

5 See the report by Palestine Legal, 'The Palestine Exception to Free Speech: A Movement Under Attack in the U.S.' https://palestinelegal.org/the-palestine-exception (accessed 10 December 2017).

6 Foreign states have been involved in domestic counter-terrorism training in the Bay Area, such as Israeli and Bahraini police units involved in Operation Urban Shield 2011 in Berkeley that targeted Occupy protesters. The blockade of the Israeli boat at the Oakland port in protest of the war on Gaza in August 2014, in which many young Arab American activists took the lead, also highlighted the cooperation between Israeli military and police and US police in St. Louis county, Missouri where a young African American, Mike Brown, had been killed by police and militarised police forces had attacked protesters. See Massoud Hayoun, 'Oakland Activists Block Ship for Third Day', *Al Jazeera America*, 18 August 2014. Accessed from http://america.aljazeera.com/articles/2014/8/18/gaza-oakland-protest.html (accessed 28 August 2018).

7 The mass shooting at a Christmas party in San Bernadino, inspired by the Islamic State, was conducted by Syed Farook and his wife Tashfeen Malik, a Pakistani who had spent time in Saudi Arabia. Michael Schmidt and Richard Perez-Pena, 'FBI Treating San Bernadino Attack as Terrorism Case', *New York Times*, 5 December 2015. https://www.nytimes.com/2015/12/05/us/tashfeen-malik-islamic-state.html (accessed 28 August 2018).

8 See http://www.stopfbi.net/about/timeline (accessed 28 August 2018).

9 See http://www.stopfbi.net/about/timeline.

10 The Palmer Raids of 1919–20 targeted anarchists and communists, many of whom were Russian and European immigrants. Under Attorney General Mitchell Palmer and in collaboration with J. Edgar Hoover of the FBI, thousands of left activists, but also many who were just immigrants, were subjected to mass arrests and deportations as part of a post-First World War Red Scare.

11 See the Electronic Frontier Foundation's Surveillance Self-Defense Project: https://ssd.eff.org/ (accessed 28 August 2018).

12 Quote from back cover of *Manufacturing Terrorists: The FBI's Entrap and Demonize Strategy*, Dissent and Repression Comic Series, Defending Dissent Foundation, www.DefendingDissent.org (accessed 28 August 2018).

REFERENCES

Abunimah, A. (2014). *The Battle for Justice in Palestine.* Chicago, IL: Haymarket Books.

Aidi, H. D. (2014). *Rebel Music: Race, empire and the new Muslim youth culture.* New York: Pantheon.

American-Arab Anti-Discrimination Committee (ADC) (2008). *Report on Hate Crimes and Discrimination Against Arab Americans.* Washington, DC: American-Arab Anti-Discrimination Committee Research Institute.

Associated Press (2012). 'AP's Probe into NYPD Intelligence Operations', *Associated Press.* Accessed from www.ap.org/Index/AP-In-The-News/NYPD (accessed 8 July 2012).

Badiou, A. (2005). *Metapolitics* (translated by Jason Barker). London: Verso.

Barrows-Friedman, N. (2014). *In Our Power: U.S. students organize for justice in Palestine.* Charlottesville, VA: Just World Books.

Bayat, A. (2010 [2013]). *Life as Politics: How ordinary people change the Middle East.* Stanford, CA: Stanford University Press.

Downs, S., & Manley, K. (2014). *Inventing Terrorists: The lawfare of preemptive prosecution.* Albany, NY: Project Salam and National Coalition to Protect Civil Freedoms.

Dubal, V. (2012). 'The Demise of Community Policing: The impact of post-9/11 federal surveillance programs on local law enforcement', *Asian American Law Journal*, 19: 35–59.

Foucault, M. (1995). *Discipline and Punish: The birth of the prison* (translated by Alan Sheridan). New York: Vintage Books.

Khabeer, S. A., & Alhassen, M. (2013). 'Muslim Youth Cultures'. In J. Hammer & O. Safi (eds), *The Cambridge Companion to American Islam* (pp. 299–311). New York: Cambridge University Press.

Kumar, D. (2012). *Islamophobia and the Politics of Empire.* Chicago, IL: Haymarket.

Kundnani, A. (2014). *The Muslims are Coming: Islamophobia, extremism, and the domestic War on Terror.* London and New York: Verso.

MacArthur, A. P. (2006/2007). 'The NSA Phone Call Database: The problematic acquisition and mining of records in the United States, Canada, the United Kingdom, and Australia', *Duke Journal of Comparative and International Law*, 17: 441–481.

Maira, S. (2007). 'Deporting Radicals, Deporting La Migra: The Hayat Case in Lodi', *Cultural Dynamics*, 19(1): 39–66.

—— (2016). *The 9/11 Generation: Youth, rights, and solidarity in the War on Terror.* New York: NYU Press.

Mendieta, E. (2011). 'The Politics of Terror and the Neoliberal Military Minimalist State: On the inheritance of 9-11', *City*, 15(3–4): 1–7.

Nguyen, M. T. (2011). *The Gift of Freedom: War, debt, and other refugee passages.* Durham, NC and London: Duke University Press.

Puar, J. (2007). *Terrorist Assemblages: Homonationalism in queer times.* Durham, NC: Duke University Press.

Sherman, J. (2009). '"A Person Otherwise Innocent": Policing entrapment in preventative undercover counterterrorism investigations', *University of Pennsylvania Journal of Constitutional Law*, 11: 1475–1500.

Silva, K. (2016). *Brown Threat: Identification in the security state* (pp. 25–51). Minneapolis, MN: University of Minnesota Press.

Sirin, S., & Fine, M. (2008). *Muslim American Youth: Understanding hyphenated identities through multiple methods.* New York and London: NYU Press.

5

ASIO and the Australia–Timor-Leste solidarity movement, 1974–79

Bob Boughton

In May 2002, Timor-Leste (East Timor) became the first country to achieve independence in the twenty-first century, ending over four hundred years of colonial rule which began when the Portuguese arrived in the sixteenth century. The first government was led by FRETILIN, the political party which had launched the independence struggle in 1974, following the fall of the fascist regime in Portugal, only to face an armed invasion and brutal military occupation by its giant neighbour, the Republic of Indonesia in December 1975. By the time of the 1975 invasion, FRETILIN leaders had been working with solidarity activists in Australia for over a year as well as with other international solidarity and liberation movements, and this formed the basis for an association which continued throughout the war and beyond. The work of the period covered in this chapter, between 1974 and 1979, is sometimes overshadowed in studies of the role of international solidarity in the independence struggle (e.g., Fernandes, 2011), partly because of the great upsurge in activity after the Indonesian military massacre of student protesters at the Santa Cruz cemetery in Dili in 1991. Before 1991, many of the most influential Australian solidarity activists were members of communist and socialist organisations, and had a radical anti-imperialist, anti-colonialist ideology. This perspective was shared by key FRETILIN leaders with whom they worked closely, often in clandestine and semi-clandestine ways (Da Silva, 2011).

Australia's secret intelligence services closely monitored the activities of the Australian solidarity movement and its FRETILIN allies from 1974 onwards. The Australian Security Intelligence Organisation (ASIO) played a particular role, because it already had in place an extensive surveillance network and technology for monitoring the Communist Party of Australia (CPA) (McKnight, 1994), FRETILIN's strongest and best-organised ally. Targets of this surveillance included all the FRETILIN members who visited Australia, namely José Ramos-Horta, Abílio Araújo, Roque Rodrigues, Estanislau da Silva; the key solidarity organisations, including the CPA-initiated Campaign for an Independent East Timor (CIET), Melbourne-based Australia East Timor Association (AETA), and solidarity groups in Darwin, Brisbane, Perth and Adelaide, as well as all the main individual CPA members involved in solidarity work. The scale of this surveillance was massive. In a note on one of the files which have now been released and are held in the AETA Office in Melbourne, ASIO reported it had assembled 13 volumes of information on CIET alone between 1974 and 1979 (ASIO, 23 March 1984). A volume could contain as many as 200 separate pages. Over the same period, many personal files on individual activists undertaking this work were created or expanded.

Less than one decade earlier, the US Central Intelligence Agency (CIA), had shared information on Indonesian communists with the same military regime which was now invading Timor, leading to the deaths of many thousands of PKI (Indonesian Communist Party) activists and supporters at the hands of militias and security forces (Simpson, 2017). It is not yet clear whether or not similar information was exchanged between Australia and Indonesia about FRETILIN, though some recent research points in that direction (Job, 2015). However, in late 1978, a clandestine radio link between FRETILIN leaders in the mountains and solidarity movement activists operating from northern Australia was compromised, and a major part of the FRETILIN leadership died in the encirclement operation that followed. This chapter utilises extracts from partially released ASIO files and the recollections of some surviving FRETILIN and Australian activists to tell a story about this period, and to draw out some contemporary lessons.

I write, not as a so-called 'neutral' academic observer, but as a long-time participant in the solidarity movement. A few years ago, my thirty-something son wandered into an exhibition at the Sydney Police

Museum to be confronted by a 1975 photo of his long-haired 24-year-old not-yet-father during a demonstration against the Indonesian invasion of East Timor. The photo had been taken and filed by an ASIO officer tasked with recording the activities of known Sydney CPA members. While I was a member, having joined only a few months previously, I was not the main subject of the photo. Standing quite near me was a member of the CPA National Committee, the late Denis Freney, who at the time was the CPA's leader of the party's solidarity work with independence movements in the Pacific region (NLA, n.d.).

As I now know from my experience as an 'activist researcher' (Choudry, 2013) in the popular education movement in the Asia Pacific (Boughton & Durnan, 2017), ASIO's interest in the CPA, Denis Freney and the CPA's connections with FRETILIN, the independence movement in East Timor, was part of a much longer history. This history has involved the surveillance, disruption and repression of radical anti-capitalist and anti-imperialist social movements in Australia, not just by ASIO, but by a range of associated security agencies and police forces. In this chapter, I trace some of the complex web of connections across individuals, parties and movements, and back and forth in time, which are the skeleton of a history. This account is based on my recollections of the period, from conversations with other comrades both in Timor-Leste and Australia who were directly involved, from published accounts of this work by participants, journalists and academics, and from reviewing some of the archival material now becoming available, including released ASIO files. The PhD theses of two Timorese scholars who were active members of the Resistance (Cabral, 2002; Da Silva, 2011) have also been invaluable.

This story has three purposes. First, to reveal a small part of what is largely hidden, even now, about the operations of Australia's 'secret state' and its complicity, within living memory, in war crimes and genocide in our region; second, to recover some of another lost story – the story of how a group of well-organised and disciplined political activists learned to operate from within Australia, East Timor and in several other countries, to build and maintain an active campaign of solidarity with the national liberation struggle of the Timorese, and third, to encourage contemporary activist researchers to dig further into this story, which remains highly relevant to current issues and struggles in our region.

In 1974, the 'Carnation Revolution' in Portugal ended decades of fascist rule, and set in motion a rapid decolonisation process in

Portugal's so-called 'external territories', including Angola, Mozambique and Guinea-Bissau, and the tiny half-island territory known then as Portuguese Timor. In Australia, anti-colonial and anti-imperialist activists, many of whom were CPA members, had long supported the independence struggles in Africa, and they quickly set about building relations with the new political forces emerging in Portuguese Timor, only a few hundred kilometres from Darwin, in Australia's Northern Territory. In 1974, Freney made his first visit to Timor's capital Dili, where he met independence leaders and offered support. These activities were reported in the files of Australia's internal security agency, ASIO, and passed on to other intelligence agencies and the Department of Foreign Affairs. ASIO's long history of surveillance of CPA activities, supposedly to prevent 'subversion' within Australia, today seems almost comical in its anti-communist paranoia (Burgmann, 2014), but there were significant economic and geo-strategic interests at work. The Australian state had two clear objectives concerning Portuguese Timor. The first was to protect and consolidate its relationship with the bulwark of anti-communism in South East Asia, namely the Republic of Indonesia. The second was to ensure as much control as possible of the rich oil and gas fields in the sea between the island of Timor and Australia (McGrath, 2017).

In recent years, Australia's so-called 'intelligence community' has both come out of the shadows, and multiplied, in terms of its component organisations. In the mid-1970s, according to Dr Jim Stokes of the National Archives Office:

> The only agency of which most Australians were aware was the Australian Security Intelligence Organisation (ASIO) ... ASIO's main targets were the Communist Party and other organisations believed to have Communist links ... The other three agencies were almost unknown to the general public. The Joint Intelligence Organisation (JIO) and the Defence Signals Division (DSD) were located deep within the Defence Department. JIO used covert and published sources to produce strategic assessments, while DSD intercepted foreign electronic communications from a network of stations operated by the armed forces. DSD's functions were still not acknowledged officially ... Lastly there was the Australian Secret Intelligence Service (ASIS), which was not acknowledged officially ... ASIS undertook covert intelligence gathering outside Australia and was responsible to the Minister for Foreign Affairs.
>
> (Stokes, n.d.)

JIO, part of the Australian military's intelligence arm, is now called the 'Defence Intelligence Organisation'. DSD, now called the 'Australian Signals Directorate', is of particular importance in this story because it operates the Shoal Bay Receiving Station near Darwin:

> Shoal Bay ... has two primary roles: the interception of satellite communications and the interception of high frequency signals ... As Australia's principal source for interception of Indonesian military and civilian communications, Shoal Bay has had a particularly [*sic*] role in Australian government understanding of Indonesian military activities in East Timor from 1975 to 1999, an understanding usually withheld from the Australian public.
>
> (Nautilus Institute, n.d.)

Furthermore, all four Australian intelligence agencies (ASIO, JIO, DSD and ASIS) were (and are) part of an international network of cooperation, established under the "Five Eyes" Agreement whereby the intelligence communities of the UK, the US, Canada, Australia and New Zealand shared signals intelligence with each other, creating what Edward Snowden called 'a supra-national intelligence organisation that doesn't answer to the laws of its own countries' (NDR, 2014). According to a *UK Defence Reporter* article:

> The secretiveness of the alliance is so severe that the treaty that created it was not in the knowledge of Gough Whitlam, then Prime Minister of Australia, as late as 1973 and it did not come to the public attention until 2005. Only in June 2010, the full text of the UKUSA Agreement was released by the British and American governments and for the first time officially recognised.
>
> (Tossini, 2017)

The year 1975 was a significant one in Australia's political history: the first Labor government for over two decades was ejected from office by the Governor-General in a so-called 'constitutional coup' (Head, 2016). While there has been much speculation on the role of the intelligence community in this, Whitlam's actions on East Timor had been perfectly aligned with a policy that foreign affairs officials had pursued since well before his election, namely to favour integration of East Timor into Indonesia. This would have disastrous consequences for the Timorese, whose first-ever period of independent government lasted less than one month, before a massive military invasion on 7 December 1975 by the Indonesian Army drove the government from Dili into the mountains, from where it began what would be a 24-year-long war of national liberation (Cabral, 2002).

Indonesia had begun sending its troops into what was still Portuguese Timor, the sovereign territory of a European power, in September, with the full knowledge of Australian officials, who were alerted to this by JIO. While this was denied by Australian officials publicly, the full-scale invasion was no surprise for FRETILIN or its international supporters, who had already begun preparations for the war that would follow. This included moving key FRETILIN leaders, including the current PM, Marí Alkatiri, and the FRETILIN Foreign Minister, José Ramos-Horta, out of the country, to establish a government-in-exile and build an external wing to maintain diplomatic and solidarity links, from Australia, Mozambique, Angola and Portugal.

Meanwhile, Warwick Neilley, a CPA member who was working in the Darwin office of the North Australian Workers Union, had purchased simple two-way radios tuned to the frequency used by, among others, the Royal Flying Doctor Service, and had taken them into Timor. This was to allow FRETILIN to maintain contact between the diplomatic external wing (known by its Portuguese acronym DEF) and those who had remained inside to lead the armed struggle; and communicate events inside to the outside world.

Following the invasion, the radio operation, as it is now remembered by activists, evolved fairly rapidly into three distinct kinds of activities. The first involved monitoring from Darwin of FRETILIN radio broadcasts from inside Timor-Leste, broadcasts sometimes addressed to the population inside, and on other occasions, to the international audience. Second, there was a 'semi-secret' two-way communication, whereby FRETILIN leaders inside would dialogue with people in Australia, including, for example, sympathetic parliamentarians like Labor's Ken Fry, or, on at least several other occasions, with UN and other diplomatic officials. This channel was also used by FRETILIN leaders who came to Australia, including the DEF leader at that time, Abílio Araújo, and Foreign Affairs Minister José Ramos-Horta. The third operation was completely clandestine and involved two-way communication in code between operators inside Timor and in Darwin, through which internal and external resistance leaders shared information and orders.

In Darwin, the overall operation was managed by Brian Manning, a CPA member and activist in the Waterside Workers Federation (now Maritime Union of Australia), whose recollections of this work were published in 2001, alongside those of several other Australian radio operators who assisted between 1975 and 1978. (Manning, 2003; Elenor, 2003). Freney, meanwhile, who was based in Sydney, organised the distribution of the material received via the radio link. The public material was translated and published via media releases and in the solidarity network's own newspapers, mainly *East Timor News*, digitised copies of which can be seen on the CHART website (CHART, n.d.(b)). The secret material was sent on to the DEF group based in Mozambique, under the leadership of Marí Alkatiri. Another CPA national official, Joe Palmada, was responsible for security, which included recruiting operators from 'unknown' members like Chris Elenor, and giving them false identities and other strategies deemed necessary to maintain the operation clandestinely.

The CPA did not come to this work with any illusions regarding the Australian state and its commitment to 'open democracy'. Formed in 1920, and for its first 25 years, an active member of the Comintern, the CPA had at various times been declared illegal, and had been forced itself to operate as an 'underground' or 'clandestine' organisation. This included two periods of illegality within the memory and experience of several of its current senior leaders, one in 1940 when it opposed the 'phoney war', and another in 1950, when the then conservative Prime Minister Robert Menzies made it an illegal organisation – a decision later overturned by the High Court and confirmed in a Referendum. In both periods, the CPA had continued to operate, publishing and distributing its newspapers and pamphlets through clandestine networks, despite some leaders being jailed. More importantly, the CPA had developed strong links with communist parties throughout the region, including one of the most significant, the Communist Party of Indonesia (PKI), of which several hundred thousand members and supporters had been murdered ten years earlier, in actions led by some of the same Indonesian generals who led the invasion of Timor.

As experienced CPA leaders, Manning, Freney and Palmada were well aware of this history. Manning, who had been in the Northern

Territory since the 1950s, had been active in the formation of the Northern Territory Aboriginal Rights Council, which campaigned against the repressive legislation then in force restricting the movement and civil and political rights of Aboriginal people. He also played a key role mobilising union support for the historic walk-off by Aboriginal pastoral workers from the Wave Hill cattle station in 1966–67 (Boughton, 1999; NMA, n.d.). Much of this work had to be carried out clandestinely and semi-clandestinely, to avoid the draconian laws then in place to ensure Aboriginal labour discipline. This history also meant that Manning, like Freney, was already a 'person of interest' to ASIO, with his own extensive file.

The key to the whole operation, however, was not the Australian communists and activists, but rather the members of FRETILIN, inside and outside the country. For example, much of the radio communication was in Portuguese or Tetum, and so a Timorese comrade had to be present when messages were being received. One of the Timorese radio operators, Estanislau Da Silva, who came to Australia for this purpose from Mozambique, where Alkatiri was based, was arrested and deported, after Commonwealth Police raided one of the bush locations, presumably acting on intelligence provided by ASIO and its associated entities. In other aspects of the solidarity operation, money raised by FRETILIN members in Mozambique and Angola was smuggled into Australia by CPA member, Mark Aarons, to help fund the work. FRETILIN external leaders including Ramos-Horta, Roque Rodrigues and Abílio Araújo undertook speaking tours in Europe and in Australia and other countries, to help build the solidarity movement and to lobby for diplomatic support, especially in Portugal (Cabral, 2002; Da Silva, 2011).

All this activity was subject to surveillance and disruption, as can be seen clearly from the ASIO files on CIET. Historians and people involved in solidarity work have accessed only a very small amount of the information held in these files, so the full story of what they contain could take many years to uncover. Among some of the most interesting documents that I came across are communications between ASIO and the Joint Intelligence Organisation (JIO), demonstrating that domestic intelligence gathering by ASIO was part of a larger operation by the Australian and international intelligence communities.

The interests these agencies sought to defend were imperialist, bound up, as many now admit, with the extension of western capitalism's control of the strategic resource of oil, and its interests in controlling shipping lanes essential for world trade (McGrath, 2017). Anti-communism, dressed up as the defence of liberal democracy and human rights, was actually an ideological cover for the defence and extension of capital's control over the strategic resources and trade routes essential to its continued growth. The same forces which backed the 1965–66 genocide in Indonesia were now continuing that same process in East Timor, ensuring that the region in which Australia was a vital base would remain open for business. The CPA was a target of the intelligence agencies, not because it was communist and aligned with hostile foreign powers, which, by this time, it was not, having severed its links with Chinese and Soviet communist parties years earlier. Its danger arose from its unequivocal opposition to capitalism and imperialism, and from an experienced cadre, which had, over its 55-year history, learned what kind of organised resistance it took to defend and extend the influence of their organisation and the international movement of which they saw themselves a part.

In reviewing the ASIO files, it became apparent that the security agencies had uncovered and perhaps even fostered divisions within the solidarity movement in Australia between CPA activists and supporters and more 'liberal' organisations and activists who did not agree with the CPA's anti-imperialist analysis of the geopolitical situation. These activists, associated with some church groups and non-government organisations (NGOs) believed that the CPA's explicit anti-imperialism was alienating a potential support base within Australia for Timorese independence, including within the Australian Labor Party. Interestingly, similar divisions had opened up along similar lines in the previous decade, over the way to build mass support for the Aboriginal rights struggle in Australia, with some church groups and NGOs encouraging Aboriginal leaders to disassociate themselves from the CPA (Brian Manning, personal communication). Among the criticisms that more liberal activists made of the CPA was that it operated as a disciplined and united force within the broader movement, and did not share all the information it obtained via its clandestine and semi-clandestine operations. The irony here is that it was just this capacity for disciplined and clandestine operation which made the CPA an invaluable ally for FRETILIN, which, like the CPA leadership, had no illusions about the nature of western imperialism and its openness to purely democratic and legal means of resistance.

In March 1978, a leader of the more 'liberal' tendency, David Scott, travelled to Mozambique to meet Marí Alkatiri and the DEF, returning in early April. He took with him a position paper, summarised by Da Silva as follows:

> First, there was a large reservoir of public support for FRETILIN and the East Timorese people, but it has proved very difficult to convert that latent support into political action. Second, part of the cause of this was 'the direct link between FRETILIN and the Communist Party of Australia through Denis Freney and ETNA, [which] is often mentioned by conservative (and moderate A.L.P) politicians and journalists as a reason for not supporting FRETILIN.' Third, there was a 'power politics dispute between the CPA and the Australian Labor Party'.
>
> (Da Silva, 2011, p. 245)

Freney went over shortly afterwards, at FRETILIN's request. It is clear from the released files that both trips were the subject of ASIO surveillance reports, in which unidentified agents speculated on a leadership struggle going on in the solidarity movement. These reports reveal that the intelligence agencies had informants inside the solidarity movement. The question then arises: who were these informants, and were they actively fomenting disputes themselves?

A key lesson from this period is that, in the face of imperialist aggression, effective solidarity may require clandestine work. If it does, then there are many techniques and skills developed over past decades which may need to be revived and re-learned. To illustrate this, I have used some extracts from the memoir of one of the operators, Chris Elenor, published on the *Rough Reds* website (Elenor, 2003). The overall secrecy and security of the operation was the first consideration:

> Joe [Palmada] explained the Party … needed a person to disappear from Sydney for six months to do this underground work. It would involve isolation, some physical risk and possible arrest. I would have to leave following training within a couple of weeks …
>
> [I] would stage a sudden departure to Western Australia … Contact would be through an address in Perth. In reality after driving the vehicle (at not more than fifty miles an hour) to Darwin, I was to immediately set about securing a base. I was to shun open contact with Brian Manning and keep contact to a minimum, however he had found a ramshackle demountable on an out of the way block which would make a suitable base.

Basic equipment had to be bought and equipped, relying on the CPA's existing networks:

> I eventually found a Telecom Landrover ute [which] was checked over and purchased by someone else in the network and delivered to Harry Hatfield's, a metalworker comrade, for a few modifications. As an optional extra, Landrovers could have an extra fuel tank fitted for long range operations. Harry made a tank that was indistinguishable from the genuine accessory and fitted it complete with fuel line and tap to the Landrover. Access was from inside the cab, and once the disguising mud film and four screws had been removed from the lid, there was room in the tank for the radio, aerials, power cables, code books and other transmitting paraphernalia. In the bottom was an asbestos mat to keep heat radiating from the exhaust pipe running alongside away from the radio equipment.

He also had to acquire new skills:

> I met Andrew Waterhouse (another CPA comrade) at the Café Sport in Leichhardt … he said we were going away for a few days. I had to learn how to operate the radio, some electronics for trouble shooting, and as immediate homework, the international alphabet. He took me to a safe house in the Blue Mountains and we started work on radio theory and electronics. Andrew was very skilled in this and was constantly learning from the experience of the operation, refining the gear and working to get a stronger, more reliable radio signal into East Timor.

The technology of course was very different:

> Denis was the Sydney connection in the pipeline and the coded and plain text messages and tape recordings would flow between us via Australia Post boxes in Darwin and Sydney, registered in other than our own names. The coded messages were then sent on via an old telex machine Denis had acquired, cheaper than international phone calls.

Importantly, as the operation was disrupted several times between 1976 and 1978, some lessons only came with experience:

> DSD [had] used direction-finding equipment to pinpoint the location of the previous transmitter and … all transmissions would need to be kept to under half an hour. This had been the downfall of the previous operation.

> They had camped and transmitted from the one spot for too long, and even had a vege garden going when he visited them ...

Finally, and perhaps most importantly, the knowledge of the experienced local activists was essential: 'Brian Manning, a wharfie in Darwin, had located a possible base and had some safe transmitting sites in mind, based on his local knowledge.'

These extracts, and the much fuller accounts from Manning, Elenor and Freney listed in the references below, illustrate that the 'pedagogy of mobilisation' (Holst, 2002, p. 87) is a sophisticated curriculum, involving not just an individual acquiring certain technical skills, but an organisation learning from experience how to deploy the resources of its widely distributed membership, while maintaining sufficient security to ensure minimal disruption of an operation by the security forces. In this case, a communication network had to be established which reached from inside FRETILIN-controlled areas of occupied Timor, deep in the mountains, across the sea to Darwin, from where further links were made to activists and supporters in Australia and to the media, and also, at the same time, via another channel, to the FRETILIN leadership in exile in Mozambique, Angola and Portugal. Moreover, communication was in at least four languages. In Timor, the resistance communicated in Portuguese and Tetum (Cabral & Martin Jones, 2008). In Australia, the communists were all English-speaking. The fourth 'language' was the code used for the secret channel.

There is another, darker, lesson from this operation. Despite the experience both FRETILIN and the CPA brought to their work, and developed further over time, they did not succeed in preventing it from being compromised, with eventual disastrous results. From the very beginning, the Indonesian military and intelligence apparatus, key members of which had been trained in the US, saw the prime target as the 'communists' in the FRETILIN leadership, which included Nicolau Lobato, and a group which had been studying in Portugal at the time of the revolution there, where they had enjoyed close relations with both the Portuguese left and anti-colonial leaders from the Portuguese territories in Africa. In 1978, the Indonesian military launched Operation Skylight, a campaign to capture and kill the surviving members of the leadership identified with this more 'radical' political and economic agenda. As described by Estevao Cabral:

> On December 3, 1978, Alarico Fernandes, the then Minister of Information and Internal Security surrendered to ABRI [Indonesian Armed Forces] in a vain attempt to secure peace negotiations. On surrendering to the Indonesians, Fernandes took with him all the equipment belonging to Radio Maubere, the National Radio of the RDTL [Democratic Republic of East Timor]... As a result of his departure, FRETILIN's communication with the world outside East-Timor was completely severed.
>
> Prior to his surrender, Fernandes had been involved in the launch of Operation Skylight by the Indonesian army which was designed to capture the 'so-called the communist-wing, to whom responsibility was attributed for the continuation of the war'. The main target of this operation was Nicolau Lobato ... [now] President of the party. Fernandes had located [his] whereabouts ... in the hills near Maubisse, in the southern part of East-Timor. After this, ABRI pursued Lobato relentlessly in that region.
>
> ... after a six hour gun-battle, which commenced just before dawn, he was captured and killed by units of Timorese battalion 744, on December 31, 1978. Thus, in the words of a FRETILIN report of the early 1980s 'by the end of 1978, the political leadership of the National Resistance faced a deep crisis'. Areas that FRETILIN had used as its strongholds and supply bases were lost. Its infrastructure could no longer function properly and other means of struggle had to be developed.
>
> (Cabral, 2002, pp. 266–267)

While the full story is still unclear, it seems that the Indonesians had taken control of the radio operation for some time before this became known in Australia, either because they had already captured Fernandes, or because he had defected. Whatever the reason, messages had begun coming through which did not follow the usual protocols, creating suspicions among the external leadership that there was an internal power struggle which was supported by some of their own number, including their Foreign Minister, Ramos-Horta. The conflicts around these events, and lingering doubts as to whether or not some of their key leaders were betrayed, continue to affect relations among the older Resistance leaders who now form part of the governing group in an independent Timor-Leste. These divisions have since been reproduced within the international solidarity movement, especially as it grew significantly from 1991 onward, and were still having an effect during the post-independence political crisis of 2006, discussed below.

We can also learn from this period how anti-communism operated throughout the Cold War as the fundamental ideological framework, through which imperialism defended its interests and attacked those who would oppose them. Anti-communism was *the* hegemonic ideology in this period, in the way that anti-terrorism has become in more recent years. Simply to name an individual, an organisation, or a political demand as 'communist' or 'communist-inspired' was sufficient, across large sections of the population, not only in Australia but perhaps even more so in Indonesia, to discredit the target so named. It was also sufficient to dehumanise people labelled in this way, and justify the total denial of their civil and political rights, up to and including their right to life. Indonesia's Suharto dictatorship had mastered the art of anti-communist propaganda, and deployed it to great effect internally, and in all its dealing with FRETILIN (Cabral, 2000). But it was also a key element in the geo-strategic context. In Suharto's meetings with the US President Ford just prior to the invasion, and with Australian Prime Minister Whitlam, the key point he repeatedly made was that FRETILIN was communist, and that independence could lead to increased communist influence in the region.

The fourth lesson, or set of lessons, that we can take from the events of this period concerns how we understand the limits of democracy in a country like Australia. There is no doubt that, compared with Suharto's Indonesia at the time, or occupied Timor-Leste, or Portugal prior to the Carnation Revolution, Australian democracy creates significant space for the development of movements for change. However, this space can very quickly come under close surveillance and, if the actions of social movements and political organisations are deemed to threaten so-called 'national security interests', then this surveillance will become active disruption. Moreover, behind the scenes, in documents that only became public thirty years after they have had their effect, government ministers, officials and their corporate allies are engaged in very different conversations from those they have on the public record. These conversations, and the background analyses based on their intelligence gathering efforts, are shared with their counterparts in other governments in other countries, some of which operate in conditions where repression is not nearly so subtle. The events of 1975–78 clearly demonstrate a level of collaboration and complicity among Australian politicians and officials in what became a genocidal and totally illegal invasion of the sovereign territory of another country, less than two hours travel from our northern shores.

My analysis also raises a deeper question, namely the contradictory relationship that this history reveals between two different traditions and conceptions of international solidarity. One of these is liberal solidarity, which is based on international law and human rights. The other is the solidarity of international socialism. In November 2006, long-time Australian Timor-Leste solidarity activist Pat Walsh made this statement:

> The nature of this solidarity (with Timor-Leste) in Australia has changed over the years. Originally it was largely ideologically driven and related to FRETILIN, but today it is a broader phenomenon that embraces a cross-section of partnerships in both societies and includes business, professionals, and local and national government in its ranks. This is *a welcome development and a model for other countries.* It is consistent with *a human rights approach*, particularly in support of the *right of self-determination* – a right which is still being realised; it is in tune with the successful inclusive ethos that President Xanana Gusmao injected into the Timor project many years ago; and it ensures the diversified mix of inputs that nation-building in Timor requires.
>
> (Walsh, 2007; emphasis added)

This is not, as Walsh suggested, a new approach. In fact, as the intervention by Scott and Tanter described above shows, it had long been the position of a significant element within the Australian solidarity movement, especially among people associated with aid NGOs. This liberal view of solidarity plays down the importance of global capitalism, and in particular the imperialist ambitions of what Samir Amin calls 'the triad' – the US, Japan and Europe – in determining geopolitical change within the Asia-Pacific. As I have sought to show here, socialist, anti-imperialist solidarity work is different. It exposes the historical continuity between the destruction of the PKI in Indonesia and the invasion of Portuguese Timor, both of which were supported by the US and its allies in order to contain anti-colonial and national revolutions spreading through South East Asia in the wake of the Chinese victory and the successes being won in Vietnam. The anti-communist ideology which justified the massacre of PKI supporters in Indonesia was once again used to justify the suppression of FRETILIN in Timor. The solidarity which the CPA espoused and practised gained its meaning and urgency from the party members' understanding of these processes.

This understanding was built over decades of links with anti-colonial and national liberation movements, since the 1920s and 1930s, when CPA leaders met and studied with their counterparts in the Asian communist parties of China, Vietnam, India and the Dutch colonies which would later become Indonesia (Boughton, 1997).

This tradition of socialist, anti-imperialist solidarity informed the CPA's work in the 1930s opposing the Menzies government's export of pig-iron to Japan, which was already invading China. It continued into the 1950s and 1960s, opposing the imperial ambitions of the triad in Malaya, Korea, Vietnam, Cambodia and Indonesia. It was also behind the CPA's support of the Southern Africa Liberation Centre in Sydney which provided material and political support to the anti-apartheid movement in South Africa, and the independence movements in Zimbabwe and the ex-Portuguese colonies, Angola, Mozambique and Guinea-Bissau. On the other hand, social democratic and liberal democratic parties as we know them in the West, in the Global North, do not operate clandestinely, or engage in armed struggle. So, when people in Australia or the UK or the US say that FRETILIN was a nationalist party or a social democratic party, they are ignoring what is perhaps the most significant aspect of FRETILIN's true nature in 1975. FRETILIN was an *anti-colonialist* party, a party of national liberation; and its natural allies and the parties from which it learned most in the early years of its existence were other national liberation parties and revolutionary parties. They were the parties which had the experiences, skills and traditions of clandestine work and armed struggle that FRETILIN needed. That is why they formed an alliance with the CPA, because it was part of an international movement which had been working successfully with national liberation movements since the 1920s, and which had its own experience of illegality and operating clandestinely.

Finally, it would be a great mistake to think that the role of intelligence and security agencies in defending imperialist interests in the region has diminished or become more benign in the last decade. After Timor-Leste became independent, Australia's security apparatus continued to play a significant role in attempts to limit the new FRETILIN government's access to oil and gas resources in the Timor Sea, including bugging Prime Minister Alkatiri's offices under cover of an NGO aid operation, during negotiations over the maritime boundary between the two countries. This was directly related to the Australian government's partnership with a major oil company, Woodside Petroleum, which had benefited from previous arrangements negotiated between Australia and Indonesia when Indonesia was illegally occupying the country (McGrath, 2017; Fernandes, 2017). There are indications from secret cables that Wikileaks published from the US embassy in Dili during the 2006–07 political crisis, and from published reports from observers in Timor-Leste at the time, that the US, Australia and Indonesia were all intervening in this crisis in an effort to have the FRETILIN government removed from office (Anderson, 2006; Martinkus, 2006; Lao Hamutuk, 2017). Analysis of the events of these later periods, however, is beyond the scope of this chapter.

CONCLUSION

The CPA ceased operating as a political party at a final Congress in 1991, and its membership and resources were transferred to a new organisation, the SEARCH Foundation, which has continued the CPA's tradition of international solidarity work. In May 2000, I was privileged to be chosen to be a participant in a SEARCH delegation invited to the FRETILIN cadres Conference in Dili, the first above-ground conference to be held in-country since 1975. Sadly, in the 17 years that have elapsed since then, four of my comrades who were part of that delegation have died: Brian Manning, Pippa Duncan, Rob Durbridge and Graeme Larcombe. At least two other radio operators, Neville Cunningham and Cosmos Bryson, have also died. So too have many more of our FRETILIN comrades who had survived the war. This leads me to reflect on what will happen in the next 15 years, as the rest of us reach the end of our lives. The members of that delegation had begun our solidarity work forty years ago, and our relationships with our FRETILIN comrades were initially built in our twenties and thirties. So, the question the chapter finishes with is this: are today's solidarity movement activists building relationships which will survive another forty years? If not, then we should do something about it, now. Because there is nothing more certain than that international solidarity will be needed then, just as much as it was forty years ago and has been ever since. As our FRETILIN comrades say, *A luta continua!*

For activists working today in international solidarity, the lessons from this earlier period are that disciplined semi-clandestine action requires an organisation to lead and coordinate the work – if not a party, then something which shares some of its features. Second, this work will need to deal with opposition, not only from security agencies, but from more liberal tendencies within the wider movement. Third, to counter these more liberal tendencies, there is a need to develop and promote detailed historical and concrete analysis of the role of imperialism in relation to the movement or movements being supported. Fourth, international solidarity means accepting and supporting the priorities and strategies of the leadership of the 'front-line' movement, something which many in the Global North find difficult. Finally, however 'free' one's own society might appear, the 'secret state' will still be operating in the shadows, and the consequences for those living and working under the regimes the 'secret state' sustains in other countries can be deadly. One can therefore never assume that international solidarity work to confront these forces can be done without huge risk.

REFERENCES

Anderson, T. (2006, December). 'Timor Leste: The second Australian intervention', *Journal of Australian Political Economy*, 58: 62–93.

ASIO (Australian Security Intelligence Organisation) (1984, 23 March). 'Memo. Subject: Royal Commission Enquiry. When did ASIO cease interest in the Campaign for an Independent East Timor?' Copy obtained by author, from files held in the office of Australian East Timor Association, Melbourne.

Boughton, B. (1997). 'Educating the Educators: The Communist Party of Australia and its influence on Australian adult education', Doctoral dissertation. La Trobe University, Bundoora Victoria. Accessed from www.academia.edu/19259023/Educating_the_Educators_The_Communist_Party_of_Australia_and_Its_Influence_on_Australian_Adult_Education (accessed 28 August 2018).

Boughton, B. (1999). 'The Communist Party of Australia's Involvement in the Struggle for Aboriginal and Torres Strait Islander Peoples' Rights 1920–1970'. In R. Hood & R. Markey (eds), *Labour and Community. Proceedings of the Sixth National Conference of the Australian Society for the Study of Labour History* (pp. 37–46). Wollongong: ASLH Illawarra Branch, Department of Economics, University of Wollongong.

——, & Durnan, D. (2017). 'Popular Education Pedagogy & South-South Solidarity. An Asia Pacific Perspective'. In A. v. Kotze & S. Walters (eds), *Forging Solidarity. Popular Education at work* (pp. 39–48). Rotterdam: Sense.

Burgmann, M. (ed.). (2014). *Dirty Secrets: Our ASIO files.* Sydney: New South Publishing.

Cabral, E. (2000). 'The Indonesian Propaganda War Against East Timor'. In P. Hainsworth & S. McCloskey (eds), *The East Timor Question. The struggle for independence from Indonesia* (pp. 69–84). London and New York: I.B. Taurus.

—— (2002). 'FRETILIN and the Struggle for Independence in East Timor 1974–2002: An examination of the constraints and opportunities of a non-state nationalist movement in the late twentieth century', Doctoral dissertation. Lancaster University, Lancaster, UK.

——, & Martin-Jones, M. (2008). 'Writing the Resistance: Literacy in East Timor 1975–1999', *International Journal of Bilingual Education and Bilingualism*, 11(2): 149–169.

Choudry, A. (2013). 'Activist Research and Organizing: Blurring the boundaries, challenging the binaries', *International Journal of Lifelong Education*, 33(4): 1–16. Accessed from doi: 10.1080/02601370.2013.867907 (accessed 27 August 2018).

CHART (Clearing House for Archival Records on Timor) (n.d.(a)). 'Resistance Radio 1975–1978'. Accessed from https://timorarchives.wordpress.com/2016/04/21/resistance-radio-1975-1978/ (accessed 1 February 2018).

—— (n.d.(b)). *East Timor News* 1977–1985. Accessed from https://chartperiodicals.wordpress.com/2010/09/01/etn/ (accessed 5 February 2018).

Da Silva, A. B. (2011). 'FRETILIN Popular Education 1973–78 and Its Relevance to Timor-Leste Today', Doctoral dissertation. University of New England, Armidale, Australia.

Elenor, C. (2003). '*Calling Fretilin*'. In H. Alexander & P. Griffiths (eds), *A Few Rough Reds: Stories of rank and file organising* (pp. 12–26). Canberra: Australian. Accessed from http://roughreds.com/rrone/elenor.html (accessed 28 August 2018).

Fernandes, C. (2011). *The Independence of East Timor: Multi-dimensional perspectives – occupation, resistance, and international political activism.* Brighton, Portland and Toronto: Sussex Academic Press.

—— (2017). 'Asia-Pacific: Espionage against East Timor and the need for parliamentary oversight', *Alternative Law Journal*, 42(1): 71–73. Accessed from doi:10.1177/1037969X17694796 (accessed 27 August 2018).

Head, M. (2016). 'ASIO, the "protest years" and Whitlam's dismissal', *Alternative Law Journal*, 41(3): 195–199.

Holst, J. (2002). *Social Movements, Civil Society and Radical Adult Education.* Westport, CT: Bergin & Garvey.

Job, P. (2015). 'The anti-FRETILIN hit list, secret briefings and the co-option of Australian foreign policy, 1974–1975', paper presented at the Timor Leste Studies Conference 2015. Volume 2. *Timor Leste 1975: 40 Years On.* Dili, Timor Leste.

Lao Hamatuk (2017). Cables sent from the United States Embassies in Dili, Canberra, the Vatican and Lisbon, plus U.S. State Department memos about Timor-Leste, released by Wikileaks. Updated 11 July 2012. Revised

25 August 2017. Accessed from www.laohamutuk.org/reports/Wikileaks/WikileaksDiliIndex.html (accessed 5 February 2018).

Martinkus, J (2006). 'Of coup plots and shadowy foreigners', *New Zealand Herald*, 22 June. Accessed from www.etan.org/et2006/june/24/22jmart.htm (accessed 28 August 2018).

McGrath, K. (2017). *Crossing the Line: Australia's secret history in the Timor Sea.* Carlton: Redback Quarterly.

McKnight, D. (1994). *Australia's Spies and Their Secrets.* St Leonards, NSW: Allen & Unwin.

Manning, B. (2003). 'Charlie India Echo Tango calling Timor Leste', In H. Alexander & P. Griffiths (eds), *A Few Rough Reds: Stories of rank and file organising* (pp. 12–26). Canberra: Australian. Accessed from http://roughreds.com/rrone/manning.html (accessed 28 August 2018).

National Library of Australia (NLA). (n.d.). 'Guide to the Papers of Denis Freney. MS9535'. Accessed from http://nla.gov.au/nla.obj-327185516/findingaid (accessed 28 August 2018).

NMA (National Museum of Australia). (n.d.). 'Brian Manning, Collaborating for Aboriginal Rights'. Accessed from http://indigenousrights.net.au/people/pagination/brian_manning (accessed 5 February 2018).

Nautilus Institute. (n.d.). 'Shoal Bay Receiving Station'. Accessed from https://nautilus.org/publications/books/australian-forces-abroad/defence-facilities/shoal-bay-receiving-station/ (accessed 4 February 2018).

NDR (2014). Transcript of NDR interview with Edward Snowden. Accessed from www.ndr.de/nachrichten/netzwelt/snowden277_page-2.html (accessed 28 August 2018).

Simpson, B. (2017). 'Newly Declassified U.S. Embassy Jakarta Files Detail Army Killings, U.S. Support for Quashing Leftist Labor Movement', *National Security Archive Briefing Book.* Accessed from National Security Archive website: https://nsarchive.gwu.edu/briefing-book/indonesia/2017-10-17/indonesia-mass-murder-1965-us-embassy-files (accessed 28 August 2018).

Stokes, J. (n.d.). 'A Background to the History and Recordkeeping of the Royal Commission on Intelligence and Security (1974–77), also known as the Hope Royal Commission'. Accessed from www.naa.gov.au/collection/publications/papers-and-podcasts/intelligence-and-security/rcis-stokes.aspx (accessed 5 February 2018).

Tossini, J. V. (2017). 'The Five Eyes. The Intelligence Alliance of the Anglosphere', *UK Defence Journal.* Accessed from https://ukdefencejournal.org.uk/the-five-eyes-the-intelligence-alliance-of-the-anglosphere/ (accessed 28 August 2018).

Walsh, Pat (2007, February 15). 'Reflections on solidarity with East Timor', *APSNet Policy Forum.* Accessed from https://nautilus.org/apsnet/reflections-on-solidarity-with-east-timor/ (accessed 28 August 2018).

6

The plantation-to-plant-to-prison pipeline

David Austin interviewed by Aziz Choudry

In the 1960s and 1970s, Canadian state security carried out active surveillance on a range of Black organisations and individuals across Canada. As in many other locations across North America, Montreal was a hotbed of Black politics, some of which was loosely classified by the Royal Canadian Mounted Police (RCMP) as radical activity. Drawing on this historical moment, along with recent data on the Black prison incarceration rate, this interview probes the relationship between Canadian state security practices that were rooted in what David Austin refers to as 'biosexuality' – a prevailing fear of the Black presence and activity rooted in the history of slavery and colonialism in the Americas and its attendant racial codes[1] – and the contemporary reality of racial profiling and Black incarceration in Canada and the US.

Among other things, biosexuality is also rooted in economics. Since the collapse of slavery in the nineteenth century, North American Blacks have sought various means of procuring employment in light of the collapse of the 'security' attached to their being tied to the plantation. At various moments in both Canada and the US, Blacks were part of the vanguard of the labour movement, for example, John A. Robinson in the Order of Sleeping Car Porters in Canada, Randall Robinson and the Brotherhood of Sleeping Car Porters in the US, both in the early 1900s; and the League of Revolutionary Black Workers in Detroit in the 1960s.

In essence, Black labour and Black groups sought to self-organise within the context of precarious economic possibilities and a decidedly hostile socio-political environment. Blacks had shifted from being producers of surplus labour on the plantation (of course, this challenges Marx's assumption that only workers produce surplus labour) to surplus or superfluous labourers perceived by the state to be a serious threat to national security. The end result of this phenomenon has been growing rates of incarceration in Canada and the US – both as a result of criminal activity directly related to institutional and structural hostility towards this surplus population, and the criminalisation and harsh penalisation of Black people – the use of profiling and stop-and-search measures against Black people, and particularly Black youth, and police assault that have frequently resulted in fatal shootings. The argument here is that the criminalisation of Black people involves measures that are directly related to surveillance and security measures tied to the inherent belief that being Black represents a security threat that is to be monitored, policed, and when deemed necessary, detained.

Finally, the interview probes the question of resistance. Within the context outlined above, what does it mean to resist, and how does resistance occur, or what form does/can it take? Tied to this question is the question of where Black resistance fits within the context of broader societal change.

Aziz Choudry: How do we understand 'national security' and resistance from a critical historical perspective in relation to the lives and struggles of Black folks in North America? Much of what is discussed in academic contexts and in activist literature doesn't really get at its colonial roots, so maybe that's a place to start.

David Austin: Clearly, in terms of how state security functions, it affects and has historically affected a range of people. What I have focused on is how Canadian state security, and state security in general, has impacted and shaped the lives of people of African descent as a way of not simply going back into the historical record, but as a way of thinking about those issues in the contemporary context. It is important to think about state security processes as, in part, having evolved out of policing Black bodies and minds within the context of slavery, for the purpose of disciplining and punishing slaves in relation to their labour. We're talking about a process in which Africans were transported from one part of the world to another for the specific purpose of exploiting their labour, and in which a specific apparatus is developed in order to ensure that they engage in that work. This is important in terms of thinking about the use of Black labour today in the penal system in which prison labour is being exploited by corporations.

Part of what I have focused on is how the codes that have been inherited from that historical period have been continued today, in slavery's afterlife. Under slavery, there was this constant fear of slave rebellion that partly accounts for the preoccupation with containing rebellion that went along with the need to discipline and control slaves and maintain the slave order in order to exploit their labour. There was also a constant fear of preventing forms of Black and white solidarity (David Roediger[2] talks about this). All of this is tied to how we think about those questions today in terms of what solidarity means, impediments to solidarity, and the conscious actions and decisions taken to prevent forms of solidarity between groups of people that may, otherwise, have a great deal in common despite cultural differences. So what we find in the 1960s is that, in the aftermath of slavery in which Black labourers who were responsible for producing surplus labour and surplus value – I'm making this point as a way of rethinking or revising Marx's conception of the working class in which the working class is tied to capitalism in Europe and modern technology and machinery (the means of production) in the factory context which of course centres the European working class. But of course, to state the obvious, slaves used their labour, and as C. L. R. James and Fernando Ortiz, the Cuban historian of slavery, pointed out, Black slave labour produced surplus value which translated into profits, which was crucial to the development of modern capitalism. This free labour made a profound contribution and was crucial to the development of modern capitalism. It was alongside this process that the security and surveillance apparatus was developed to maintain the slave regime and infrastructure. We cannot separate the process of slavery from the emergence of modern capitalism and we cannot separate that process from the history of colonialism in terms of forms of coercion and violence enacted upon Black folks from this context. They were connected then, but are somehow disconnected in our minds today, when we talk about the prison industrial context and the rates of incarceration of Black folks in the US, Canada and the UK.

What we have in the post-slavery period is emancipation without freedom and the question became – what do you do with a population that was a source of surplus labour that produced great profits under slavery and modern capitalism but is now superfluous, or no longer necessary? These emancipated slaves are of course potentially restless and restive, and a source of rebellion, and they find themselves further policed and under the scrutiny of surveillance. So in the post-emancipation period, we have this Du Boisian problem of what to do with the emancipated slave who is yet unfree. The modern response to that problem has been the prison industrial complex in which Blacks are housed in prisons in disproportionate numbers. But of course, they are not simply being housed in prisons but increasingly used as a source of cheap labour. Surveillance, repression and prison – and prison labour has become the solution. It's as if the whole thing has come full circle, as Black labour is now used as a free producer of surplus value, as productive labour in prisons.

AC: How do we think about the question of resistance in relation to this?

DA: The whole point of discipline and punishment is to prevent resistance of this restless, 'free' population. Then the question becomes, how do we as political people respond to this and think about the role of the population that has been marginalised and dispossessed in processes of social transformation? How do we organise in our/those communities in ways that translate that anger and frustration and resentment towards the structures that have created these circumstances? How do we go beyond critique of the system and towards political conversations, popular education conversations on how change comes about?

Resistance comes in many forms, but a fundamental question concerns the relationship between people who have the time and space to think about these questions – intellectuals – and so-called 'ordinary' people. In community work, there is that tension between addressing day-to-day questions about survival, living and existing, and on the other hand, addressing how to change the structural conditions that contribute to dispossession, desperation and marginalisation. How do we begin the conversation on what change means and how do we bring it into being? How do we talk about structural power, create the space for these conversations outside of academic environments? When I worked as a youth worker in Montreal, we tried to carve out that space with youth who were looking for answers by exposing them to Fanon, for example, as a way of explaining the internecine violence that was occurring around them and as a way of breaking down these pseudo-conceptions of 'Black on Black crime' in the media. What does Fanon have to say about the psychological and social forces at play that influence this violent phenomenon? How can this experience be channelled and translated into politics and thinking and acting to bring about change on a local community level in ways that connect with other local movements engaged in similar work – whether in the UK or Bangladesh, creating the basis for a broader and even international movement? How do we connect the local with the international and avoid the prevailing parochialism that separate groups that have a great deal in common, but without overlooking the differences between them?

Again, for me, this involves acting on a local level where things matter most to people, while being conscious of what is happening and connecting the dots with what is happening elsewhere, in other parts of the world. This represents the genuine makings of an internationalist movement as opposed to abstractly talking about internationalism.

As youth workers, we were reading Freire and thinking about popular education and how we dialogue as opposed to simply speaking to members of the community, learning and thinking about what these young women and men were going through, which included being constantly monitored and harassed by the police. Of course community organisations, like NGOs, are beholden to state and private foundation grants, so we also need to think about how groups and movements have functioned without this kind of support and examine their successes and failures. How did SNCC [Student Non-violent Coordinating Committee] function? How did the Black Panther Party [BPP] and other groups function? How did they organise at the community level – healthcare, breakfast programmes, after-school programmes, etc. – how did they do this? How did the League of Revolutionary Black Workers in Detroit organise? How do we break from the grant model of organising and, in general, existing models and their limitations and towards models that genuinely facilitate freedom, allowing us to break with what is and to imagine what can be?

Revisiting those movements as well as various thinkers within the context of how power functions, and in order to think about how we organise for change, this is, I think, an important step in the right direction.

AC: Going back to the idea of the plantation-to-plant-to-prison pipeline in North America, what are the economic interests tied to state security in Canada and the US? Is there continuity and change in terms of how this has or hasn't shifted over the years?

DA: It's all tied to economics in one form or another. When we think about various moments in the history of Black migration – in the US from the South to the North fleeing micro police states in the South (lynchings, chain gangs, etc.); you have the Harlem Renaissance and the migration to the northern US and Canada in search of economic opportunities. There is always this tension because there is the desire for labour but the people whose labour is desired are considered undesirable. And when the need for that labour is not in the same demand, the question, again, becomes what do you do with the superfluous population that is no longer tied to the plantation in the South or in the Caribbean and that is not needed to the same degree in the North? This permanent sense of being the Other, outsider, or the immigrant is tied to this, as is policing.

This brings to mind Giorgio Agamben's notion of the refugee's permanent state of exception, a permanent state of emergency in which everyday rights and entitlements are suspended.[3] But while Agamben references the liminal status of refugees, Blacks have been living in a permanent state of dispossession, the permanent refugee.

As capitalism's needs shift, at times in need of more labour in times of relative economic boom, and less labour in times of crisis, the desperate need to police, for surveillance, and to incarcerate people of African descent waxes and wanes, to a degree, although as a whole the process is sustained and consistent. These shifts tell us something about the simultaneity of progression and regression: the fact that we can have advancements in terms of the level of education and a growing Black elite for example, but on the other hand, increasing numbers of Blacks who are locked away in the prisons, tied up in the judicial system, high drop-out and unemployment rates, etc., a phenomenon that plays itself out in the UK, Canada and the US in similar proportions. In Quebec for example, this has historically meant that, despite being more highly educated than the average, including graduate-level degrees, people of African descent have found themselves less employable, and in some instances confront higher rates of unemployment than high school-educated Quebecers.

At what point do we have a conversation about the system itself? And at what point do we begin to name alternatives, for the disenfranchised and dispossessed, of which people of African descent are disproportionately represented – as are Indigenous Peoples? When do we have a serious conversation about what is this thing called 'socialism', or about alternatives to the prevailing economic system? How do we begin to imagine another kind of society in which human beings can live and interact as human beings? For me, shorn of all the baggage tied to Europe, the word 'socialism' still has resonance and meaning because it speaks to an alternative, in theory, a society shorn of hierarchical structures; a society in which people own their labour and are invested in the politics that shape and determine their life chances. That should sound good to anybody concerned with social change. How do we think about this in practice as a viable alternative? Clearly, there are conversations to be had about what the politics of the left have meant for people of African descent, a left that has failed to seriously consider the plight of Black folks, not to mention Indigenous folks, beyond narrowly defined class concerns and economics. Clearly, any notion of social change or socialism that doesn't take into consideration how race has been an impediment to building a genuine left or socialist alternative is not going anywhere.

AC: What are some of the specific forms of knowledge and learning that have been produced in terms of Black organising and struggles in Canada that allow people to push past this liberal notion of state security and to get at the nature of the state in a more serious way?

DA: I think we're at a point where the level of conversation or the point of departure for these political-economic questions is well out of sync with the reality and lacks a sense of urgency in relation to where we actually are. To be fair, we've had the Black Lives Matter (BLM) movement that has injected a sense of political-intellectual urgency that is important not to dismiss, and their point of departure in terms of appreciating the convergence of gender, race, and class and power, internationalism is perhaps in advance of the previous generation. This said, we learn things as we go along and there's something to be said for conversations between the younger, older and 'in-between generation' as someone referred to me the other day, a context in which the older generation learns from the younger, or at least should, but there are still things that the younger can learn from the older. BLM has played a profoundly important role. We are also seeing the potential to subvert the movement as it becomes more accepted. What we learn from the 1960s and 1970s – the things that stand out for me – is that in one form or another, they were all talking about a kind of socialism or socialistic society. To get beyond the word and closer to its meaning, they were talking about a more egalitarian society, a non-capitalistic society in terms of its social and economic relations, a society that was not colonial or imperialistic in terms of Canada's or the US's relationship with other parts of the world. That was their point of departure, and this is profoundly significant when we think about where some of those conversations begin today, particularly in terms of those narratives that suggest that solidarity doesn't matter any more and that politics is simply about representation. For the Black internationalist left in the 1960s and 1970s, their point of departure was that we cannot speak about equality for some at the expense of others, and beyond thinking about the symbolic significance of having a Black face in the White House, there would have been no space or tolerance for a structure, and the person at the head of that structure, that dropped bombs on people overseas and neglected society's most dispossessed at home while bailing out the banks in a moment of economic crisis; there would be no space or tolerance for the general commitment to neoliberal policies in which the same level of social, economic and political neglect that was practiced by previous administrations is continued. So, the politics of that moment, with all of its problems in terms of thinking about gender, sexuality, and all kinds of questions in that very masculine moment that were really not on the agenda, were clear on how power functioned locally and internationally. If we are going to accept the romance of that time and the iconic symbolism of that moment, we also have to be able to appreciate the politics and the fact that the BPP, Angela Davis, George Jackson, etc., were speaking to, in some form or another, some kind of socialism, even when many of them were quite clear that they were not speaking about some outmoded European forms of socialism. They were also internationalists. You had the Third World anti-colonial solidarity and radical politics of Lorraine Hansberry; and Maya Angelou was living in Ghana and returned to the US to work with Malcolm X; James Forman, like Malcolm X, travelled across the African continent; Walter Rodney taught in Tanzania and was very familiar with various forms of African socialism, including the Ujamaa experiment under Nyerere's leadership.

AC: What are the differences between how this plays out in Canada and the US in relation to the plantation-to-plant-to-prison pipeline idea with the focus on the security and surveillance state?

DA: It's tricky because, on the one hand, Canada exists in the shadow of the US and has historically been a junior 'soft power', but when we look at the historical relationship between Canada and the Caribbean, for example (Peter Hudson's[4] work on Canadian banks speaks to this), the myth of Canadian innocence is so strong that it shields the reality that Canada has been both an imperial power and an imperial intermediary. When Rodney was in Montreal in 1968 and delivered his presentation on 'African History in the Service of Black Liberation' at the Congress of Black Writers,[5] one thing he said as someone from Guyana, was that bauxite, the major mineral used in the manufacture of aluminium, is mined in Guyana and manufactured in Arvida, Saguenay Lac-Saint Jean, Quebec, not far from Montreal. He named that as a way of saying that Canada is not the innocent peacekeeping nation it makes itself out to be on the world stage. Clearly, Canada is not the imperial power that the US is and has been, but there was slavery in this country and we live with all of its attendant racial codes today. We have the myth of reconciliation with Indigenous Peoples and yet they live under colonial circumstances that are reproduced in various ways, including in relation to the recent conversations about the Keystone oil pipeline. So, the myth of Canadian innocence is almost as strong as the myth of American exceptionalism – the idea that anyone can achieve in the US if they exercise their will and pull themselves up by the bootstraps. Proportionately, they are equally pernicious. There are entire sections of prisons in Canada with large numbers of people of African descent. So there are differences in terms of absolute numbers, and the national narratives are different, but proportionately, the differences are not that significant. When you see how people live in the historically Black Preston districts,[6] for example, in Halifax, and consider the overall situation among Black folks out there, and how Black folks whose history goes back more than two centuries in Nova Scotia and essentially still live in a de facto segregated and grossly unequal society, what does their lived experience, in contrast to the national narrative, tell us about Canada? There are differences in terms of the respective histories – even though it is important to acknowledge the continuities in the histories – all of that is true. But in practice – and Barrington Walker's book[7] is important in this sense in Ontario, as is Afua Cooper's book in relation to Quebec and slavery in New France[8] – the lived experiences have not been that much different when we make allowances for the particularities is terms of size, etc.

AC: This book [this volume] focuses on what we have or haven't learned in terms of surveillance regarding progressive organising and struggles in liberal democracies. What lessons can be learned from reflecting on the plantation-to-plant-to-prison pipeline in the North American context in order to think about these kinds of questions today? What do you think people should learn from experience?

DA: History for me is congealed experience that allows us to go back and benefit from that concentrated experience that is captured in whatever narrative or book or archive in order to learn something about the present. And when you look at these security files and read accounts of what happened in a particular meeting or event, some of which were private or closed events, we realise the extent to which these groups were infiltrated, and we should be prompted to think about how surveillance functions today. That's the importance of that history. If you are engaged in a politics that challenges the status of how things are or to organise to bring about change in some form or another, you should not be surprised when the very power that you are confronting does everything in its power to prevent you from achieving your goal. This is when we get beyond the romance of the 1960s–1970s and the BPP and Black Power, for example, and recognise how they were destroyed. This history can be about trying to come to terms with the pitfalls, mistakes, challenges that movements confront and have confronted historically so that we can benefit and learn from that congealed experience and potentially avoid some of the same mistakes and challenges. We are not supposed to be surprised that in any movement we find agents and provocateurs whose mission is to disrupt and destroy movements. And this is particularly so today when authorities have the technology at their disposal to carry out surveillance more effectively. The question then becomes, what strategies and tactics should be adopted or adapted to engage in processes of change? How do we organise for change in the current conjecture or context? Part of the answer to this involves having an appreciation of the fact that power does not simply cede power. Power will do everything in its power to disrupt, destroy and detain those who attempt to challenge it. For me, that's the big lesson.

Some things, some understanding, comes with time, and this is why we need the intelligence and experience of youth connected with the experience of the older generation, engaged in an ongoing conversation. That's how experience gets shared. In the absence of that, actions are often taken that negatively affect lives, and some lives are more affected than others because of the ways in which race functions in this society. If you engage in a process whose end goal is to fundamentally change the world that we live in for the better, you have to anticipate that there are challenges involved in that and you have to be sure that that's where your convictions lie, because it is not something to play with, and lives are at stake.

NOTES

1 David Austin, *Fear of a Black Nation: Race, sex, and security in Sixties Montreal* (Toronto: Between the Lines, 2013), pp. 11, 167, 182, 187.
2 David R. Roediger, *The Wages of Whiteness: Race and the making of the American working class* (London: Verso, 1999).
3 Giorgio Agamben, *Means Without End: Notes on politics* (Minneapolis: University of Minnesota, 2000), pp. 4–6, 8–9. and Giorgio Agamben, *Homo Sacer: Sovereign power and bare life* (Stanford, CA: Stanford University Press, 1998), pp. 15, 119.
4 Peter Hudson, 'Imperial Designs: The Royal Bank of Canada in the Caribbean', *Race and Class*, 52(1) (July-August 2010): 33–48.
5 See Walter Rodney, 'African History in the Service of Black Revolution'. In David Austin (ed.), *Moving Against the System: The 1968 Congress of Black Writers and the making of global consciousness* (London: Pluto Press, 2018), pp. 127–142.
6 Black Loyalists who fought for the British Crown during the American War of Independence were settled in East and North Preston after the

war. Historically, the areas have been plagued by sparse economic resources and all of the attendant problems that accompany this today.

7 Barrington Walker, *Race on Trial: Black defendants in Ontario's criminal courts, 1858–1958* (Toronto: University of Toronto Press, 2010).

8 Afua Cooper, *The Hanging of Angélique: The untold story of Canadian slavery and the burning of Old Montreal* (Toronto: HarperCollins Publishers, 2006).

7

Forgetting national security in 'Canada'[1]

Towards pedagogies of resistance

Gary Kinsman

This chapter explores two instances of the social organisation of forgetting of national security state practices and resistance to this in 'Canada'. These involve the political limitations of organising efforts against repressive state legislation and for an apology for state national security injustices.

The first occurs under the guise of resisting what was often referred to as police state measures (Bill C-51 the Anti-Terrorism Act) in 2015. The second occurred in 2017 with the apology to LGBTQ2S+[2] people for the purge campaigns and 'historical injustices' committed against us. These relate in differing ways to the social amnesia created about histories of national security and state repression and what can be learned from resistance to them and the activist knowledges resistance produced. In both cases, these organising efforts, and especially state responses, end up staying on the surface of national security ideology, developing only internal critiques of aspects of these practices, while preventing national security itself from being put into question (Kinsman, Buse & Steedman, 2000). I focus here on the pedagogical implications of these efforts. Engagement with national security is always about knowledge and learning. Unfortunately, in these two instances, it has largely been a pedagogy from above that gained hegemony. What could have been used to undermine national security ends up being transformed and used to shore it up, even if in modified form. I contrast this with the exploration Patrizia Gentile and I develop in *The Canadian War on Queers* (Kinsman & Gentile, 2010) of critical analysis of national security and learning from resistance to security practices.

TAKE ONE: MOBILISATIONS AGAINST BILL C-51 – FROM NATIONAL SECURITY TO PRIME MINISTER HARPER AS THE PROBLEM

In 2015, Stephen Harper's Conservative government introduced new legislation as part of its intensification of security practices. Passed with the support of the Liberal Party as the Anti-Terrorism Act, it built upon existing national security practices that were already strengthened in the 'war on terror' (Kinsman & Gentile, 2010, pp. 429–458), while broadening them. Key features included: an expansion of national security to prevent interference with the 'economic or financial stability of Canada';[3] the criminalisation of speech acts having nothing to do with violence; making measures such as the no-fly list even more secretive; compelling government agencies to share information with the Royal Canadian Mounted Police (RCMP – the federal police); making existing practices of preventative arrest even worse, and giving the Canadian Security Intelligence Service (CSIS) the power to operate as police while maintaining its status as an intelligence agency (BCCLA, 2015). The pro-capitalist character of Canadian national security was made more explicit with this targeting of movements that interfere with Canadian 'economic and financial stability', building on practices that target Indigenous and ecological opposition to the tar sands and pipelines, as well as other Indigenous struggles and direct action based organising in global justice, student and workers' struggles.

In the mobilisation against this legislation dominated largely by liberal and social democratic forces, the long history of national security practices was largely forgotten as there was a focus on this being about Harper and his attack on freedom of speech. For instance, one flyer for a significant coalition demonstration on 14 March 2015 in Toronto declared: 'Don't Let Stephen Harper's Terror Bill Destroy Our Rights' (Stop Bill C-51, 2015 flyer).

This points to the *moment* of anti-Harper politics which largely framed this organising effort and was central to its limitations. The Harper government shifted state policies further to the right in several areas, which led to an exaggerated focus on his individual responsibility for these changes in the resulting organising efforts. This led to not seeing continuities with earlier national security practices and the common interests of the Canadian national security state that linked the Conservative government and the Liberal opposition. The implication sometimes seemed to be that national security policing prior to this legislation was not a significant problem, and there was little attempt to fight against these changes in the context of a broader battle against national security.

While this anti-Harper focus was useful in undermining popular support for the legislation, it did not allow people to learn from the history of resistance to earlier national security policing. The organising was against excesses but not against national security itself. It did not prepare people for the ways in which the Liberal government elected in 2015 would maintain the legislation's basic features.

The Liberals voted for the Bill, wanting to support strong national security measures, but said they would get rid of its excesses and lack of oversight if elected (Hall, 2016). In June 2017, they finally introduced legislation (Bill C-59), which left most of its components intact while reining in and clarifying only a few of the powers granted to security agencies. It also raised new concerns through an expansion of security powers relating to cyber-surveillance (CCLA, 2017).

TAKE TWO: THE APOLOGY – FROM THE CANADIAN WAR ON QUEERS TO A RETURN TO THE NATION AND NATIONAL SECURITY

On 28 November 2017, the Liberal government issued an official apology (PMO, 2017) to LGBTQ2S+ people for a series of injustices, especially the national security campaign that led to thousands of members of the public service and the military being purged from the 1950s to the early 1990s, once they were identified as 'homosexuals' or 'sex deviates' (in the military) during the Canadian war on queers (Kinsman & Gentile, 2010; We Demand an Apology Network (WDAN), 2016). This was justified on the grounds that 'homosexuals' were a threat to national security, since we suffered from a 'character weakness' that made us vulnerable to blackmail by foreign agents. As we detail in our book, people directly affected by the purge campaign said the only people who tried to blackmail them were the RCMP and other security forces trying to get the names of people who were 'homosexual' in the public service and the military (Kinsman & Gentile, 2010).

This apology came about in part because of the growing self-organisation of those directly affected by the purge campaigns, especially in the We Demand an Apology Network (WDAN) and the support this gained first in the New Democratic Party (NDP), then among the Liberals and in the mass media (WDAN, 2016). A space was created through the organising of WDAN (2016; 2017), through EGALE's *Just Society* report (EGALE, 2016), and through the class-action suits launched against the government, for more people to break the silence by telling their stories of being purged, and of surveillance and harassment. Possible lines of rupture with the national security state opened up.

However, through a series of shifts, the apology is transformed: from an apology from below to an apology from above. This also has to do with the apology social form itself, which suggests that once an apology is given, what occurred can be forgotten (S. Maynard, 2017), and with the contradictions of relying on a politics of recognition from state agencies (Coulthard, 2014).

The statement read by Prime Minister Justin Trudeau was transformed for many through saying 'we are sorry' into a re-assertion of the 'nation', with no major questions regarding national security being raised. This was done through the eclipsing of a pedagogy of resistance from below and the mobilisation of a pedagogy of patriotism and the triumph of the 'Canadian values' of 'diversity' and 'inclusion' drawn from state multiculturalism. In multiculturalism as state policy, formal and cultural rights are granted to various ethnic and other groups while the substantive social and class basis for oppression continues. There are major problems with pedagogies of multiculturalism, inclusion and diversity[4] that forget the history of settler colonialism, anti-Black racism and slavery, racist immigration policies, and more (Bannerji, 1995, 2000; Thobani, 2007; R. Maynard, 2017; Walcott, 2016).

PEDAGOGIES FROM ABOVE AND OF RESISTANCE

The pedagogical implications of this organising in both instances never put national security in question. Rather than an active remembering of the history of repression and making groups of people into 'others' that is central to national security, and a remembering of our multifaceted resistance to these practices, it instead became a pedagogy from above based on forgetting this resistance. This occurs both when focusing on the problem being an individual rather than national security itself and in an apology being used to let some previously otherised people back into the nation. Instead, pedagogies of resistance allowing us to remember not only state violence but also our diverse resistance to it is a much more critical and empowering way to proceed. This allows not for the shoring-up of national security but for its subversion through the expansion of resistance.

'WE' ARE THE CRISIS OF NATIONAL SECURITY

In response to these instances of the active social organisation of forgetting, I offer a different pedagogy based on the resistance of remembering. In part, capitalism and oppression rule through what Patrizia Gentile and I call the 'social organisation of forgetting' which is based on the eclipsing of our historical and social memories (Kinsman & Gentile, 2010; Gentile, Kinsman & Rankin, 2017). This is what leads to the assertion that national security practices – without excesses and with 'oversight' – are 'good' and that there are no basic problems with 'national security'. This forgetting is crucial to how social power works in our society. We no longer remember past struggles that won us the social gains, social programs and human rights, as well as limitations placed on the national security state, that we often take for granted. We have been forced to forget where we have come from; our histories have never been recorded and passed down, and we are denied the social literacy that allows us to relive our past and, therefore, to grasp our present (Kinsman & Gentile, 2010, p. 21).

'Canada' is not a unitary entity, but is instead criss-crossed with struggles over colonisation, racialisation, class, gender, sexuality, the environment and more. Canada's national security is defined by those with political and class power who define *their* interests as the 'national interest'. It is *their* security that is being defended in national security. It is our various movements for social and ecological justice that challenge *their* national security.

Drawing on Holloway's (2005, 2010, 2016) affirmation that 'we'[5] are the crisis of capitalism, I argue that 'we' in our various movements are the crisis of national security. 'We' are the 'national security risks' that they are fighting against. We need to resist their national security since their 'security' is based on our insecurity, oppression and exploitation. *Their* national security is a threat to the security and progress of our movements.

Memory has a social and historical character. But many of us lack a historical sense of our lives because we have been denied a language of social literacy that allows us to remember our experiences, especially given the secretive character of national security practices in Canadian history and the pervasive mythologies of Canadian multiculturalism, inclusion and diversity that can prevent us from remembering actual histories of colonisation, racism, repression and violence. This lack of historical memory makes it hard to remember social aspects of our pasts and their implications for our historical present (Kinsman & Gentile, 2010, p. 37).

Focusing on Harper, the mainstream organising against Bill C-51 did not lead us to remember the long history of national security repression, nor fully grasp how the problem was not simply Harper but Canadian national security itself. This also allowed Trudeau's Liberal government to continue these national security practices with only minor modifications. The apology process for the purge campaign has been able to largely portray the campaign as a 'mistake' that has now been corrected so that queer people can join the nation, the military and national security: and we can forget about the experience of being made into national security threats. But heterosexual hegemony (Kinsman, 1996) remains largely intact, even as queer and to some extent trans people are granted formal rights. But there are also those left behind or excluded from the 'rights' revolution, including queer and trans people of colour, two-spirit people, queer and trans homeless and poor people including queer and trans youth expelled from their families, sex workers and more, and there is much remaining oppression (Dryden & Lenon, 2015).

Drawing on work for *The Canadian War on Queers*, which documented the national security campaign against gay men and lesbians in Canada from the late 1950s to the early 1990s, I analyse national security as an ideological practice that is always about defining the 'nation' as well as the 'enemies' of the 'nation', and forgetting or justifying actual national security repression. We always need to ask which nation and whose security is being defended (Kinsman, Buse & Steedman, 2000). It is crucial to not take national security for granted.

National security is always based on the exclusion of some groups of people identified as 'other,' or as the 'enemy' within, from the very fabric of the 'nation-state'. Meanwhile, other groups are included at the centre of this nation-state. While national security often violently excludes, it is also *productive* of the character of social power in the nation-state. Crucial to pedagogies of resistance is recognition of not only 'repressive' but also 'productive' dimensions of national security.

In the context of the war on queers, while queers were expelled from the nation, heterosexuality in a relational fashion was placed at the centre as the national, normal, secure and safe sexuality. The other side of this was the construction of heterosexual hegemony and the social relations of the closet forced on many queer people.

ISLAMOPHOBIA, WHITE SUPREMACY AND NATIONAL SECURITY

In the context of the 'war on terror', while those identified as Arab and Muslim are expelled from the nation in a relational fashion, white and 'Christian' identified people are placed at its centre. This is a 'nation' built on the colonisation of Indigenous Peoples and anti-Black racism and racist immigration policies. This provides a basis for white supremacy and what is often referred to as 'Islamophobia'.[6]

The importance of these struggles was highlighted at a Toronto demonstration I attended with over 6,000 people protesting against Islamophobia and white supremacy following the murders of six men at Quebec City's Islamic Cultural Centre (Hussan, 2018; *Global News*, 2018). In the context of a broader speech against white supremacy, on 4 February 2017, Yusra Khogali of Black Lives Matter-Toronto (BLM-TO) called Justin Trudeau a hypocrite and 'a white supremacist terrorist' for maintaining racist immigration and refugee policies, the colonisation of Indigenous Peoples and a racist and white supremacist state and society. When she said this in context, most of the crowd was with her, but the mainstream media almost immediately attacked her credibility, dislocating what she said from the context in which she spoke. Unfortunately, most left and social movement activists did not defend her. As a result, the cycle of mobilisation initiated by the Toronto January 21, 2017 Women's March Against Trump, which saw thousands of people in movement and making political connections, began to be undermined.

This construction of Trudeau as qualitatively different from Harper played a role in limiting opposition to the continuation of national security policing under the Liberal government and in support for the apology from above. While there are significant differences in style and policy between Trudeau and Harper, this has been mobilised to obscure their common commitments to the national security state and maintaining capitalist, racist and patriarchal social relations. In not seeing this, the relevancies of national security come to trap us within the ideological codes of nation and national security (Kinsman & Gentile, 2010, p. 33).

PEDAGOGIES OF RESISTANCE

It is important to remember and to learn from experiences of struggle that have obstructed national security and forced shifts in its practices. People are never simply the passive 'victims' of national security but often actively navigate and resist these practices. Even before an organised movement emerged, gays were able to obstruct national security campaigns in the early 1960s. David's story from 1964 in Ottawa describes national security surveillance to identify men in the bar and resistance to this at the Lord Elgin basement tavern which was then a meeting ground for men interested in having sex with other men:

> We even knew … that there was somebody in some police force … who would be sitting in the bar. And you would see someone with a … newspaper held right up, and if you … looked really closely you could find him holding behind the newspaper a camera, and these people were photographing everyone in the bar … We always knew that when you

> saw someone with a newspaper held right up in front of their face … that somebody would take out something like a wallet and do this sort of thing [like snapping a photo] and then … everyone would then point over to that person …. And I am sure that the person hiding behind the newspaper knew he had been found out.
>
> (Kinsman & Gentile, 2010, p. 1)

This resistance was part of a broader practice of non-collaboration with the RCMP that developed in gay networks in Ottawa in the early 1960s, and forced the RCMP to shift strategy. It could no longer rely on gay informants outside the public service and had to rely more on local sexual policing, threatening to lay criminal code charges against people so that they would give up people's names. It also participated in the 'fruit machine' detection research commissioned by the Canadian government to try to find a 'scientific' way to determine people's sexualities so that 'homosexuals' could be denied employment or purged (Kinsman & Gentile, 2010).

In the rest of this chapter, I go into more detail on the limitations of mainstream opposition to Bill C-51 and the apology from above. Throughout, I paint into the picture pedagogies of resistance.

RESISTING THE INTENSIFICATION OF NATIONAL SECURITY POLICING

As mentioned, Bill C-51 intensified important aspects of the national security regime. The breadth of opposition to Bill C-51 undermined some of the initial public support through its focus on Harper's attack on civil liberties, but did not prevent it from passing nor did it prepare people for what would be needed after the Liberals were elected.

I was uneasy with the rhetoric used in this organising, and at its lack of recognition of the long history of national security attacks on Indigenous Peoples, the left, the unions, immigrants, Black activists and other people of colour, feminists, lesbians and gays and queer movements, the global justice movement, anti-poverty activists, the radical wings of ecology movements and those identified as Muslim and Arab.

The roots of these national security attacks go back to the formation of policing as part of the colonisation of Indigenous Peoples. The attacks on people of colour, Arabs and Muslims pre-date 9/11. Indigenous land defenders, direct action anti-poverty activists, Black activists, global justice activists and environmental activists have been accused of being 'terrorists' long before Harper. Activists have been targeted before for social and economic disruptions that threaten the 'national interest' (Kinsman & Gentile, 2010). There is not that much new here, although Bill C-51 made these practices more formalised and clearly mandated.

A different, more deeply-rooted politics was prefigured at a Toronto event with over two hundred people, facilitated by No One Is Illegal Toronto, called 'C-51 Can't Stop Us! Fighting Colonialism, Islamophobia and Surveillance' (30 March 2015). The event included recognition of the earlier and continuing histories of national security policing practices against Indigenous communities through a presentation by Judy Da Silva from Grassy Narrows (Asubpeeschoseewagong First Nation), as well as the experiences of those placed under security certificates when Mohammad Mahjoub spoke.[7] Security certificates allow for indefinite detention and regulation of non-permanent residents (Kinsman & Gentile, 2010, pp. 447–448). This was followed by activists from various movements calling for defying Bill C-51 through deepening our struggles.

Syed Hussan read a powerful and poetic manifesto calling for the breaking of Bill C-51:

> The purpose of C-51 … they say, is to defend Canada … This Canada sprung forth into the world through the theft of Indigenous lands. Its birth a blood bath whose stains cannot be washed away by apologies … And in the hands and jails of this Canada, too many of us have been terrorists, too many of us criminal. And so today, either we proudly declare We Are All Terrorists. Or we insist in one loud voice that there are no terrorists … A brutal, vicious, greedy Canada has been breathing down on us for too long. It is our enemy. In the words of June Jordan, let us become a menace to our enemies.
>
> (Hussan, 2015)

This organising was based on ripping open the ideology and practice of national security and identifying that 'we' are the crisis of national security. It was a brilliant instance of a pedagogy of resistance, since it both remembered the long history of national security policing, as well as our histories of resistance and was based on amplifying resistance. It is unfortunate it was not picked up more broadly in the organising against

Bill C-51. National security participates in producing colonialism, racism and capitalism, and breaking it creates openings for Indigenous, anti-racist and anti-capitalist struggles.

While criticising Bill C-51, the moderate anti-Harper opposition focused on the need for more limited forms of security policing that would not target 'legitimate' protest but would instead focus only on forms of protest and subversion that were not legal, such as many direct action protests. To be effective, opposition to Bill C-51 needed to take apart the division between 'good' and 'bad' protestors that state responses and protest policing introduced (Kinsman, 2006). To accept this division is playing by their rules and is like struggling with one hand tied behind our backs, ruling out forms of organising that are often the most effective. The tactics they lay out as 'proper' are the ones that often have little impact and that contain our struggles. We also need to remember the histories of militant struggles that have won gains for us in the past. To say that only 'good' protests are allowed is to refuse to learn from history and to deny our movements effective strategies and tactics for winning victories.

For these reasons, we must deepen opposition to state security legislation through questioning national security in more profound ways. We need to commit to breaking the Anti-Terrorism Bill and Bill C-59 through continuing our movements to challenge capitalist and oppressive economic and financial stability. We should also remember that the central targets of this legislation are Indigenous land defenders, activists organising against the tar sands and associated pipelines, and Muslim and Arab people. We need to intensify our solidarity with these groups and struggles.

This forgetting of national security practices has also occurred in the official response to the 'historical injustices' faced by LGBTQ2S+ people.

FROM AN APOLOGY FROM BELOW TO THE APOLOGY FROM ABOVE

There are two stories of the apology to LGBTQ2S+ people. The apology from below is based on a history of resistance to national security. The apology from above affirms a modified patriotic national security. The state-oriented apology from above actively attempts to submerge the apology from below. Given my long-standing involvement in demands for a state apology including in WDAN, formed in 2015, which pushed for a state apology, a broad redress process and the expungement of criminal code convictions for consensual same-sex activities (2016, 2017), I also draw on my own experiences.

In the last week of November 2017, I was thrown into the midst of this active social battle over interpreting the apology (Kinsman, 2017a, 2017b). I attended an Ottawa reception at the Lord Elgin Hotel organised by lawyer Doug Elliot, one of the lawyers for the class-action suit for redress against the federal government, and Diane Pitre, one of many in attendance who were purged from the military; the reception was held for participants in the class-action suit.

Elliot, referring to our opening story in *The Canadian War on Queers*, talked about the history of RCMP surveillance in the Lord Elgin's basement tavern in the 1960s. While mentioning that RCMP operatives would hide behind newspapers to take photos of the men in the bar, he forgot to say that it was common for the men there to turn the tables on the agents. He did not mention that this was not only a site of surveillance, *but* more importantly a site of resistance. This eclipsing of the history of queer resistance would become more profound the next day.

Elliot then told people at the reception that 'you did nothing wrong, you just wanted to serve your country.' This appeal to Canadian patriotism would also become more intense the following day. This appeal to nation and the affirmation of how supposedly wonderful Canada is for all LGBTQ2S+ people is what Jasbir Puar and others call 'homonationalism' (Puar, 2007; Dryden & Lenon, 2015; Alwad, 2015).[8] Unfortunately, some queer left critics of the apology tend to reduce the apology simply to 'homonationalism', ceding this terrain entirely to the apology from above and eclipsing the long history of queer resistance to national security.[9]

What made my experience of the apology so contradictory was the rupture between WDAN's grass-roots concerns based on the experiences of those directly affected by the purge campaign, and the attempt to transform this resistance into an apology from above that forgets this resistance.

This was accomplished rather successfully in a number of overlapping ways. A year after WDAN's formation, EGALE, a major Canadian LGBT rights organisation, produced the *Just Society* report (EGALE, 2016) arguing for a wide-ranging apology, redress and the expungement of criminal code convictions for consensual same-sex sexual activities. While including some useful proposals, the report had significant limitations with an exaggeration of the 1969 criminal code reform which was only a limited and partial decriminalisation. It suggested instead that the then Prime Minister Pierre Elliot Trudeau (Justin Trudeau's father) was pushing for equality for gays and lesbians; and used a quote framing the report from P. E. Trudeau's 'Just Society' speech, advocating individual rights but opposing the collective movements of self-determination of Indigenous Peoples and the people of Quebec (EGALE, 2016, p. 7).[10] This occurred in the absence of any significant movement organising among queer and trans people on these and other questions (Maynard, 2017).

These practices intensified when the people who had been purged from the public service and the military were then excluded from the government's own Advisory Council that helped to advise on the apology (Kinsman, 2017d). The commitment to the apology and setting up of an Advisory Council with very limited forms of consultation itself became a state management device curtailing further queer protest. For instance, once the government agreed that the apology would be before the end of 2017, WDAN's efforts approaching Pride Committees to pressure the Liberal government ended and the only possible remaining course of action became making a submission to the Advisory Council and to the governmental Secretariat on LGBT issues (WDAN, 2017).

These practices continued through the efforts of lawyers for the class-action suit articulating people's needs to a still heterosexist legal regime linked to the Canadian nation-state;[11] through the work of the Liberal government itself (the LGBT Secretariat, the Prime Minister's Office, the speech writer) managing to combine patriotism with the apology, and through much of the mainstream media coverage, especially but not only the work of *Globe and Mail* journalist John Ibbitson.

While many important stories of the purge campaigns were told in the media, they were often framed as in Ibbitson's 25 November 2017 *Globe and Mail* feature which, after a series of illuminating interview excerpts with people directly affected by discrimination, ended in the following 'homonationalist' fashion: 'with this apology Canada will have gone further to secure and advance the rights of sexual minorities than any other country in the world. In that sense, the apology is really a celebration. There has never been a time and place where it was so okay to be queer' (Ibbitson, 2017). Most media stories also tended to construct those purged as 'victims' and did not focus on queer histories of resistance to national security.

These practices shifted the apology process towards an apology from above, and worked on the continuing patriotic commitments of many of the people directly affected in WDAN, and among those signed up for the class action suit, especially those purged from the military.

The next day – 28 November – I arrived on Parliament Hill to hear the prime minister's apology. As Justin Trudeau started to read the apology, I had mixed feelings: elation that it was finally happening, but also sadness for all those who died in the decades before it took place. Patrizia Gentile and I had asked in a 1998 research report for a state apology and compensation (Kinsman & Gentile, 1998).

Around me in the parliamentary gallery sat many people who had been purged by the Canadian government. In this context, it was moving to hear the prime minister finally take responsibility for the Canadian war on queers. Some of the language was clearly shaped by WDAN's submission (2017) to the Advisory Council and the vital advocacy work of former NDP MP Svend Robinson[12] on that body who made sure that these important concerns were addressed. But in very important ways, Trudeau's apology didn't go far enough. After a while, hearing 'we are sorry' over and over rang hollow.

It was also a very white apology, not going nearly far enough in addressing the colonisation of Indigenous nations or the racist character of Canada and sexual regulation. It simply accepted Canadian nation and state formation. It was only an apology to Canadian citizens in a language defending Canadian borders against Indigenous nations, and refugees, migrants and undocumented people, many of whom are people of colour. It was kept well within the framework of national security and the 'nation' which it was careful not to put in question. Instead, the apology was used to construct a notion of Canadian-ness identified with diversity and inclusion, as in '[f]or all our differences, for all our diversity, we can find love and support in our common humanity … We're Canadians, and we want the very best for each other, regardless of our sexual orientation or gender identity and expression' (PMO, 2017).

A very brief reference to being a partner for 'queer people of colour, and others who suffer from intersectional discrimination' (PMO, 2017) lacked any clear commitment to fighting colonialism, racism, sexism, or class exploitation. This is an appropriation and a complete misuse of intersectionality as non-critical analysis. There is no addressing of how sexual, gender, racialising, gendered and class forms of oppression and exploitation are made in and through each other in a mutually determined fashion (Bannerji, 1995, 2000).

In the only attempt to account for why the purge campaign happened, Trudeau stated, 'You see, the thinking of the day was that all non-heterosexual Canadians would automatically be at an increased rate of blackmail by our adversaries' (PMO, 2017). But the active agency behind the purge was not the 'thinking of the day', which implies no real state responsibility for what took place. This was certainly not the thinking of gay and lesbian activists in the 1960s and 1970s who challenged such views. Instead this 'thinking' was actively put in place by the Canadian national security regime when we were targeted as national security risks for suffering from a 'character weakness' (Kinsman & Gentile, 2010). It was these state agencies that threw queer and gender non-conforming people outside the fabric of the 'nation', making us into national security risks. This analysis needs to be extended, putting in question national security when it is otherising any group of people including currently with Indigenous, Muslim and Arab people.

There are also many appeals to the nation and to patriotism in the apology including 'To those who wanted to serve, but never got the chance ... you should have been permitted to serve your country ... You were not *bad* soldiers, sailors, airmen and women ... You served your country with integrity. You are professionals. You are patriots' (PMO, 2017). This was directed to those people impacted by the purge campaign as they attempted to incorporate us back into the mainstream of a still heterosexist, transphobic, racist, sexist and class-divided Canada. We forget at our peril what we learned from being expelled from the fabric of the nation about the character of Canadian state relations.

The social basis for the reception of this apology from above with its appeal to the nation and to national security is partly shaped by the emergence of the neoliberal queer (Kinsman, 2016, 2017c) who is accommodated to capitalist and racialising relations and state formation. This white middle-class social layer has had an impact on groups like EGALE and some people involved in WDAN. We have to recognise the current complicities of some queers (largely, but not entirely, white and middle-class men) in national security campaigns against people of colour and 'subversives'. For instance, Doug Elliot, chair of the Just Society Committee of EGALE, and leading class-action suit lawyer, spoke vehemently against BLM-TO's disruption of the 2016 Toronto Pride parade (Elliot, 2016). He argued that this protest was 'the most reprehensible thing I have seen' at Pride, that this 'hijacking of the parade' was a 'complete betrayal', and that 'the homophobes have treated us better than this' (Elliot, 2016). This protest by BLM-TO – a queer- and trans-led group – was directed at getting the Pride Committee to address the needs of Black and other people of colour, and Indigenous people within Pride as well as excluding institutional police contingents from Pride until police racism and violence towards people in the Black community ends (CBC, 2016). In part, this response is based on forgetting the Canadian war on queers, as some people shifted from having been national security risks into becoming defenders of national security against people of colour, Indigenous Peoples and 'subversives', including many queer and trans people.

The apology itself was largely symbolic. The substance was provided by the agreement in the class-action suit which will bring about some redress for the people who were purged who are still alive (Agreement in Principle, 2017; Final Settlement Agreement, 2018). This also underlines how people had to go to court to get any justice from the government. People affected by the purge campaign will have to decide whether this agreement meets their needs. One concern is the partial nature of the public release of the state documents that organised this purge campaign. It is vital that the historical silencing surrounding the purge be overcome. The final settlement leaves this all up to a Research Project within Library and Archives Canada 'but does not warrant that the Research Project will identify, access and/or release all of Canada's documents relating to the LGBT Purge' (Final Settlement Agreement, 2018, p. 176).

Substance is also in the expungement legislation for convictions for consensual same-sex sexual practices (Bill C-66) that was introduced on 28 November 2017 which has major limitations. This includes that the bawdy house legislation under which hundreds of men in the 1970s and 1980s were charged is not covered. 'Indecent act', another charge used against men having sex with men is also not included. Nor are the obscenity sections that were used against lesbian and gay publications and bookstores, and the charge of 'vagrancy' used against trans and gender non-conforming people included. Furthermore, the age of consent used is 16 which is higher than the heterosexual age of consent set at 14 for this time period until 2008, and the onus is on the individual to take the initiative to apply including proving it was consensual activity which can be very difficult given the state of records and documents in court cases (Active History, 2017; Gentile et al., 2018). Despite major calls for changes in the Bill from queer, AIDS and sex worker activists at the Senate hearings on the bill, EGALE supported Bill C-66 without any amendments (Roy, 2018). This legislation was proclaimed into law in June 2018 (Government of Canada, 2018). In the legislation (Bill C-75) directed at repealing historically unjust and unused laws while the anal intercourse section is finally repealed, the bawdy house law, indecent acts and other sections of the criminal code that criminalise consensual sexual and gender activities are maintained (Another Flawed Bill, 2018).

THE APOLOGY FROM BELOW: A HISTORY OF RESISTANCE

But there is another *better* history *for* the apology that the apology from above forgets. The apology did not simply come from the goodness of journalist John Ibbitson, Justin Trudeau, or the Liberal government, as some have suggested. This is instead the story of decades of queer resistance to the purge campaigns which creates the social basis for this official apology. This goes back further than the actions of the men turning the tables on RCMP surveillance at the Lord Elgin in 1964 mentioned earlier. It includes the We Demand demonstration on Parliament Hill in 1971 which called for an end to the purges and was itself put under the surveillance of the RCMP, given that our movement in the 1970s was seen by the Canadian state as a threat to national security. This was predictably not mentioned in the apology but raised in the points for an apology from WDAN (2017).

It includes the protests in Montreal and Ottawa that forced the sex police to back off in their repression of lesbian/gay establishments, partially justified on national security grounds, in the 1975/76 pre-Olympic 'clean-up' campaign; the advocacy of the National Gay Rights Coalition/ Canadian Lesbian and Gay Rights Coalition in the 1970s; and those who went public with struggles against the purge campaigns including Gloria Cameron, Barbara Thornborrow, Darl Wood, Michelle Douglas (Kinsman & Gentile, 2010, pp. 232–240, 412–413) and Paul-Emile Richard.

Later, the growing number of people coming forward to talk publicly about their experiences of being purged and to push for justice led to the formation of WDAN. When the government announced in spring 2017 that the apology would happen within their mandate which could mean as late as 2019, WDAN with EGALE issued a joint media release saying this was unacceptable. WDAN also approached Pride Committees across the country raising questions about the blank cheque given to Justin Trudeau to walk in Pride parades when he would not commit to meeting our important demands. Within a week, the government committed itself to the apology by the end of 2017. This was part of that long arc of resistance coming from below.

In this sense, the apology is an important victory for this history of resistance which is why the feelings of those who were purged when hearing the apology must be affirmed. With all its limitations, this is something we won.

The state pedagogy from above of nation and patriotism wants us to forget this resistance and the critical perspectives it raises about national security. Rather than accepting being incorporated as patriotic citizens into Canada as it currently exists, we need to continue to transform society to ensure not only freedom for queer, trans and two-spirit people but also for all oppressed and exploited peoples.

This also reminds us of what remains to be done. This includes getting rid of the gay and other discriminatory blood bans (Dryden, 2015; GotBlood2Give, 2018); ending the criminalisation of HIV+ people[13] and sex workers; opening the borders to not only queer and trans refugees and migrants but to all people fleeing persecution; ending the criminal code sections that continue to be used to criminalise our consensual sexualities; ending all practices enforcing the two-gender binary and the oppression of trans and non-gender -conforming people; ending the homelessness and poverty that impacts on many queer, trans and two-spirit people; ending the colonisation of Indigenous sexual and gender practices and developing real nation-to-nation relations with Indigenous nations; the ending of all forms of racism including anti-Black racism and racist policing; the ending of the heterosexist and transphobic terror that all too many queer and trans young people still face in the schools and on the streets, and so much more.[14] This requires an orientation that puts not only sexual and gender policing in question but also national security.

To do this, we need to resist the socially organised forgetting of the apology from above. The movements for queer and trans liberation in the context of broader social justice movements must continue. There is clearly a need for the development of a broader pedagogy of resistance against the national security pedagogy of forgetting in the interests of the 'nation.'

TOWARDS PEDAGOGIES OF RESISTANCE

In this chapter, I examined two areas where national security could have been challenged but was instead largely shorn up. The problems come from focusing on an individual state leader and removing new national security measures from the history of national security and resistance to it. In the apology, there is a shift from the queer resistance that led up to it and its replacement with a commitment to a modified national security committed to the nation. Crucial to moving beyond these limitations are pedagogies of resistance that allow us to actively remember and to build on the resistance of people in the historical past and present to the many injustices of national security.

NOTES

1 Throughout this chapter, I trouble 'Canada' as a settler colonial state and society. From its beginning, the 'nation' and 'national security' have been defined against Indigenous Peoples.
2 This stands for Lesbian, Gay, Bisexual, Trans, Queer, Two Spirit and more; often I use 'queer' and 'trans' to refer to these various groups. On this use of 'queer', see Kinsman & Gentile, 2010, p. 5.
3 This is more explicit but was already present regarding national security (Kinsman & Gentile, 2010, p. 421) before Bill C-51 including in the 1994 Treasury Board statement on 'national interest' (Kinsman & Gentile, 2010, p. 41).
4 We always need to ask on whose terms are people being included (and who has already been included) and who is diverse and who is at the centre and is not defined as 'diverse' (Bannerji, 1995, 2000).

5 Holloway uses 'we' to refer to working-class and oppressed people in struggle and certain compositions of struggle. 'We' is a project that people can come to be involved in and to identify with (2005, 2010).

6 Islamophobia, like the formulation homophobia it builds on, can carry with it individual and psychological connotations. Instead, we need to get at social practices and relations.

7 Mohammad Mahjoub was arrested on a security certificate in 2000. He has not been charged with any offence in Canada and CSIS refused to provide any evidence to substantiate its claims.

8 Despite its insights, homonationalism as a conceptualisation needs to be more historically and socially grounded. On some of this, see Kinsman, 2016, 2017c; Gentile and Kinsman, 2015.

9 There are still some tendencies in this direction in Steven Maynard (2017), but in general his analysis is far more complex.

10 The EGALE *Just Society* report states referring to the 1969 reform that, '[w]hile Mr. [Pierre Elliot] Trudeau launched our communities on a trajectory toward equality, subsequent events illustrate that his pioneering amendments to the Criminal Code were not nearly enough' (EGALE, 2016). The 1969 criminal code reform was, however, only a limited partial decriminalisation of two offences used against sex between men in a limited private realm, and only when it involved two consenting adults aged 21 and over – all other activities remained criminalised. This is why charges actually increased after the 1969 reform. It is even suggested in the report that '[t]he administration of the Criminal Code … was still executed in a manner that was contrary to Mr. Trudeau's stated intentions' (EGALE, 2016), as if Trudeau intended to do more with the 1969 criminal code reform than it was designed to accomplish. Under this scenario, it was simply individuals in the police and the criminal justice system who undermined Trudeau's laudable efforts. While some of this language may be excused given tactical attempts to overplay the impact of the reform to persuade Prime Minister Justin Trudeau to take concerns over apologies and redress for those who were criminalised, and purged from positions in the public service and the military seriously, it goes much deeper than this. Doug Elliot repeats this same kind of argument when he argues in *The Fruit Machine* film (Fodey, 2018) that the purge campaigns intensified following the 1969 reform, since managers in the military and public service knew that the campaign's days were numbered, despite Trudeau's continuing and overt commitment to these national security practices. In May 2018, EGALE also awarded Justin Trudeau its first Leadership award (EGALE 2018) for the apology, signalling clear support for the Liberal leader.

11 The social form of law is not only tied into capitalist social relations but also to capitalist nation-state formation (Corrigan & Sayer, 1985, 1981).

12 Svend Robinson was the first Member of the federal Parliament (1979–2004) to come out as gay in 1988 and was a tireless advocate for the rights of lesbians and gay men (Mann, 2017).

13 There was a limited shift on this on 1 December 2017 at the federal and Ontario levels, but far more is needed. See HALCO, 2017. https://www.halco.org/2017/news/hiv-criminalization-governments-of-canada-and-ontario-make-important-announcements

14 On some of this, see the Canadian Centre for Gender and Sexual Diversity, Pink Agenda 2017.

REFERENCES

Active History (2017). 'Bill 66, Gay Historians Speak Out'. Accessed from http://activehistory.ca/2017/12/c66/ (accessed 10 January 2018).

Agreement in Principle (2017). Accessed from http://lgbtpurge.com/wp-content/uploads/2017/11/Final-AIP-signed.pdf (accessed 10 January 2018).

Alwad, J. (2015). 'Queer Regulation and the Homonational Rhetoric of Canadian Exceptionalism'. In O. Dryden & S. Lenon (eds), *Disrupting Queer Inclusion, Canadian Homonationalism and the Politics of Belonging* (pp. 19–34). Vancouver: UBC Press, 2015.

Another Flawed Bill, (2018), 'Another Flawed Bill: Gay and lesbian historians on C-75'. Accessed from http://radicalnoise.ca/2018/06/12/another-flawed-bill-gay-and-lesbian-historians-on-bill-75/ (accessed 4 July 2018).

Bannerji, H. (1995). *Thinking Through: Essays on feminism, Marxism and anti-racism.* Toronto: Women's Press.

—— (2000). *The Dark Side of the Nation: Essays on multiculturalism, nationalism and gender.* Toronto: Canadian Scholar's Press.

BCCLA (British Columbia Civil Liberties Association) (2015, March 11). '8 Things You Need to Know About Bill C-51'. Accessed from: https://bccla.org/2015/03/8-things-you-need-to-know-about-bill-c-51/ (accessed 27 August 2018).

CBC News (2016, July 6). '"Black Lives Matter Toronto Recaptures Pride's Activist Roots": Pride has its origins in activism and protesting injustice, write two of its original organizers'. Accessed from www.cbc.ca/news/canada/toronto/black-lives-matter-toronto-pride-kinsman-1.3665829 (accessed 27 August 2018).

Canadian Centre for Gender and Sexual Diversity (2017). *The Pink Agenda.* Accessed from http://ccgsd-ccdgs.org/wp-content/uploads/2017/07/THE-PINK-AGENDA.pdf

CCLA (Canadian Civil Liberties Association) (2017). 'Ten Things You need to Know About Bill C-59'. Accessed from: https://ccla.org/ten-things-need-know-bill-c-59/ (accessed 27 August 2018).

Corrigan, P., & Sayer, D. (1981). 'How the Law Rules: Variations on some themes from Karl Marx'. In B. Fryer et al. (eds), *Law, State, Society* (pp. 21–53). London: Croom Helm.

—— & Sayer, D (1985). *The Great Arch: English state formation as cultural revolution.* Oxford: Basil Blackwell.

Coulthard, G. (2014). *Red Skins, White Masks: Rejecting the colonial politics of recognition.* Minneapolis, MN: University of Minnesota Press.

Dryden, O. (2015). 'A Queer Too Far: Blackness, "gay blood," and transgressive possibilities'. In O. Dryden & S. Lenon (eds), *Disrupting Queer Inclusion, Canadian Homonationalism and the Politics of Belonging* (pp. 116–132). Vancouver: UBC Press.

—— & Lenon, S. (eds) (2015). *Disrupting Queer Inclusion, Canadian Homonationalism and the Politics of Belonging.* Vancouver: UBC Press.

EGALE, Canada Human Rights Trust (2016). 'The Just Society Report, grossly indecent, confronting the legacy of state sponsored discrimination against LGBTQ2SI communities'. Accessed from https://egale.ca/wp-content/uploads/2016/06/FINAL_REPORT_EGALE.pdf (accessed 27 August 2018).

—— (2018). 'Prime Minister Justin Trudeau to accept the 2018 Egale leadership award'. Accessed from https://egale.ca/prime-minister-justin-trudeau-to-accept-the-2018-egale-leadership-award/ (accessed 27 August 2018).

Elliot, D. (2016). OMNY Radio, Toronto. Accessed from https://omny.fm/shows/kelly-cutrara/gay-rights-lawyer-doug-elliott-on-pride-parade-dis#description (accessed 10 January 2018).

Final Settlement Agreement, (2018). Accessed from http://lgbtpurge.com/wp-content/uploads/2018/04/Final-Settlement-Agreement.pdf (accessed 4 July 2018).

Fodey, S. (2018). *The Fruit Machine*, Sandbay Entertainment.

Gentile, P., & Kinsman, G. (2015). 'National Security and Homonationalism, the QuAIA Wars and the Making of the NeoLiberal Queer'. In O. Dryden & S. Lenon (eds), *Disrupting Queer Inclusion, Canadian Homonationalism and the Politics of Belonging* (pp. 133–147). Vancouver: UBC Press.

——, Hooper, T., Kinsman, G., & Maynard, S. (2018). 'Fix Bill C-66: Gay and lesbian historians speak out'. Accessed from http://ccgsd-ccdgs.org/wp-content/uploads/2018/04/Fix-Bill-C-66-2.pdf (accessed 4 July 2018).

——, Kinsman, G., & Rankin, L. P. (eds) (2017). *We Still Demand! Redefining resistance in sex and gender struggles.* Vancouver: UBC Press.

Global News (2018, January 5). 'Muslim Group Asks for Day of Remembrance'. Accessed from https://globalnews.ca/news/3947951/muslim-group-asks-for-day-of-remembrance-for-1st-anniversary-of-quebec-mosque-shooting/ (accessed 10 January 2018).

GotBlood2Give website. Accessed from https://gotblood2give.weebly.com/ (accessed 29 July 2018).

Government of Canada (2018). Royal Assent of Bill C-66. Accessed from www.canada.ca/en/public-safety-canada/news/2018/06/royal-assent-of-bill-c-66-expungement-of-historically-unjust-convictions-act.html (accessed 4 July 2018).

HALCO (2017, December 1). 'HIV Criminalization: Governments of Canada and Ontario make important announcement'. Accessed from www.halco.org/2017/news/hiv-criminalization-governments-of-canada-and-ontario-make-important-announcements (accessed 10 January 2018).

Hall, C. (2016, May 17). 'Trudeau Tracker, the Anti-Terrorism Bill', *CBC News*. Accessed from www.cbc.ca/news/politics/trudeau-tracker-anti-terrorism-bill-1.3586337 (accessed 27 August 2018).

Holloway, J. (2005). *How to Change the World Without Taking Power: The meaning of revolution today*. London: Pluto Press.

—— (2010). *Crack Capitalism*. London: Pluto Press.

—— (2016). *In, Against and Beyond Capitalism: The San Francisco lectures*. Oakland, CA: PM Press.

Hussan, S. (2015, April 1). 'Those That Fight It Are Called Terrorists, and Those That Survive It Are Called Criminals'. Accessed from http://rabble.ca/blogs/bloggers/hussan/2015/04/those-fight-it-are-called-terrorists-and-those-survive-it-are-called-c (accessed 27 August 2018).

—— (2018, January 25). 'I Went to the Canadian Mosque Where Six Muslims Were Killed: On the ways we counter collective forgetting'. Accessed from www.canadalandshow.com/visiting-the-quebec-city-mosque-where-six-muslims-were-killed/ (accessed 27 August 2018).

Ibbiston, J. (2017, November 24). 'How will LGBTQ Canadians take Trudeau's Apology? Eight views on Canada's injustice', *Globe and Mail*. Accessed from www.theglobeandmail.com/news/national/lgbtq-canada-apology/article37071384/ (accessed 27 August 2018).

Kinsman, G. (1996) *The Regulation of Desire: Homo and hetero sexualities*. Montreal: Black Rose.

—— (2006). 'Mapping Social Relations of Struggle: Activism, ethnography, social organization'. In C. Frampton, G. Kinsman, A. Thompson & K. Tilleczek (eds), *Sociology for Changing the World* (pp. 133–156) Halifax: Fernwood Publishing.

—— (2016). 'From Resisting Police Raids to Charter Rights: Queer and AIDS organizing in the 1980s'. In W. K. Carroll & K. Sarker (eds), *A World to Win: Contemporary movement and counter-hegemony* (pp. 209–232). Winnipeg: ARP Books.

—— (2017a, December 5). 'The Apology from "Above" and "Below" – Expanded version'. Accessed from http://radicalnoise.ca/2017/12/05/the-apology-from-above-and-below-expanded-version/ (accessed 10 January 2018).

—— (2017b, December 1). 'How Canada's Historic Apology to LGBT People Falls Short'. Accessed from www.dailyxtra.com/how-canadas-historic-apology-to-lgbt-people-falls-short-81945 (accessed 10 January 2018).

—— (2017c). 'Queer Resistance and Regulation in the 1970s: From liberation to rights'. In P. Gentile, G. Kinsman & L. P. Rankin (eds), *We Still Demand! Redefining resistance in sex and gender struggles* (pp. 139–162) Vancouver: UBC Press.

—— (2017d, September 27). 'Why I Could Not Sign the Contract and Confidentiality Agreements to be on the Advisory Council for the Apology'. Accessed from http://radicalnoise.ca/2017/09/27/why-i-could-not-sign-the-contract-and-confidentiality-agreements-to-be-on-the-advisory-council-for-an-apology/ (accessed 10 January 2018).

—— & Gentile, P. (2010). *The Canadian War on Queers: National security as sexual regulation.* Vancouver: UBC Press.

—— & Gentile, P., with the assistance of Heidi McDonell and Mary Mahood-Greer (1998). '"In the Interests of the State": The anti-gay, anti-lesbian national security campaigns in Canada', Preliminary research report, Sudbury: Laurentian University.

——, Buse, D. & Steedman, M. (eds) (2000). *Whose National Security? Canadian state surveillance and the creation of enemies.* Toronto: Between the Lines.

Mann, A. (2017, December 13). 'Canada's First Openly Gay MP on the Long Road to an Apology for LGBT People', *Xtra!*. Accessed from www.dailyxtra.com/canadas-first-openly-gay-mp-on-the-long-road-to-an-apology-for-lgbt-people-82509 (accessed 10 January 2018).

Puar, J. (2007). *Terrorist Assemblages: Homonationalism in queer times.* Durham, NC: Duke University Press.

Maynard, R. (2017) *Policing Black Lives: State violence in Canada from slavery to the present.* Halifax, Winnipeg: Fernwood Publishing.

Maynard, S. (2017). 'To Forgive and Forget? Homonationalism, hegemony, and history in the gay apology'. Accessed from http://activehistory.ca/papers/to-forgive-and-forget-homonationalism-hegemony-and-history-in-the-gay-apology/ (accessed 27 August 2018).

PMO (2017). 'Remarks by Prime Minister Justin Trudeau to Apologize to LGBTQ Canadians'. Accessed from https://pm.gc.ca/eng/news/2017/11/28/remarks-prime-minister-justin-trudeau-apologize-lgbtq2-canadians (accessed 27 August 2018).

Roy, M. (2018) 'Presentation for the Just Society Committee of EGALE, Senate Human Rights Committee, (18 April)'. Accessed from http://www.cpac.ca/en/programs/in-committee-from-the-senate-of-canada/episodes/61703468 (accessed 27 August 2018).

Thobani, S. (2007). *Exalted Subjects: Studies in the making of race and nation in Canada.* Toronto: University of Toronto Press.

Stop Bill C-51 (2015). Leaflet for the Toronto action as part of the National Day of Action to Stop Bill C-51.

Walcott, R. (2016). *Queer Returns: Essays on multiculturalism, diaspora and Black Studies.* London, Ontario: Insomniac Press.

WDAN (We Demand an Apology Network) (2016, June 8). The We Demand an Apology Network submission on the urgent need for an official state apology and redress for those affected by the anti-gay/anti-lesbian purges in the public service and the military. Accessed from http://lgbtpurge.com/wp-content/uploads/2017/03/We-Demand-An-Apology-Network.pdf (accessed 27 August 2018).

—— (2017). 'Points Needed in an Apology'. Accessed from http://209.59.164.201/~ccgsdccdgs/oldsite/wp-content/uploads/2017/11/Points-needed-in-an-official-public-state-apology-pdf (accessed 27 August 2018).

8

Prevent as far-right Trojan horse

The creeping radicalisation of the UK national security complex

Nafeez Ahmed

The post-9/11 era has seen governments becoming increasingly militarised as a direct response to the threat of terrorism. This tendency toward militarisation has involved an inexorable expansion of state social control powers, through the exercise of domestic and foreign-facing institutions associated with 'national security'.

A number of research problems emerge here. Firstly, the expansion of Western policing powers at home and abroad must be understood in its historical context. Western policing powers in foreign theatres have traditionally expanded in the context of imperial social relations.

Secondly, the interconnections between multiple Western states within a wider global system of unequal power helps us to grasp the phenomenon overall as a global one, relating to dynamics and structures not exclusive to any one nation-state.

Thirdly, Britain's role can be better understood in terms of the British state's legacy as a former colonial power, currently operating as the junior surrogate of hegemonic US power in a post-war world system under the contours of an Anglo-American framework of order.

Fourthly, against this backdrop, a perspective of the radicalisation of the British national security complex can emerge as a symptom of a wider global process related to the dynamics of the international system constructed by the US and Britain – a system that in many ways is rapidly unravelling. The unravelling of this system is responsible for both the escalation of the phenomena of terrorism, and the radicalisation of Western (and British) state responses to it.

With these points in mind, we will proceed by grounding this analysis in the knowledge produced by communities, chiefly (though not exclusively) Muslim communities targeted by Prevent, on how state security practices have affected them and their capacity to engage in society as citizens. This knowledge leads us to a recognition of both continuity in the targeting of these communities over nearly two decades, whereby these policies have continued relentlessly, as well as change through a process of discernible radicalisation, in which the targeting of these communities has become at once more entrenched and wide-ranging. This then leads us to explore the most recent configurations of national security-based power projection within the UK under the Conservative government. This will be contextualised against the history of the expansion of military policing powers as a largely imperial strategy of social control to suppress indigenous resistance and insurgencies.

We will then connect this with alarming evidence of the Conservative government's transatlantic connections with far-right and neo-Nazi movements tied to the Trump administration as well as to political parties in Europe. This analysis helps situate the radicalisation of Britain's right-wing political establishment in relation to the creeping radicalisation of counter-terrorism and counter-extremism strategy, which increasingly constructs and targets 'suspect communities' in different ways, including Muslim communities, certain ethnic diaspora communities, Black and ethnic minority communities, and activist political groups.

Reframed in this way, the radicalisation of the UK national security complex appears as an effort by a section of the Anglo-American establishment to respond to escalating structural crises in an unequal world system in which traditional neo-imperial power relations are unravelling under the weight of multiple interlocking system failures. Those system failures manifest in increasing socio-political and economic dislocations, fuelling the emergence of specific terrorist and insurgent groups in several Muslim-majority nation-states of strategic importance to Anglo-American interests. In turn, the resulting escalation of extremist narratives and activity provides justification for the radicalised expansion of the national security complex as it seeks ever-widening military and policing powers at home and abroad.

These powers, though ostensibly targeted at specific threat groups, are applied wholesale across entire communities and societies. This has created massive distrust between the British government, wider society, and sections of some of these communities. A range of studies drawing on knowledge produced in and by communities targeted by Prevent illustrate that this breakdown of trust has not only fundamentally damaged the state's capacity to detect real terrorist threats, but has led to contradictory responses from sections of these communities: non-engagement; critical engagement; and slavish assimilation. The tensions between these ways of engaging the increasing radicalisation of the state have, in turn, undermined effective and cohesive strategies of response which might serve to transform these regressive and dangerous system dynamics, circumventing the possibility of creating new more positive relationships.

COMMUNITY KNOWLEDGE OF COUNTER-EXTREMISM: PREVENTING DISSENT

In December 2016, the British government published its First Annual Report on its National Security Strategy and Strategic Defence and Security Review (NSS and SDSR) which had been adopted in 2015. It highlighted the unprecedented expansion of domestic surveillance and policing powers under the new 'Prevent duty', but also demonstrated the context of this expansion in relation to Britain's global national security strategy (HM Government, 2016). The report celebrated the expansion of Prevent through the statutory recognition of the 'Prevent duty' in the Counter-Terrorism and Security (CTS) Act 2015, which obligates public authorities to prevent people from being drawn into terrorism.

The CTS Act established a statutory duty on all public sector workers – teachers, lecturers, nurses, doctors and other professionals – to prevent extremism in their institutions. This could only be done by monitoring users of those services – anyone including nursery children, school children, university students, medical patients, and so on – for signs of being at risk of radicalisation. The 'Prevent duty' placed the Home Office's Channel Programme, a scheme originally coordinated by the Metropolitan Police in parts of Britain, on a national legal footing. Under the programme, individuals identified as extreme, or being 'at risk' of extremism, are referred to Channel, which makes an assessment to determine whether the referred individual requires an intervention to deradicalise them, and the kind of intervention they will make.

In 2013, a former Channel coordinator at a local authority told me that the risk-profile indicators used to identify vulnerable individuals who might be in need of a deradicalisation intervention were too vague to be of use in genuinely uncovering someone at risk of becoming involved in terrorist activity. Another key problem with the programme is that, as referees are required to consent to an intervention, Channel is structurally designed to cater primarily to referrals who would be open to receiving support from UK authorities – whereas those most at risk of engaging in or sympathising with terrorism would be more likely to simply reject an intervention. Channel's efficacy toward reaching and deradicalising those most at risk is therefore questionable. The greater probability is that it will focus on people who are unlikely to participate in terrorism at all, while allowing those who are to slip through. Senior Metropolitan Police and Home Office officials in charge of the Channel programme acknowledged this at an invite-only Channel training exercise. The same local authority Channel coordinator also confirmed that the programme functioned as a covert intelligence gathering exercise. Officially, the government and police claimed that people who are referred to Channel are not kept on a database. However, the former Channel coordinator confirmed that the programme maintained a secret logging system to store all names and profiles of those referred, contrary to public claims (N. M. Ahmed, 2013).

The CST Act retroactively legalised the storage of this information by requiring local authorities to produce risk assessments of people suspected of being drawn into violent as well as non-violent extremism, and establishing procedures for 'internal and external information sharing' about 'vulnerable individuals' between relevant agencies (N. Ahmed, 2015a). The Conservative government's definition of extremism is so broad as to potentially include anything remotely critical of 'British values' as defined by government policy. In 2010, the coalition government widened the definition of 'preventing terrorism' to include challenging non-violent ideas 'that are also part of a terrorist ideology', and thus comprising a form of 'non-violent extremism'. By 2015, this approach was solidified: 'Extremism is vocal or active opposition to fundamental British values, including democracy, the rule of law, individual liberty and mutual respect and tolerance of different faiths and beliefs' (May, 2015). Under this view, 'non-violent extremism' could potentially encompass any ideas which the state deems 'can create an atmosphere conducive to terrorism and can popularise views which terrorists exploit' (HM Government, 2015).

These amorphous definitions provide the government with the power to categorise thought, speech and activism as extremist, or 'at risk' of extremism, simply for contesting, opposing, or undermining British government policies, bearing on the conceptualisation and practice of 'democracy' and the 'rule of law' at home and abroad. Activity critical of these policies can be construed as being opposed to 'British values' as defined by the state and its practices. Whatever the intent behind Prevent, its inherent structure functions as a mechanism for state intrusion into the social, political and cultural policing of the communities predominantly targeted by Prevent. This is enabled by the ideological foundations of the Prevent paradigm, which essentially recast social, political and economic challenges into psychological and ideological problems to do with the individual and their 'vulnerability', by adopting a scientifically groundless theory of radicalisation that largely evacuates its social, economic and political conditions (Kundnani, 2012). Counter-extremism guidance prepared by local authorities has thus ended up flagging up risk factors with little meaningful connection to terrorism, such as the 'unexpected growing of a beard', outpourings 'about governmental policies, especially foreign policy', or belief in government conspiracies (McGovern, 2016).

The knowledge produced from communities on the frontline receiving end of Prevent policies bear out that their impact is further profoundly politicised and racialised. In its submission to the British government's Prevent guidance consultation process in January 2015, the London-based activist collective, the Campaign Against Criminalising Communities (CAMPACC), noted that anti-terror legislation had been abused by the government to support 'oppressive regimes allied with the UK' and to persecute opponents of those regimes inside Britain. CAMPACC highlighted 'Turkey's oppression of Kurdish separatists, Sri Lanka's oppression of Tamil minorities, Israel's attacks on the democratically elected Hamas government of Gaza, etc. More recently, these powers have been used against UK Kurds suspected of joining the anti-ISIS resistance in Syria.' CAMPACC thus criticised the Prevent agenda for manufacturing 'a rationale for systematic surveillance of "non-violent extremism"', which in particular 'treats Muslims as a suspect community which must undergo pervasive surveillance and demonstrate its allegiance to "British values" – which are contradicted by UK foreign policy especially in relation to Iraq, Afghanistan and Palestine' (CAMPACC, 2015).

The Federation of Student Islamic Societies (FOSIS), one of the oldest British Muslim civil society organisations operating as an umbrella group for Muslim student societies, reports experiencing great difficulties in challenging executive abuse in the implementation of counter-terrorism policy. The shift to a concern about 'non-violent extremism', coupled with 'wide discretionary powers that are sustained and deployed through constructing categories of suspicion in which Muslim identity plays a central role', created conditions in which the typical social welfare activities of university Islamic societies could 'become interpreted as indicators suggesting the potential for radicalisation'. Consequently, the cooperation with communities required to make UK counter-terrorism strategy effective erodes due to distrust among subject communities (Choudhury, 2017). These experiences of distrust and alienation are reflected across Muslim communities who have come into contact in some way with Prevent. One study of British Muslim undergraduate students found 'limited general understanding and negative characterisations of Prevent, with perceptions of this policy being ineffective and inappropriate for higher education contexts' (Kyriacou et al., 2017).

The preoccupation with preventing radicalisation of young Muslims in particular has led to a toxic climate in which 'entire Muslim communities, from children to adults, have become "suspects"'. Whereas racialised ignorance was a frequent schooling experience before the 7/7 attacks in London, testimonials of young Muslim pupils reveal that the aftermath of those attacks has seen this racialisation metamorphose under the imperatives of a government-led securitisation agenda, leading discourse over 'Pakis' to convert into narratives about 'the dangerous "would-be" terrorists' (Saeed, 2017).

A range of organisations representing such frontline experiences confirm the discriminatory impact of Prevent on Muslim communities. Both the National Union of Teachers and the National Union of Students highlight the Prevent duty's disproportionate focus on Muslim students, alienating Muslims and ethnic minorities while fostering distrust between classmates, often through reinforcement of racialised stereotypes through the lens of 'national security' (F. Whittaker, 2016; McVeigh, 2015).

Yet Prevent's approach also means that while remaining rooted in a racialised preoccupation with the 'Muslim threat', its expansion from a focus on 'violent' to 'non-violent' extremism has made its broad risk-analysis framework increasingly applicable to various forms of political activism. During its focus on 'violent extremism', Prevent programmes were originally established only in local authorities with Muslim populations of 2 percent or higher. This imagination of the pre-criminal space was racialised and localised by equating the threat of violent extremism with the physical demography of Muslim populations. With the shift to 'non-violent' extremism, the 'Prevent duty' is now applied through national networks of healthcare and education provision, comprising a fundamental expansion of the imagination of the pre-criminal space warranting generic unimpeded surveillance (Heath-Kelly, 2017).

Although the government has gone to pains to disavow culpability for instances where political activism has ended up being demonised in local Prevent training, in reality this overarching conceptual and ideological structure is conducive to doing so. For example, local Prevent lesson plans in Leicester portrayed Suffragettes as extremists due to the use of violence by elements of the movement in pursuit of women's rights. The teaching materials compared Suffragette tactics of protest, resistance and damage to property to those adopted by the Nazis and terrorists (Hooper, 2018b). The 'value' of democracy thus promoted under the Prevent duty is a peculiar conceptualisation which evacuates its core meaning by denying the contestation of ideas and political struggles – such as the struggle to expand suffrage – integral to democracy. Democracy instead is subliminally posited as separate from the very political struggles that created it. The 'shared value' of democracy that emerges under Prevent's ideological mantle is premised on suppressing and suspecting the legitimacy of political dissent (Wolton, 2017).

Communities targeted by Prevent have, through the transmission and documentation of their experiences by NGOs, academics and journalists, demonstrated that the widening and entrenchment of Prevent has occurred in the context of serving an unaccountable configuration of state power which seems designed to undermine genuine democratic inclusion.

NEO-IMPERIAL LOGICS FROM COUNTERINSURGENCY TO RACIALISED EMERGENCY

This radicalisation of the Prevent strategy should not be surprising, however. The increasing application of Prevent through domestic education reflects the extent to which education abroad has traditionally been deployed to serve Western military and security objectives across the Global South. Under Prevent, these imperial strategies to subjugate local populations in the South have returned to be deployed to monitor, control and suppress marginalised communities in a form of 'internal colonialism' (Novelli, 2017).

This symbiotic connection between the UK's domestic Prevent programme and foreign policy priorities is structured through a broader national security paradigm, the contours of which are visible from the government's First Annual Report on its 2015 NSS and SDSR, cited earlier.

While that paper set out the Conservative government's rationale for Prevent, it also established the direct links between the challenges Prevent is supposed to address and the UK's wider national security policies. The document endorsed the Prevent agenda's expansion, noting that 'The Prevent statutory duty has prompted a significant step forward in the delivery of Prevent work. Almost 550,000 frontline staff have attended Prevent training to identify those vulnerable to radicalisation.' It also celebrated the passing of the Investigatory Powers Act 2016, for bringing 'together the powers available to law enforcement and the security and intelligence agencies to acquire communications and communications data', and establishing those powers 'on a single, clear statutory footing'. The Open Rights Group has described the legislation as the 'most extreme surveillance law ever passed in a democracy' (Z. Whittaker, 2016).

The document cements the ideological link between Britain's previously illegal, now retroactively justified, national surveillance infrastructure, and the perceived desirability of simultaneously extending Prevent as a nationwide safeguarding mechanism for allegedly vulnerable individuals. Seen through the lens of the dynamics described above – in which the principal casualty of Prevent is political dissent that directly challenges government policies – the document further connects this domestic counter-extremism agenda with Britain's wider foreign policy posture, in the context of its national security priorities.

For instance, it cites regional counter-extremism goals as a basis for consolidating Britain's alliance with Gulf regimes. 'We have maintained our strong relations with partners in the Gulf region', the report declares, noting a 'deepening and broadening' of relationships through the first UK-Gulf Cooperation Council Summit in December 2016. Multiple objectives of this strategy include 'cutting off the supply and availability of firearms to criminals and terrorists', protecting 'UK citizens and the flows of energy and trade in the region', as well as 'enhancing our support to the defence and security export sector'. To these ends, the document refers to 'detailed planning and preparations for a more permanent and substantial military presence in the Gulf'.

The extent to which counter-extremism is a serious priority, however, is questionable, given that the document systematically evades credible evidence of Gulf regime sponsorship of Islamist militancy around the world. One example is a July 2016 report from the UK foreign affairs parliamentary committee, noting alarming evidence supplied by the Ministry of Defence of 'financial donations' to Islamic State (ISIS) from wealthy donors inside Gulf states, including from Gulf royal families. According to the report, British Foreign Office officials confirmed that 'some governments in the region may have failed to prevent donations reaching ISIL [ISIS] from their citizens' (Donaghy, 2016). That evidence dovetails with a leaked classified 2014 memo by then US Secretary of State Hillary Clinton, citing US intelligence sources confirming that 'the governments of Qatar and Saudi Arabia ... are providing clandestine financial and logistic support to ISIL [ISIS] and other radical Sunni groups in the region' (McKernan, 2016). The implication is that Britain's 'national security' strategy is to cement its regional partnerships with regimes which the Anglo-American national security community has identified as the central source of financial support for violent extremism.

More broadly, the national security strategy document notes that the government has set up a new £1.3bn Prosperity Fund to enable the UK 'to deepen relationships with countries across the globe'. The fund will use Official Development Assistance resources to promote 'reforms' in support of economic growth in 'developing countries'. Such reforms refer to largely neoliberal policies of privatisation, deregulation and liberalisation, which will create 'opportunities for international business, including UK companies'. Such UK aid practices have already helped

101 mostly British companies extend control over $1 trillion worth of Africa's oil, gold, diamonds, coal and platinum (Curtis, 2016).

'National security' thus appears as a catch-all category legitimising a wide range of domestic and foreign policy priorities which adhere to a neo-imperial logic designed to facilitate the interests of British transnational companies across the defence, energy and resource sectors, with close ties to the British state. To that extent, the UK's counter-extremism strategy, including the Prevent agenda at home, appears as an evolution from Britain's historic legacy of colonial strategies to manipulate potentially subversive populations abroad. Those counter-insurgency strategies were derived by Colonel Frank Kitson as 'low intensity operations' to suppress indigenous resistance to British imperial rule, labelled as 'subversion and insurgency' consisting of 'political and economic pressure, strikes, protest marches, and propaganda, and ... the use of small-scale violence'. 'Security' measures to be adopted as part of Kitson's counter-insurgency toolkit comprised systematic surveillance, intelligence gathering, psychological warfare and intimidation against entire populations in order to separate them from insurgents. Legal frameworks would be deployed to legitimise these practices – in Kitson's own words: 'the law should be used as just another weapon in the government's arsenal' (Levidow, 2017).

The counter-insurgency connection is not a mere historic antecedent, or even an intriguing parallel, but rather an active driver of governmental counter-terrorism approaches. UK counter-extremism strategy encompassing Prevent draws directly on UK military counter-insurgency doctrines as applied in foreign war theatres such as Afghanistan and Iraq (Sabir, 2017). Prevent is thus indelibly connected with the neo-imperial logic of British foreign policy, bringing that logic to bear on domestic population groups perceived as vulnerable to dissenting against the direction of UK foreign policy.

Broader drivers of the radicalisation of the UK national security complex, then, must be found not simply in the British national security apparatus, but in the context of Britain's role as junior partner in a US-dominated world order which, however, faces multiple crises. US hegemony itself faces a fundamental geopolitical crisis, in which US unipolarity is rapidly giving way to a fractious multipolar system, in which the activities and growth of rival powers increasingly constrain US capacity to project power and economic influence (Grygiel &

Mitchell, 2017). This geopolitical crisis overlaps with a deeper global economic crisis, erupting with fervour since the 2008 financial crash but preceding that and continuing unameliorated since then, through which the structural fragility of global capitalism has heightened competition within the transnational capitalist class, while also deepening faultlines between that and the global working class (Robinson, 2017).

Both those processes represent the unravelling of the military-political and economic foundations of Anglo-American neo-imperial power. This unravelling is being further underpinned by the impact of a convergence of biophysical crises across environmental, ecological and energy systems (N. M. Ahmed, 2010). These biophysical crises have and will continue to inflame geopolitical tensions across the Middle East and North Africa, while also exacerbating global economic malaise, and straining US and British military-political reach (N. M. Ahmed, 2017).

Against these global trends, the radicalisation of the Anglo-American national security complex is a strategic response to these multiple, interlocking systemic crises. Rather than recognising these crises for what they are – systemic crises symptomatic of the existing structure of Anglo-American power itself – US and UK national security agencies respond through discursive strategies focusing on their most immediate manifestations in the form of escalating geopolitical violence within the Muslim-majority regions of the Middle East, North Africa and Central Asia, which are also the locus for core neo-imperial Anglo-American interests (as articulated in the Conservative government's first annual report on the new UK national security strategy) in energy, trade, arms sales and defence contracts. Those discursive strategies increasingly construct 'Islam' and 'Muslims' as threats to, and within, an Anglo-American-dominated Western European world order (or 'civilisation'). To a significant extent, the historical record suggests that this discursive strategy is not simply a case of reactionary cultural hysteria, but a deliberate response on the part of key elements of the Western European national security complex (Skoll, 2016). The consistent direction of US intelligence practices, for instance, in relation to surveillance and entrapment of Muslim terrorism suspects reveals that it has systematically empowered key anti-Muslim ideologues within the 'Islamophobia' industry (Marusek, 2018).

Such practices, radicalised further in the aftermath of ongoing global economic malaise, have empowered extreme right-wing discourses and groups – focusing obsessively on 'Islam' and 'Muslims', along with other problematised racial constructs including 'migrants', 'gypsies' and 'asylum seekers' – as fundamental civilisational threats, across both Western Europe (Askanius & Mylonas 2015) and the United States (Hell & Steinmetz, 2017). Yet these are not merely fringe processes belonging primarily to the purview of far-right populist groups. Indeed, the discursive strategies of Islamophobic actors increasingly manufacture the appearance of 'a seemingly mainstream political position by framing racist standpoints as a defence of Western values and freedom of speech'. Consequently, 'Islamophobic discourse is strengthened by xenophobic currents within mass media, and by the legitimisation of intellectuals and political actors', leading to a situation 'where racist attitudes towards Muslims are easily disseminated into the public debate, fuelling animosity against European Muslims' (Ekman, 2015). The expansion of Prevent as a discriminatory state-control mechanism targeted disproportionately across Muslim communities as well as across activist political communities is therefore part of a wider process by which Anglo-American power has become entwined with the formerly fringe far right.

DISCURSIVE TRANSMISSION: POLITICAL LEGITIMISATION OF FAR-RIGHT EXTREMISM

Considerable evidence has emerged demonstrating that Britain's Conservative Party and the US Republican Party have deliberately fostered strategic alliances with far-right political parties across Western Europe. Thus it is not a coincidence that the racialised shift toward an amorphous 'non-violent extremism' targeted through a Muslim-centric, surveillance-oriented 'Prevent duty' was spearheaded by a Conservative Party which simultaneously cultivated strategic alliances with a range of neo-Nazi political movements in Europe, many with alarming ties to European and American 'counterjihad' networks.

These were the findings of an investigative report that I prepared, commissioned by Tell MAMA UK, which monitors and campaigns against anti-Muslim attacks and movements. The investigation identified direct linkages between the Conservative Party and neo-Nazi political movements in Europe, with ties to the same 'counterjihad' network that had inspired Norwegian far-right terrorist Anders Breivik.

This movement's modus operandi is a historical ancestry connected to Nazi collaborators during the Second World War combined with a tactical opposition to Nazism developed in the post-9/11 period, focusing on the threat categories of 'Islam' and 'Muslims' (N. M. Ahmed, 2016).

The European Conservatives and Reformists Group (ECR) is the coalition of right-wing political parties in the European Parliament which is officially chaired by the UK Conservative Party. Several parties that have been members of the coalition at various times have alarming neo-Nazi sympathies and connections: the German AfD (Alternative for Germany), the Danish People's Party and the Finns Party.

From 2014 to 2016, the AfD was a member of the ECR until its expulsion three months after AfD leaders called for German border police to shoot refugees. Even before then, the AfD's senior leadership had a strong history of connections with Nazi collaborators; and the party was and remains allied with the notorious European anti-Islam street movement, Pegida, which has also had a widening neo-Nazi support base and leadership (Hoerner, 2015; Thran & Boehnke, 2015; DW, 2015b). These connections were among the reasons that then Prime Minister David Cameron originally opposed the appointment of the AfD to membership of the ECR. He was overruled by his own Tory MEPs, demonstrating the creeping radicalisation of sections of the party's membership.

Since 2014, Danish MEP Morten Messerschmidt has also been a member of the ECR. Until late 2016, Messerschmidt represented the Danish People's Party (DPP) in the European Parliament, but resigned from that post over allegations of misuse of funds. From 2014 to 2016, Messerschmidt held a senior role in the ECR as Vice Chair. The DPP also has close ties to the Danish Pegida movement, which was founded by Nicolai Sennels, a former DPP parliamentary candidate (DW, 2015a). Messerschmidt, who remains a member of the ECR despite his DPP resignation, is a convicted racist with ties to both Sennels, and the notorious *Gates of Vienna* website, which inspired the actions of convicted Norwegian far-right terrorist Anders Breivik. Breivik cited the *Gates of Vienna* blog 86 times in his manifesto. The blog was highlighted by the UK anti-racism body, Hope Not Hate, for its alarming extremist content, which includes references to anti-Muslim paramilitary operations during a civil war with European Muslims, a guide to amateur bomb-making, and predictions of an inevitable race war within Europe between Muslims and their neighbours (Elgot, 2015). Messerschmidt conducted an interview with Sennels published on the *Gates of Vienna* blog in October 2009. He conducted a further interview with Sennels in November 2011, in which he predicted that Europe would be overrun by a civil war with Muslims within twenty years (N. M. Ahmed, 2016).

Another ECR member since 2014 is Jussi Halla-aho, leader of the Finns Party in Finland. A member of the extreme right-wing Finnish nationalist association, *Suomen Sisu* (Finnish Power), since 2011, Hallo-aho is another convicted racist (Gardner, 2014; Äystö, 2017). The original policy statement of *Suomen Sisu* (now deleted) advocated a white-supremacist ideology comparable to that of the Ku Klux Klan and the American Nazi Party (Tessiere, 2013). Breivik quoted Hallo-aho in his manifesto from an article he had contributed to the *Gates of Vienna* blog called 'Multicultural Discourse in Finland and Sweden'. The blog describes Hallo-aho as having contributed two guest essays to the website. The *Gates of Vienna* blog also quotes and features Hallo-aho as a key ideological influence (Bodissey, 2008; mtv.fi, 2011; GoV, 2014).

These members of the Tory-chaired ECR represent what Breivik referred to as the 'Vienna school', with reference to the anti-Muslim ideology promulgated by the *Gates of Vienna* blog, the individuals it cites and promotes, and the authors that contribute to it. Although Cameron's personal opposition to the AfD is a matter of record, the far-right extremist 'Vienna school' appeared to have a direct influence on his emerging cohesion and counter-extremism policy. Documents obtained under the Freedom of Information Act by the BBC's Secunder Kermani revealed that Ameet Gill, Director of Strategy at the Office of the Prime Minister, had engaged in written correspondence with former Dutch MP, Ayaan Hirsi Ali. She has been identified as a major voice in the global far-right 'counterjihad' network, according to Nick Lowles, a ministerially appointed UK government advisor who sits on the UK government's cross-departmental working group on anti-Muslim hatred. Government sources claimed that the correspondence with Hirsi Ali concerned David Cameron's counter-extremism strategy. Ali herself, who has demanded a Western-led war to 'crush' Islam, was cited in Breivik's manifesto as a source of inspiration, and later appeared to sympathise with Breivik's self-justification that he 'had no other choice but to use violence' because 'all outlets to express his views were censored' (Khalid, 2016).

Although Ameet Gill moved on after Theresa May became prime minister, the influence of the 'Vienna school' inside parts of the Conservative

Party appears to have continued. Compelling circumstantial evidence of this comes from the persistent influence of the Henry Jackson Society (HJS), a right-wing British think-tank. The HJS masquerades as a reputable cross-party organisation, but is actively aligned with far-right extremists. In November 2017, HJS directors Alan Mendoza and Douglas Murray spoke at the 'Restoration Weekend' conference in Florida, organised by the David Horowitz Freedom Center, listed as an extremist organisation by US hate-group monitor, the Southern Poverty Law Center. Event participants included key figures in US white nationalist movements, including Ann Coulter, Robert Spencer, David Horowitz, Steve Bannon, Sebastian Gorka, Milo Yiannopoulos, among others. Bannon and Gorka, of course, held senior positions in the Trump administration, while others such as Coulter, Spencer and Horowitz have been flagged as leaders in a global network promoting anti-Muslim hatred, according to an analysis by Lowles for Hope Note Hate. Spencer and Horowitz (the former 162 times) are quoted in Breivik's manifesto (Lowles, 2015; Khalid, 2016; Hooper, 2018a; Lobe, 2011). Mendoza and Murray's platform-sharing with leading US white nationalist figures is a recent incident in a longer history. Murray has himself endorsed a range of harsh anti-Muslim policies, including a ban on Muslim immigration to Europe (N. Ahmed, 2015b).

Yet HJS has retained an inordinate level of influence on government counter-extremism policy. Under Cameron, a No. 10 Downing Street extremism report was caught plagiarising significant sections of text from an HJS report (*THE*, 2015). In 2017, court documents from a legal challenge by British citizen Dr Salman Butt to overturn the Home Office labelling him an extremist, revealed that the Home Office's Extremism Analysis Unit (EAU) based its analysis of counter-extremism trends partly on information provided by HJS subsidiary project, Student Rights, through a 'weekly digest' sent to the Home Office. The documents, consisting of witness statements from senior Home Office officials, also confirmed that the Home's Office Research Information and Communications Unit (RICU) cited information from the Centre for Social Cohesion (CSC), a think-tank previously led by Douglas Murray which was subsumed into HJS (Cage, 2017).

HJS's continuing ideological influence on the highest levels of the Conservative government was made further apparent from Prime Minister May's initial senior cabinet appointments. Home Secretary Amber Rudd, International Development Secretary Priti Patel, and

Brexit Secretary David Davis had all sat for years on HJS' Political Council until their ministerial appointments, resigning from their HJS posts only after receiving media inquiries about the government's associations with an anti-Muslim think-tank (N. Ahmed, 2016).

While retaining high-level influence on British government policy, HJS has simultaneous ties to a transatlantic far-right network heavily influenced by the so-called 'Vienna school'. HJS represents an intellectual clearing house for an Anglo-American neoconservative movement, bringing together political, economic and military elites from across the US and UK, many of whom have direct affiliations to the American and British military-industrial complexes, national security agencies and defence establishments (Griffin et al., 2015).

CONCLUSIONS

The British state is the site of an intensifying struggle in which parliamentarians, political lobbies and private institutions with direct ties to far-right extremists and white nationalists in Europe and the US have attempted to influence UK government national security policies. This has involved using the mantle of 'national security' to push through doctrines of radicalisation associated with surveillance-oriented policy recommendations which tend to justify a racialised preoccupation with Muslims as 'suspect' communities, while also absorbing all sorts of radical political activity into the same orbit of generalised suspicion.

Evidence from the Conservative Party's alliance with neo-Nazi affiliated white nationalist political parties in the European Parliament demonstrates that the party has become increasingly sympathetic to views, language and policy positions adopted by the far-right 'Vienna school' ideology which inspired Breivik. On the other hand, the capacity of individuals and think-tanks which overlap with influential figures in the 'Vienna school' to influence government counter-extremism policy and strategy at a high level demonstrates that the radicalisation of this strategy over the last few years under Conservative rule is a direct consequence of an entryist strategy by which far-right ideologues have attempted to enter into the corridors of power to determine policy.

In the US and across Europe, the convergence between the far-right and mainstream political parties, as well as state security agencies, is by no means an entirely novel phenomenon. Yet the historically specific transatlantic relationships documented here demonstrate an increasing capacity to encroach on mainstream policy making, not merely from the background, but through ideological leverage on key political influencers. This influence has been exerted through the lens of 'national security', and unearths the role of a global network of far-right groups with ties to both the incumbent Republican and Conservative administrations in the US and UK respectively. While there has been continuity with previous such relationships, the scope of these relationships has undertaken a qualitative leap. The key factors driving this radicalisation process appear to be: a new transnational operating space for the far right opened up by the Internet and social media; renewed transnational coordination across European and US 'counterjihad' networks oriented around the far-right's so-called 'Vienna school'; the failure of traditional national security policies in ameliorating Muslim world crises (while actually contributing to them); along with the inability of the political class to respond effectively to the entrenchment of global economic malaise. The danger is that government policy-making related to counter-extremism is becoming radicalised as a result of the creeping adoption of concepts originating from a transatlantic nexus of extreme-right political organisations and parties. British counter-extremism ideology has increasingly become the subject of extensive efforts of discursive transmission by which these actors have sought to infiltrate 'Vienna school' concepts into state policy, using the language of national security as a mechanism. National security has thus become an ideological smokescreen for this process of discursive transmission.

In this context, the extension and consolidation of the UK Prevent paradigm from violent extremism to non-violent extremism can be understood, in itself, as a process of radicalisation, by which the British state has come increasingly under the influence of far-right ideology. This process has involved the move from a racialised preoccupation with specific Muslim communities to a nationalised focus on generally subversive cultural and political behaviours which extends the rubric of surveillance across public authorities and institutions, but is structured in such a way that they tend to encompass, in particular, Muslims, Black and ethnic minorities, and young people. It has also accompanied a consolidated alliance with some of the same Muslim regimes such as Saudi Arabia, Qatar and Turkey, implicated in leaked and official documents as being at the forefront of the direct financing of terrorist groups like ISIS.

This raises the question of the structural causes of the vulnerability of the British state to such radicalisation. The scope of British national security ideology as articulated in recent official documents indicates that one core driver is the escalating breakdown in traditional Anglo-American national security structures abroad, which are unable to contain the impact of multiple social, political and economic crises in key foreign theatres, especially Muslim-majority ones. As these crises converge and escalate, many of which are the direct consequence of Anglo-American national security policies, the resultant crises are being exploited to consolidate and expand those policies. The radicalisation of British counter-extremism strategy is, then, a symptom of a deeper governmental shift toward the absorption of the ideological values and vision of the far right.

Against this background, Muslim, Black and ethnic minority, and activist communities face limited strategies of response. Current strategies have failed to ameliorate the radicalisation of the British state. To some extent, the approach to date has only seen the acceleration of this radicalisation. It has focused for the most part on rejecting the legitimacy of Prevent outright, and demanding an overhaul of all extant counter-extremism strategy. While this is an understandable response, it is one that is predictably viewed by the state as obstructive, and ends up cementing the divide between state and subject communities. It also cements the divide within subject communities along an internal neo-imperial 'bad Muslim'/'good Muslim' dichotomy. The result is that a range of civil society groups opposed to Prevent become categorised by the state as 'bad Muslims', while others working in alignment with government counter-extremism priorities are labelled as 'good Muslims', as exemplified in one HJS report which broadly depicts critics of Prevent as either extremist themselves, or having 'extremist connections' (Sutton, 2016).

This has a toxic impact within these communities, creating a fundamental divide between civil society groups critical of the British state, and others whose primary focus involves either building resilience to extremist recruitment efforts within communities, or bringing different faith communities together. This has led to parallel forms of seemingly mutually exclusive activism, expressed in scepticism of British state institutions, and another which attempts to build a positive and inclusive sense of British citizenship identity. The government's Prevent strategy reinforces this dichotomy by imposing a very specific ideology of the 'good citizen', focused on uncritical acceptance of state-defined values of democracy which, however, are defined in such a way as to be fundamentally inimical to the forms of political dissent and struggle that constitute preconditions for genuine democracy.

Hence a range of important civil society groups all providing a public service in their own right – from legitimate criticisms of government policy to legitimate work to strengthen community resilience against Islamist militancy – end up working at cross-purposes. The outcome of this 'divide and rule' scenario is that the British state continues on a self-defeating trajectory of far-right radicalisation, Islamist militancy continues to grow undeterred, while subject communities become fragmented amidst disempowering in-fighting. This also results in a polarisation in which critics of Prevent find themselves increasingly alienated from a capacity to engage mainstream policy makers, which thus further entrenches the same circles of established influencers, many with far-right connections. Thus Prevent-funded organisations which do positive work in communities are seen as untrustworthy by parts of those communities, simply due to their affiliations with government under (legitimate) perceptions of the Prevent programme's disfigurement in the context of the encroachment of a national security complex increasingly influenced by far-right ideology.

An alternative strategy could be explored, involving a combination of approaches from civil society with a quite intentional view to transform the way subject communities and related civil society groups relate to the state. Multiple approaches by different groups should be coordinated, rather than developed in isolation and at cross-purposes, encompassing both evidence-based critical scrutiny of counter-extremism strategy; and evidence-based activism to build community resilience to Islamist militancy. This requires strategic collaboration and creative engagement between anti-Prevent critics, and organisations which work within and under Prevent. While the latter need to be able to hear and learn from the former; the former need to be able to recognise the need for the latter, in order for both camps to meaningfully address deep-seated social, political, cultural and economic challenges across communities.

While it would be foolish to presume that doing so would in itself generate immediate change, the only conceivable mechanisms by which the underlying premises and orientation of Prevent might be challenged and transformed is by opening it up to critical scrutiny through a process of sustained direct engagement. One potential first step to achieve this is to open up new conversations between anti-Prevent groups and community networks which receive Prevent funding.

REFERENCES

All URLs accessed during August 2018.

Ahmed, N. (2015a, 13 February). 'Preventing Dissent', *INSURGE Intelligence* (blog). Accessed from https://medium.com/insurge-intelligence/preventing-dissent-27efd26191a9

—— (2015b, 3 June). 'White Supremacists at the Heart of Whitehall', *Middle East Eye*. Accessed from www.middleeasteye.net/columns/white-supremacists-heart-whitehall-789183852

—— (2016, 20 July). 'Theresa May's Cabinet Scrambles to Disassociate from Extremist Think-Tank Tied to Donald Trump', *The Canary*. Accessed from www.thecanary.co/uk/2016/07/20/theresa-mays-cabinet-scrambles-disassociate-extremist-think-tank-tied-donald-trump/

Ahmed, N. M. (2010). *A User's Guide to the Crisis of Civilisation: And how to save it*. London: Pluto Press.

—— (2013, 9 December). 'UK's Flawed Counter-Terrorism Strategy', *Le Monde Diplomatique*. Accessed from https://mondediplo.com/outsidein/uk-s-flawed-counter-terrorism-strategy

—— (2016). 'Return of the Reich: Mapping the global resurgence of far right power', investigative report. London: Tell MAMA and INSURGE intelligence. Accessed from https://medium.com/return-of-the-reich

—— (2017). *Failing States, Collapsing Systems: BioPhysical triggers of political violence*. Springer International Publishing. Accessed from www.springer.com/gb/book/9783319478142

Askanius, T., & Mylonas, Y. (2015). 'Extreme-Right Responses to the European Economic Crisis in Denmark and Sweden: The discursive construction of scapegoats and lodestars', *Javnost – The Public*, 22(1): 55–72. Accessed from https://doi.org/10.1080/13183222.2015.1017249

Äystö, T. (2017). 'Insulting the Sacred in a Multicultural Society: The conviction of Jussi Halla-Aho under the Finnish Religious Insult Section', *Culture and Religion*, 18(3): 191–211. Accessed from https://doi.org/10.1080/14755610.2017.1365736

Bodissey, B. (2008, 19 November). 'Muzzled in Finland, Part 5 | Gates of Vienna', *Gates of Vienna*. Accessed from http://gatesofvienna.net/2008/11/muzzled-in-finland-part-5/

Cage (2017). 'Blacklisted: The secretive Home Office unit silencing voices of dissent', *Cage*. Accessed from https://cage.ngo/publication/blacklisted-the-secretive-home-office-unit-silencing-voices-of-dissent/

CAMPACC (Campaign Against Criminalising Communities) (2015). 'Response to Prevent Duty Guidance: A consultation', *Campaign Against Criminalising Communities*. Accessed from http://campacc.org.uk/uploads/CAMPACC%20to%20Prevent%20consultation.pdf

Choudhury, T. (2017). 'Campaigning on Campus: Student Islamic societies and counterterrorism', *Studies in Conflict & Terrorism*, 40(12): 1004–1022. Accessed from https://doi.org/10.1080/1057610X.2016.1253986

Curtis, M. (2016). 'The New Colonialism: Britain's scramble for Africa's energy and mineral resources', *War on Want*. Accessed from https://waronwant.org/resources/new-colonialism-britains-scramble-africas-energy-and-mineral-resources

Donaghy, R. (2016, 7 December). 'IS Received Secret Funding from Gulf States: British Parliament report', *Middle East Eye*. Accessed from www.middleeasteye.net/news/received-secret-funding-gulf-states-british-parliament-report-concludes-1412204400

DW (2015a, 23 January). 'PEGIDA Denmark Takes Cue from Germany', *Deutsche Welle*. Accessed from www.dw.com/en/pegida-denmark-takes-cue-from-germany/a-18201808

—— (2015b, 25 January). 'PEGIDA, Neo-Nazis, and Organized Rage'. Accessed from www.dw.com/en/pegida-neo-nazis-and-organized-rage/a-18212964

Ekman, M. (2015). 'Online Islamophobia and the Politics of Fear: Manufacturing the green scare', *Ethnic and Racial Studies*, 38(11): 1986–2002. Accessed from https://doi.org/10.1080/01419870.2015.1021264

Elgot, J. (2015, 27 July). 'MPs Call for "anti-Muslim Paramilitary Manual" Website to Be Investigated', *Guardian*. Accessed from www.theguardian.com/technology/2015/jul/27/mps-website-anti-muslim-paramilitary-manual-investigated-muhammad-cartoons-exhibition

Gardner, S. (2014, 19 June). 'Strange Bedfellows', *Euro Correspondent*. Accessed from https://www.euro-correspondent.com/eu-insider/320-strange-bedfellows.

GoV (2014). Jussi Halla-Aho | Gates of Vienna. *Gates of Vienna*. Accessed from http://gatesofvienna.net/repression/jussi-hall-aho/

Griffin, T., Aked, H., Miller, D. & Marusek, S. (2015). 'The Henry Jackson Society and the Degeneration of British Neoconservativism: Liberal interventionism, Islamophobia and the "War on Terror"', *Spinwatch*. Accessed from www.thecordobafoundation.com/attach/spinwatch%20report_web.pdf

Grygiel, J. J., & Mitchell, A. W. (2017). *The Unquiet Frontier: Rising rivals, vulnerable allies, and the crisis of American power*. Princeton, NJ: Princeton University Press.

Heath-Kelly, C. (2017). 'The Geography of Pre-Criminal Space: Epidemiological imaginations of radicalisation risk in the UK Prevent strategy, 2007–2017', *Critical Studies on Terrorism*, 10(2): 297–319. Accessed from https://doi.org/10.1080/17539153.2017.1327141

Hell, J., & Steinmetz, G. (2017). 'A Period of "Wild and Fierce Fanaticism": Populism, theo-political militarism, and the crisis of US hegemony', *American Journal of Cultural Sociology*, 5(3): 373–391. Accessed from https://doi.org/10.1057/s41290-017-0041-y

HM Government (2015). 'Revised Prevent Duty Guidance: For England and Wales'. HM Government. Accessed from www.gov.uk/government/uploads/system/uploads/attachment_data/file/445977/3799_Revised_Prevent_Duty_Guidance__England_Wales_V2-Interactive.pdf

—— (2016). 'National Security Strategy and Strategic Defence and Security Review 2015: First Annual Report 2016'. Cabinet Office. Accessed from www.gov.uk/government/uploads/system/uploads/attachment_data/file/575378/national_security_strategy_strategic_defence_security_review_annual_report_2016.pdf

Hoerner, J. (2015, 5 January). 'Closer Cooperation between the AfD and the "Pegida" Movement Could Reshape the German Right', *LSE European Politics and Policy* (EUROPP), blog. Accessed from http://blogs.lse.ac.uk/europpblog/

Hooper, S. (2018a, 3 February). 'How Police Counter-Terror Chief Was Courted by "Islamophobic' Think Tank', *Middle East Eye*. Accessed from www.middleeasteye.net/news/exclusive-mark-rowley-police-henry-jackson-society-852933099

—— (2018b, 2 July). 'Suffragettes Compared to Nazis in Prevent-Linked "Extremism" Lesson Plan', *Middle East Eye*. Accessed from www.middleeasteye.net/news/suffragettes-extremism-respect-prevent-teach-amber-rudd-theresa-may-vote-1948640227

Khalid, W. (2016, 1 March). 'The Ayaan Hirsi Ali Problem: Why do anti-Islam Muslims keep getting promoted as "Experts"?' *Vox*. Accessed from www.vox.com/2016/3/1/11139272/muslim-pseudo-experts

Kundnani, A. (2012). 'Radicalisation: The journey of a concept', *Race & Class*, 54(2): 3–25. Accessed from https://doi.org/10.1177/0306396812454984

Kyriacou, C., Szczepek Reed, B., Said, F. & Davies, I. (2017). 'British Muslim University Students' Perceptions of Prevent and Its Impact on Their Sense of Identity', *Education, Citizenship and Social Justice*, 12(2): 97–110. Accessed from https://doi.org/10.1177/1746197916688918

Levidow, L. (2017, March). 'The UK's Counter-Extremism Agenda: Routine punishment and collective self-policing', *Green European Journal*. Accessed from www.greeneuropeanjournal.eu/the-uks-counter-extremism-agenda-routine-punishment-and-collective-self-policing/

Lobe, J. (2011, 26 June). 'Islamophobes Distance Themselves from Breivik', *Al Jazeera English*. Accessed from www.aljazeera.com/indepth/opinion/2011/07/201172611337853373.html

Lowles, N. (2015). 'The "Counter-Jihad" Movement: The global trend feeding anti-Muslim hatred', *Hope Not Hate.* Accessed from https://ia800201.us.archive.org/9/items/CounterJihadReportHopeNotHate/INTERNATIONAAL%202012%20the%20%26%238216%3BCounter-Jihad%26%238217%3B%20movement%20The%20global%20trend%20feeding%20antiMuslim%20hatred%20%20David%20Williams%20and%20Nick%20Lowles%20Hope%20Not%20Hate.pdf

Marusek, S. (2018). 'Inventing Terrorists: The nexus of intelligence and Islamophobia', *Critical Studies on Terrorism,* 11(1): 65–87. Accessed from https://doi.org/10.1080/17539153.2017.1351597

May, T. (2015, 23 March). 'A Stronger Britain, Built On Our Values', *GOV.UK.* Accessed from www.gov.uk/government/speeches/a-stronger-britain-built-on-our-values.

McGovern, M. (2016). 'The University, Prevent and Cultures of Compliance', *Prometheus,* 34(1): 49–62. Accessed from https://doi.org/10.1080/08109028.2016.1222129

McKernan, B. (2016, 10 November). 'Hillary Clinton Emails Leak: Wikileaks documents claim Democratic nominee "thinks Saudi Arabia and Qatar fund Isis"', *Independent.* Accessed from www.independent.co.uk/news/world/politics/hillary-clinton-emails-leak-wikileaks-saudi-arabia-qatar-isis-podesta-latest-a7355466.html

McVeigh, K. (2015, September 2). 'NUS Fights Back against Government's "Chilling" Counter-Radicalisation Strategy', *Guardian.* Accessed from www.theguardian.com/education/2015/sep/02/nus-fights-back-against-governments-chilling-counter-radicalisation-strategy

mtv.fi (2011, 24 July). 'Breivik Mainitsee Manifestissaan Halla-Ahon, Ahtisaaren Ja Takkulan', *Mtv.Fi.* Accessed from www.mtv.fi/uutiset/ulkomaat/artikkeli/breivik-mainitsee-manifestissaan-halla-ahon-ahtisaaren-ja-takkulan/2222138#gs.t2mVXmQ

Novelli, M. (2017). 'Education and Countering Violent Extremism: Western logics from South to North?', *Compare: A Journal of Comparative and International Education,* 47(6): 835–851. Accessed from https://doi.org/10.1080/03057925.2017.1341301

Robinson, W. I. (2017). 'Debate on the New Global Capitalism: Transnational capitalist class, transnational state apparatuses, and global crisis', *International Critical Thought,* 7(2): 171–189. Accessed from https://doi.org/10.1080/21598282.2017.1316512

Sabir, R. (2017). 'Blurred Lines and False Dichotomies: Integrating counterinsurgency into the UK's domestic "War on Terror"', *Critical Social Policy,* 37(2): 202–224. Accessed from https://doi.org/10.1177/0261018316683471

Saeed, T. (2017). 'Muslim Narratives of Schooling in Britain: From "Paki" to the "Would-Be Terrorist"'. In M. Mac an Ghaill & C. Haywood (eds), *Muslim Students, Education and Neoliberalism* (pp. 217–231). London: Palgrave Macmillan. Accessed from https://doi.org/10.1057/978-1-137-56921-9_14

Skoll, G. R. (2016). 'Construction of Fear Culture in the United States from Red Scares to Terrorism'. In *Globalization of American Fear Culture* (pp. 27–46). New York: Palgrave Macmillan. Accessed from https://doi.org/10.1007/978-1-137-57034-5_2

Sutton, R. (2016). 'Myths and Misunderstandings: Understanding opposition to the Prevent strategy', Policy Paper 7, Centre for the Response to Radicalisation and Terrorism. Henry Jackson Society. Accessed from http://henryjacksonsociety.org/wp-content/uploads/2016/10/Myths-and-Misunderstandings-PREVENT-Report-Final-29.09.2016.pdf

Tessiere, E. (2013, 25 March). 'How Ideologically Similar is Suomen Sisu to the Ku Klux Klan and U.S. American Nazi Party?', *Migrant Tales*. Accessed from www.migranttales.net/how-ideologically-similar-is-suomen-sisu-to-the-ku-klux-klan-and-american-nazi-party/

Thran, M., & Boehnke, L. (2015). 'The Value-Based Nationalism of Pegida', *Journal for Deradicalization*, 3: 178–209.

THE (Times Higher Education). (2015, 1 October). 'No 10's Extremism Report Mirrors Text of Thinktank Study', *Times Higher Education (THE)*. Accessed from www.timeshighereducation.com/news/no-10s-extremism-report-mirrors-text-thinktank-study

Whittaker, F. (2016, 28 March). 'NUT Prevent Strategy Motion: What it actually says', *Schools Week*. Accessed from https://schoolsweek.co.uk/nut-prevent-strategy-motion-what-it-actually-says/

Whittaker, Z. (2016, 17 November). 'Britain Just Passed the "Most Extreme Surveillance Law Ever Passed in a Democracy"', *ZDNet*. Accessed from www.zdnet.com/article/snoopers-charter-expansive-new-spying-powers-becomes-law/

Wolton, S. (2017). 'The Contradiction in the Prevent Duty: Democracy vs "British values"', *Education, Citizenship and Social Justice*, 12(2): 123–142. Accessed from https://doi.org/10.1177/1746197917693021

9

Political policing in the UK

A personal perspective

Emily Apple

Many people might think that living in a liberal democracy such as the United Kingdom means that there is no such thing as political policing. Fundamental human rights such as freedom of speech, association, protest and dissent are principles which we feel should be enshrined and respected. The reality is very different. Most people who have been involved in any form of political campaigning or organising can attest to this. The sheer breadth of the groups spied on by British undercover police (from anarchists to socialists; from animal rights to trade unions and family justice campaigners) has shown just how widespread this practice is.

This chapter examines political policing in the UK through personal experience. For the last 25 years, I have been involved with anti-war, anti-arms trade, and environmental protest movements. Through personal experiences and those of friends, this campaigning also led to me organising against state surveillance of protest. Surveillance of protesters takes two forms: overt and covert surveillance, although some of the aims and impacts overlap. Ultimately, the aim of political surveillance comes down to four fundamental principles: intelligence gathering, deterrence, disruption, and protection of corporate and government interests. The police and the government are reluctant to divulge the type, level and quantity of surveillance that is conducted on political protesters. Most of our information on these activities has come through the persistent work of activists and investigative journalists.

Many activists have had to take the police to court to discover the details of surveillance operations against them. This has three strands: judicial reviews and other civil cases (such as suing the police) have challenged the legitimacy of surveillance operations. Activists have also challenged police surveillance through the criminal courts after being arrested for blocking police cameras. Much of the information held about police databases and what happens to information overtly gathered by the police on protests comes from these trials (Bailii.org, 2009).

Research by activists and journalists is also the driving force behind much of what is known about undercover policing in the UK. Activist groups such as the Undercover Research Group have painstakingly built profiles of known operatives. Investigative journalists such as Rob Evans and Paul Lewis at the *Guardian* have also worked tirelessly to expose undercover officers and their tactics.

OVERT SURVEILLANCE

Forward Intelligence Teams (FIT) and Evidence Gathering Teams (EGTs) conduct overt surveillance at protests, with groups of two or three police officers, often accompanied by a civilian cameraperson. FIT policing originated in the policing of football matches in the early 1990s. But the tactics were soon adopted for protests, first appearing at the Reclaim the Streets environmental anti-roads street parties in 1995. Although FIT's tactics originated with London's Metropolitan Police, they quickly spread across the country. But FIT's objective has gone far beyond collating intelligence on their subjects. From 1995 until around 2010, they used 'harassment style policing' (Bristol Anarchist Black Cross – Prisoner Support, n.d.) to disrupt, deter and harass people away from protests.

This was achieved through a variety of tactics. Anyone attending an organising or training meeting for protests would be repeatedly photographed outside. It was impossible to attend a publicly organised meeting without being subject to FIT's gaze. On protests, their tactics intensified. Repeated and incessant photography was accompanied by following 'known' individuals throughout the day. Others were deliberately called by name. Friends of 'known' individuals were targeted for stop-and-searches and photographed repeatedly. The message from the police was clear: we know who you are and we're watching you. For example, at one protest a FIT officer told me that 'he was going to be [my] shadow' for the rest of the protest. He also claimed to have all the CCTV cameras watching me.

In 2008, former Home Secretary Jacqui Smith called for FIT to be used to tackle anti-social behaviour on council estates, describing the tactic as '[creating] an environment where those responsible for antisocial behaviour have no room for manoeuvre and nowhere to hide, where the tables are turned on offenders so that those who harass our communities are themselves harried and harassed' (Lewis, 2018).

Large numbers of people were subjected to these tactics. Files on police databases extend to politicians (Evans & Bowcott, 2014) who have spoken at events, and journalists (National Union of Journalists, 2014) who cover protests, as well as many others who have no criminal record. Using these tactics against protesters who simply wish to exercise their democratic right to dissent raises serious questions.

However, police bodies have praised the 'disruptive' element of FIT work. In 2008, during the Kingsnorth Climate Camp, an environmental protest camp at the site of a coal-burning power station, police disrupted protest by overt means. Everyone arriving at or leaving the camp was subject to stop and search, including journalists (National Union of Journalists, 2009), and children (Evans & Lewis, 2010). The policing operation was widely criticised. But a Strategic Review into policing, conducted by South Yorkshire Police, praised FIT tactics for their 'effectiveness' in 'disrupting' activists (Statewatch, 2009).

Information collated by the FIT is used on 'spotter cards', identifying people that the police are interested in and used by FIT teams to decide who to target (*Guardian*, 2009). During the protests against one of the world's largest arms fairs, Defence Security Equipment International (DSEI), in 2005, a spotter card was found on the floor, identifying suspects A to X (Apple, 2009). Those on the spotter card found themselves subject to increased surveillance, including being followed by officers during and long after a protest had finished, being targeted for stop-and-searches and vehicle checks, and being repeatedly photographed at close range.

But it's one thing to *know* about this theoretically and another to *experience* it. I was Suspect A on the spotter card found in 2005, and as I wrote when the card was publicised:

> Inclusion on the spotter cards has nothing to do with keeping tabs on domestic extremists and everything to do with harassment. If the police really believe they have grounds to monitor us there are plenty of covert methods at their disposal. In 2005, they didn't need a riot van full of cops to follow myself and my 18-month-old child after meetings. Similarly, in 2004, it was unnecessary to repeatedly use flash photography while I was breastfeeding my son.
>
> (Apple, 2009)

But while there should never be any need to police protesters in this way, subsequent revelations about undercover policing since I wrote this revealed that the police were also using undercover covert means of surveilling us. Indeed, many of the above examples of overt surveillance were carried out in the presence of undercover officers. There is further evidence that the two branches of police surveillance did not always know what the other was doing. In a Criminal Intelligence report compiled by a FIT officer from DSEI 2003, an undercover officer, Jason Bishop, is named as 'Subject Q'. This means he was identified by public order officers as a person of interest. But while FIT were surveilling him, he was also compiling his own surveillance reports on the protests.

The first time I realised I was known to the police by name was at a large anti-war march, with several thousand people. I was walking through the subway system at Hyde Park in London, and passed two police officers who identified me. At first, I thought I was imagining it. The thought that out of all the thousands of people there, these officers knew my name seemed far-fetched. But it was just the start of years of harassment from the FIT.

Every protest I went on, they were there. They called me by name and followed me, often to the pub or to meet non-political friends after protests. On the million-person march against the Iraq War in 2003, I and a couple of friends were followed for the day by over ten officers. At one point during the march, the officers were walking so close on either side of me that I was unable to walk next to my partner.

From Subject Access Requests under the Data Protection Act, I know that I am identified by the police as an 'organiser' and as 'very influential' in 'Left Wing activism', which meant that the police took these tactics further. Political policing extended to being targeted for arbitrary stop-and-searches, arrests and violence.

In 2002, the arrests averaged about once a week, mostly for offences I hadn't committed. Charges ranged from minor public order offences to higher-level offences such as violent disorder which carry an inevitable prison sentence if convicted. While, as an activist, there were times I was willing to risk arrest, it was the arbitrary arrests which had an impact. Face down on cold concrete, the sharp pinch of handcuffs and the inevitable hours in a police cell. This was often followed by ridiculous charges, and harsh bail conditions which limited my movements or whom I could contact. Then there were months of fighting court cases with the threat of imprisonment always hanging over me. But the charges rarely led to court cases. And when they did, I inevitably won.

Their tactics led to two breakdowns. During one, I ended up in hospital hallucinating cops in the place of paramedics. And while the police are only supposedly allowed to use 'reasonable force' on people they arrest, there is no such limitation on how policing affects mental health.

Serious questions therefore need to be asked about what the state is sanctioning against those who dissent when their intention is to harass and deter them away from protesting. From the evidence of those of us have organised and participated, a clear pattern emerges of the state trying to shut down and control protests. This raises fundamental problems in terms of the right of dissent and the rights of people to hold the state to account and to agitate for change. But for activists who often feel powerless, there is a positive we can take from this. The level of threat and the extreme measures the state takes to shut us down can be interpreted to illustrate that we can effect change and make a difference.

CHALLENGES

The consequences of overt surveillance and harassment have not gone unchallenged. Realising the impact that the police were having on our ability to protest and organise, a group of us set up Fitwatch in 2007. We knew that policing deterred people from attending protests – the harassment tactics meant people started avoiding street action. Our aim was to turn the tables on the FIT: photograph and follow them, publish their names and photographs on our website, block their cameras and prevent them from using their tactics against others. As *Red Pepper* magazine reported in 2008, these tactics started to make a difference:

> Until the arrival of FITwatch on the scene, a couple of coppers with some oversized camcorders sometimes seemed to be enough to put the frighteners on activists. But after a year of disrupting their invasive strategies, FITwatch says: 'FIT no longer feel safe on our demonstrations. According to their own statements, they have felt "intimidated" by our tactics, and we have at times, rendered their intelligence gathering operations "ineffective".'
>
> (Redpepper.org.uk, 2008)

Fitwatch operated nationally, targeting the Metropolitan Police FIT and officers who fulfilled the same role across England and Wales. The group aimed to engage with protesters across a variety of groups and to encourage them to act in solidarity with each other. This would mean that people would 'Fitwatch' on protests they wouldn't otherwise attend, so that challenging the police didn't mean less people engaged on the actual issues they were protesting about. This didn't always materialise – but it was something we aimed for.

FIT tactics were also challenged by Andrew Wood, a press officer from the organisation Campaign Against Arms Trade. He attended an Annual General Meeting for the company organising the London arms fair, alongside a 'known' activist. Wood was repeatedly photographed and then followed by FIT officers who tried to ascertain his identity. His image was then retained on a police database.

In 2009, the Supreme Court upheld that the actions of the officers amounted to a breach of his Article 8 rights to privacy (Bailii.org, 2009). Lord Collins described the 'chilling effect' of what happened:

> I was struck by the chilling effect on the exercise of lawful rights such a deployment would have. I was also disturbed by the fact that notwithstanding that the police had no reason to believe that any unlawful activity had taken place, and still less that Mr Wood had taken part in any such activity, when he (with Mr Prichard) walked from the hotel in Grosvenor Square where the meeting had taken place towards Bond Street Underground station via Duke Street he was followed by a police car, and then questioned about his identity by 4 police officers, two of whom then followed him on foot and tried to obtain the assistance of station staff to ascertain Mr Wood's identity from his travel card.
>
> (Bailii.org, 2009)

Alongside the image retention, the police also kept a narrative of what happened on their Criminal Intelligence database. The 'information report' contains a description of Wood and the name of his colleague, and details following the pair to the Tube station.

In a Fitwatch court case, activists were found not guilty of obstructing police photographers outside an organising meeting for the No Borders protest group. During an appeal heard at the Inner London Crown Court, the judge found that activists' human rights could have been violated by overt photography outside the meeting. The judge agreed that police did not have a 'legitimate' policing purpose in photographing attendees (Irr.org.uk, 2010). Since these cases, police are no longer visibly present outside meetings. Wood's challenge to the police is now part of police briefings on overt photography (see College of Policing, n.d.). And Fitwatch tactics of highlighting what the teams were doing were extremely effective in limiting what they do and raising awareness amongst protesters of their role.

EVERYTHING CHANGES, NOTHING CHANGES

One significant difference in the reduction of FIT on protests has been the emergence of Police Liaison Officers (PLOs). PLOs first started appearing on protests in 2010 and are now a regular feature of many demonstrations. PLOs are allegedly there to engage with protesters and help ensure any policing response is proportionate (NetPol, 2013). Attending most protests, and distinguishable by their baby-blue bibs, PLOs may have a different stated brief to FIT's. But one of their key functions remains the same: intelligence gathering.

Whereas FIT were often confrontational, PLOs attempt to be your best friend. They initiate conversation and dialogue and claim to want to help. But as a police operation against 182 cyclists participating in a Critical Mass protest against the Olympic Games in London in July 2012 showed, this is far from truthful. The PLOs who gave evidence against the nine people who were prosecuted revealed that they had undertaken intelligence-gathering roles. These included gathering information from websites and attending previous protests in plain clothes (Swain, 2013). PLOs also adopt some of the tactics of their FIT colleagues. As the police campaign group Network for Police Monitoring (NetPol) notes: 'They are often in such close proximity that they can overhear conversations between protesters. PLOs are also deployed irrespective of whether protest organisers wish to engage in communication with the police and there seems no easy way to ask them to leave' (NetPol, 2016).

A report into the policing of anti-fracking protests in Balcombe, Sussex, confirmed PLOs played a 'pivotal' role in intelligence gathering:

> [PLOS] are likely to generate high-quality intelligence from the discussions they are having with [protest] group members' and are expected to record and share this with 'Bronze Intelligence for analysis and dissemination to Silver and the rest of the Command Team (in the same way as any other intelligence)'.
>
> (NetPol, 2014b)

COVERT POLICING

While FIT teams were intimidating protesters outside their meetings and on protests, a network of undercover police officers had been infiltrating their movements, family and personal lives. Undercover officers have had sexual relationships with activists, and manipulated their relationships to get closer to the movements they infiltrated. In at least two cases, undercover officers fathered children (Evans & Lewis, 2012). It was common practice for officers to assume and steal the identities of children who died as infants for their cover names (Lewis & Evans, 2013a). The scale and breadth of this policing operation has been exposed through the investigative work of activists and journalists. But it is very clear that the information known is just scratching the surface.

The Special Demonstration Squad (SDS) was an undercover unit of the Metropolitan Police established in 1968. In 2008, its functions were amalgamated in the National Public Order Intelligence Unit (NPOIU). The exact number of police officers who have infiltrated groups is unknown, but there have been at least 144 officers and over a thousand groups infiltrated (Evans, 2017b). While all the groups infiltrated are not known, they include anarchist, environmental, animal rights, anti-war, trade unions groups and perhaps most controversially, the families of people killed in police custody. Many of those targeted had no criminal record.

A key principle in undercover policing of campaign groups is intelligence gathering. But aside from a couple of high-profile cases (Evans, 2017a), this is not intelligence gathering leading to arrests or convictions.

This raises fundamental questions about the purpose of these undercover operatives. At the moment, we have more questions than answers. What purpose did these officers fulfil by infiltrating protest groups? Was their main purpose to disrupt and subvert political actions? Were political actions more of a threat to the state and corporations than perhaps we realised?

Officers have spent years infiltrating groups, gathering information, in some cases disrupting protests and groups, but not engaging in the traditional police work of gathering intelligence, building a case and then prosecuting. This is despite undercover officers taking part in, and facilitating a variety of illegal activities including criminal damage. During my years of activism, I have been directly targeted by two undercover officers that I know about, and have known at least four others. Both the officers I knew took part in, planned and encouraged illegal actions. Out of hundreds of protests I have been on, I can only think of a handful that have been prevented by undercover officers. At the very most, the result of these operations has led to a handful of arrests and even fewer convictions. Yet during that time, there were large-scale protests, some of which ended in confrontation with the police, such as the J18 Carnival Against Capitalism, the Poll Tax Riot, and some of the student protests in 2010. Many further protests involving large-scale damage or disruption have also been successfully executed.

So what is the purpose of undercover policing? It has not been successful in the sense of traditional policing purposes: keeping the Queen's peace, maintaining law and order or securing arrests and convictions (Psi.org.uk, 1996). Indeed, it could be argued that there are cases where the presence of undercover officers has led to situations where charges have been dropped against other protesters (Apple, 2015). The extent of undercover operatives' involvement in criminal activity is unknown. Apart from a few publicised cases, many of their actions will always remain off the radar, because revealing them would involve admitting taking part in actions which could lead to imprisonment.

It is worth noting that there appears to be no discernment about the groups infiltrated. Not all groups infiltrated were engaged in unlawful protest. Some groups were infiltrated as 'gateway' organisations – that is, in order to build a profile to infiltrate the actual target group. But from the pattern of behaviour so far known, it appears that any group that even vaguely posed a threat (whether through legal or illegal means) has been a target for infiltration (Ucpi.org.uk, 2018).

IMPACT

Undoubtedly the biggest impact of the undercover policing scandal has been on those activists who have had sexual relationships with police officers. 'Jacqui' described the revelation as 'being raped by the state' (Lewis & Evans, 2013b). She had a child with undercover Metropolitan Police SDS officer Bob Lambert. She described the way it made her feel: 'It was all built on sand – your first serious relationship, your first child, the first time you give birth – they're all significant, but for me they're gone, ruined, spoiled' (Lewis & Evans, 2013b).

Many of those who had relationships with undercover officers welcomed them into their families. They attended weddings and funerals and assumed all the trappings of being a 'partner'. The Metropolitan Police has now admitted that its actions amounted to torture of those women who were duped into sexual relationships (Campaign Opposing Police Surveillance, 2017).

But less well examined is the impact on the wider movement. Given that undercover officers infiltrated over a thousand groups, there are and will be (as more cover names are released) many people affected by their actions. For some, like myself, the knowledge that we were spied on was not a surprise. We always worked on the assumption that we were. Indeed, when we were advocating targeting overt surveillance, it was done in the knowledge that our meetings were probably being spied upon by undercover operatives. Yet it was the visible officers that were making the psychological difference to our organising at the time. But this was before the revelations began about the extent of undercover policing – revelations which have done just as much damage psychologically to a lot of the people affected. Groups are still adapting to the change of environment. Some have become more closed, others more open.

This has also gone hand-in-hand with a change in surveillance culture amongst many younger activists. The prevalence of social media means that people put far more online that is available to law enforcement than ever before. Minute details of people's lives that would only previously have been available through covert means are often available for all to see without even needing a warrant. For some of us, there has also been a certain liberation in knowing that the state has spied on us with such intensity. There's nothing to hide. We can be public and vocal because we know the state already holds this massive amount of data on us.

Yet there is a huge difference between superficial knowledge that could be paranoia and knowing you are right. Finding out that the person you thought was a friend was actually a police spy is heartbreaking. It is very different knowing someone is a police spy through activist research and having it confirmed by the state. I was part of a group of activists who researched and exposed Jason Bishop as an undercover officer in 2013. In 2018, his name was confirmed by the Undercover Policing Inquiry. This confirmation felt like I was starting the whole process again in terms of grieving and trauma. As more names are revealed through the inquiry, many people will continue to go through this process.

Those of us with children are particularly hurt by the knowledge that we allowed these people into our children's lives, and that because of this, our children have police files. Mae Benedict, who was friends with undercover officer Lyn Watson, summed this up: 'It made me furious that my kid is on a police file already, and mostly it was really intrusive. Instead of details of when I *had* been found guilty of a crime, the focus instead was on me as a parent, and, by default, my child as a child of mine' (Apple, 2016a).

There is also a wider impact on dissent and protest that has yet to be dissected, because its legacy is still being experienced. Now that we are beginning to understand the breadth of the groups that have been infiltrated, this can engender an atmosphere of paranoia and mistrust and can therefore disrupt activists' ability to organise. Many are overcoming this and proving that we can still organise successfully despite this. But the impact on a new generation becoming involved in political protest is still to be evaluated. Whether the undercover police scandal has affected people wanting to involve themselves with protest groups is unknown.

Another unknown is to what extent undercover policing is still operational within protest movements. According to Metropolitan Police Assistant Commissioner Martin Hewitt, the police 'no longer carries out long-term infiltration deployments' (Apple, 2016b) on protest groups. It may take many years to find out whether this is true and what short-term or other deployments are still being carried out.

Much information the police once collated through covert means can now be gleaned on social media. But there is no definition of 'long-term', and given the police's very dubious relationship with the truth on surveillance policing, it should not be taken at face value.

THE NATIONAL DOMESTIC EXTREMIST AND DISORDER INTELLIGENCE UNIT

The glue that holds the threads of political policing and surveillance together is the National Domestic Extremist and Disorder Intelligence Unit (NDEDIU). This is a national police unit that has undergone various name changes and guises since it was founded in 2004 (Corporatewatch.org, 2014), but its purpose remains the same (Npcc.police.uk, n.d.). Built on an undefined legal concept of 'domestic extremism', the NDEDIU monitors and collates intelligence on protest groups as well as liaising with, and providing advice to, corporations who may be subject to protest. However, the working definition of 'domestic extremism' is that it 'relates to the activity of groups or individuals who commit or plan serious criminal activity motivated by a political or ideological viewpoint' (NetPol, 2014c). But, as NetPol points out, there are additional problems with the term 'serious criminal activity'.

The Regulation of Investigatory Powers Act 2000 (RIPA) (Legislation.gov.uk, 2000), which regulates the powers of public bodies to carry out surveillance, says that one of the tests of a 'serious crime' is whether someone with no previous convictions 'could reasonably be expected to be sentenced to imprisonment for a term of three years or more'. However, section 81(2b) of RIPA also includes this alternate test: 'That the conduct involves the use of violence, results in substantial financial gain or is conduct by a large number of persons in pursuit of a common purpose'.

NetPol notes that '[t]he last part of this test is very broadly and vaguely worded: by definition, criminal conduct that is neither violent nor involving financial gain can become "serious crime" when carried out by "a large number of persons in pursuit of a common purpose"' (NetPol, 2014c).

In other words, many forms of protest where there are a large number of people in pursuit of a common purpose could be covered by this definition. Examples could include a mass trespass at a power station or campaigns against fracking. These are therefore covered by the definition regardless of whether that protest has any violent intent.

It would be easy to think that with so many strands to intelligence-gathering operations that the police would be producing accurate intelligence reports on those it surveilled. But the reality is very different. Those of us who have seen the small part of intelligence records that the police have been prepared to divulge know that they are littered with mistakes, obfuscation and exaggeration. Recorded on my own files are incidences where I have been assaulted by the police and won compensation. Yet the file states that I have been violent and assaulted police officers. Thus, a picture of a threat is built where none exists.

For example, my NDEDIU file reads: 'She was violent in the custody centre at Camborne attempting to slap and punch the custody sergeant repeatedly.' In fact, I was strip-searched by force by male officers. The subsequent complaint I made was upheld; there were no grounds for the search. The police force apologised and I received compensation. Yet the narrative on my domestic extremist file still remains that I was the one who was violent.

The NDEDIU manages the domestic extremism database – and information from FIT officers, as well as regional forces are recorded on files. Even inconsequential items such as being stopped driving my car in my hometown are recorded on my domestic extremist file. Following widespread criticism, the database has been culled to 2,627 individual records (Freedom of Information request, 2014). Significantly, there is no need to have committed a criminal offence to be on the database. Association with 'known' individuals and going to certain protests is enough to warrant inclusion. The database includes journalists (National Union of Journalists, 2014) who regularly report on protests, as well as those with no criminal record. For example, John Catt, a man in his 90s, who regularly attended Smash EDO protests against the arms trade and drew sketches of them is in the database. He brought a legal challenge against the domestic extremism database regarding his inclusion. However, despite not having committed any crime, the Supreme Court found that the police acted lawfully in retaining his data because of who he associated with and the nature of some of the protests (BBC News, 2015).

DOMESTIC EXTREMISM UNITS AND CORPORATIONS

A primary purpose of the domestic extremism units is to collate intelligence in the service of corporations. As Corporate Watch explained, the National Extremism Tactical Unit (NETCU), one of the first incarnations of the units, had a dual function: 'Firstly, to provide resources to local constabularies dealing with protests; secondly, to provide an interface between companies targeted by protests and the police' (Corporatewatch.org, 2014).

This 'interface' often involves advising companies to take out High Court injunctions against activists. NETCU officers played a key role in the subsequent court cases. One protester described what happened at the hearings into a Huntingdon Life Sciences' injunction against animal rights activists:

> It was very clear to us who encountered them regularly that they were in bed with the industry, and close to main injunction lawyer Timothy Lawson-Cruttenden. We would regularly see Steven Pearl [head of NETCU] sit behind him when we were in court, and it was equally obvious that they were regularly meeting at Lawson-Cruttenden's offices, often just before hearings. In Pearl, the pharmaceutical industry and others basically had the voice of the police on their side, and as far as we could see he was willing to do whatever they needed.
>
> (Corporatewatch.org, 2014)

NETCU may be gone, but its successor, the NDEDIU, uses the same tactics and advises corporations regarding activists and High Court injunctions. In 2017, UK-based petrochemicals company Ineos was awarded an injunction against fracking protesters. Giving evidence, Ineos stated that it was advised to take out the injunction by 'senior domestic extremist officers' (Twitter.com., 2017).

BLACKLISTING

Another accusation made against the Domestic Extremism units is collusion in blacklisting. Former Chief Inspector with NETCU, Gordon Mills, attended a meeting with The Consulting Association (TCA) in 2008. Run by Ian Kerr, the TCA was responsible for blacklisting 3,213 people due to their politics or trade union activities (Smith & Chamberlain, 2015). The blacklist was used by major construction companies such as Balfour Beatty, Laing O'Rourke and Sir Robert McAlpine. Workers on the list found themselves out of jobs and unable to work. According to *The Times*, Kerr claimed that '[t]he association had close links with the police and security services, exchanging information on environmental activists and construction workers, and at least one senior officer attended a CA meeting' (Kenber, 2013). Kerr's notes from the meeting with Mills shows that he provided advice to TCA (Coburg, 2016).

THE POLICE TELL US NOTHING

We are beginning to get a much clearer picture of political policing in the UK. Work by the Undercover Research Group, activists and journalists has revealed what we know about overt and undercover policing. The police have maintained a policy of 'neither confirming nor denying' (Police Spies Out of Lives, n.d.) whether a named person is a police officer. They have continually blocked every attempt to gain justice.

The Undercover Research Group has worked tirelessly to expose and profile undercover officers. It is through its painstaking research that so much information is in the public domain. The information we have about police databases largely comes from court cases. Some comes from people like Wood and Catt who have taken the police to court. But some of it has only come to light through Fitwatch criminal trials, when activists have been accused of obstructing the police in the execution of their duty. Every piece of paper, every statement about the databases was only extracted after prolonged arguments from us or our barristers.

Other information, such as the Criminal Intelligence reports cited in this chapter have come through civil claims. Activists have also used legal mechanisms such as Subject Access Requests and the Freedom of Information Act to seek out what information is held on them and the extent of police surveillance databases. NetPol encourages and supports people to apply for their personal data. One of the important things all activists need to do is to share this information – something which NetPol does. Each piece of paper, every document, helps us to build a stronger case. Creating resources which we can all use that document how the police work, the type of information they hold, and the way they gather it, can help us challenge police surveillance and make us stronger.

WHAT DOESN'T BREAK US ONLY MAKES US STRONGER

The scope of state interference is widespread. From picket lines to protest marches, British police are not only watching what dissenters do, but they are also actively trying to disrupt and deter them from exercising their fundamental rights. Alongside this, there is evidence they are colluding with big business to ensure corporate rights trump the right to protest.

It's enough to break anyone. I am far from the only person to have suffered breakdowns because of this policing. In fact, writing this chapter has proved to be far harder than I thought, taking me down rabbit holes of memory that I thought that I had dealt with. The scars are old now but that doesn't mean they don't hurt from time to time.

The response, solidarity and support structures that activists have put in place are the reasons why so many of us keep pulling through, and why we are able, after a break, to fight another day. This support takes many forms. Fitwatch was a direct action level of solidarity. We aimed to make people safer by making protests safer. In the original Fitwatch call to action, I wrote: 'If we were being systematically tortured by the state, we would protest. Mental abuse is just as important and it is vital to the strength of our actions that we challenge this.' Through blocking cameras and taking the power away from the police, we were able to make people feel more comfortable on protests.

Police Spies Out of Lives and Campaign Opposing Police Surveillance are two groups to support those targeted by undercover policing. Both groups support those spied upon and campaign for justice for those affected. They ensure the narrative is kept in the media and stories are told on a national and international level. In campaigning, they believe full transparency is needed from the state to ensure justice. This needs to take the form of telling us the police officers' cover names, real names and releasing our files. The groups also send out a clear message that political surveillance can never be justified.

Organisations such as Counselling for Social Change (CSC) have been set up to offer free psychotherapeutic counselling to activists. I helped found CSC after having a breakdown and suffering from post traumatic stress disorder (PTSD). We were aware of how ill-equipped a lot of NHS and private counsellors were in dealing with the specific issues around trauma, burnout and activism. This was particularly relevant in terms of surveillance policing, as especially before the knowledge of undercover policing was quite so widespread, many practitioners dismissed activists as paranoid. Politically, CSC aims to put mental health firmly on the activist agenda. If we do not look after ourselves, we are not effective. If we actually want change, we need to start by ensuring we are well enough to fight for that change.

We have shown that we can come through this. We can work together, show solidarity and support each other. We will also be there to support others as they go through similar experiences. For many of us, it is one of the fundamental tenets of our political engagement and belief. The police may want to deter and disrupt our protests; they do not want people to find protest or dissent empowering or effective. And at times, it certainly feels like they are trying to break us.

But we can and must fight back, whether through direct action tactics such as Fitwatch or mutual aid solidarity structures. We can and do find ways to support each other. These things have happened to us because we want to make the world a better place. Despite the risks posed by undercover police officers, we need to make sure that our movements and organisations are accessible and welcoming to newcomers. And we need to keep going. The level of time, money and energy that has gone into spying on protesters shows the impact we can have.

Police surveillance may make things harder. Discovering the true extent of police surveillance in the UK has been sobering. However, it has also shown how worried the state is about our power to impact it and its corporate interests. We are coming out stronger from the ashes of the undercover policing scandal. We have shown that we won't give up. We will do our own research, provide our own support, and continue fighting for what we believe in. Ultimately, we can and do make a difference and this is something that we must never lose sight of.

REFERENCES

All URLs accessed 1 August 2018.

App.college.police.uk. (2013). 'Command'. Accessed from www.app.college.police.uk/app-content/public-order/command/#wood-v-commissioner-of-the-police-of-the-metropolis

Apple, E. (2009). 'My life as "Suspect A"', *Guardian*. Accessed from www.theguardian.com/commentisfree/libertycentral/2009/oct/27/police-domestic-extremists

—— (2015). 'Names of undercover police revealed, this scandal is worse than we thought', *The Canary*. Accessed from www.thecanary.co/uk/2015/12/21/exclusive-undercover-police-revealed-scandal-spreads/

—— (2016a). 'Undercover police officers spy on children, and then demand privacy', *The Canary*. Accessed from https://www.thecanary.co/uk/2016/03/23/undercover-police-officers-spy-children-demand-privacy/

—— (2016b). 'Are the police lying about undercover policing?', *The Canary*. Accessed from www.thecanary.co/uk/2016/01/20/police-lying-undercover-policing/

Bailii.org. (2009). *Wood v Commissioner of Police for the Metropolis* [2009] EWCA Civ 414 (21 May 2009). Accessed from www.bailii.org/ew/cases/EWCA/Civ/2009/414.html

BBC News (2015). 'Campaigner, 90, loses extremism case'. Accessed from http://www.bbc.co.uk/news/uk-england-sussex-31728884

Bristol Anarchist Black Cross – Prisoner Support (n.d.). 'Police harassment'. Accessed from https://bristolabc.wordpress.com/defendant-solidarity/police-harassment/

Campaign Opposing Police Surveillance (2017). 'Spycops relationships amount to torture, Met admit – Campaign Opposing Police Surveillance'. Accessed from http://campaignopposingpolicesurveillance.com/2017/12/07/spycops-relationships-amount-to-torture-met-admit/

Coburg, T. (2016). Handwritten note giving details of Woodstock meeting, *The Canary*. Accessed from www.thecanary.co/wp-content/uploads/2016/04/Handwritten-note-Details-of-Woodstock-Mtg-NETCU-6th-Nov-2008-1sm.pdf

College of Policing (n.d.). 'Public Order: Command'. Accessed from www.app.college.police.uk/app-content/public-order/command/

Corporatewatch.org. (2014). 'Re-visiting NETCU – Police collaboration with industry', *Corporate Watch*. Accessed from https://corporatewatch.org/re-visiting-netcu-police-collaboration-with-industry/

Evans, R. (2017). 'Probe into claim that police spy set fire to Debenhams could end by July', *Guardian*. Accessed from www.theguardian.com/uk-news/undercover-with-paul-lewis-and-rob-evans/2017/jan/16/probe-into-claim-that-police-spy-set-fire-to-debenhams-expected-to-end-by-july

—— (2017b). 'Undercover police spied on more than 1,000 political groups in UK', *Guardian*. Accessed from www.theguardian.com/uk-news/2017/jul/27/

undercover-police-spied-on-more-than-1000-political-groups-in-uk

—— & Bowcott, O. (2014). 'Green Party peer put on database of "extremists" after police surveillance', *Guardian*. Accessed from www.theguardian.com/politics/2014/jun/15/green-party-peer-put-on-database-of-extremists-by-police

—— & Lewis, P. (2010). 'Police admit stop and searches on 11-year-olds at Kingsnorth protest', *Guardian*. Accessed from www.theguardian.com/uk/2010/jan/12/kingsnorth-stop-search-boys-illegal

—— & Lewis, P. (2012). 'Undercover police had children with activists', *Guardian*. Accessed from www.theguardian.com/uk/2012/jan/20/undercover-police-children-activists

Fitwatch (2018). 'Fitwatch.org.uk: Fitwatch – Resisting police surveillance'. Accessed from www.fitwatch.org.uk

Freedom of Information request (2014). www.whatdotheyknow.com/request/national_domestic_extremism_and

Guardian (2009). 'Spotter cards: What they look like and how they work', *Guardian*. Accessed from www.theguardian.com/uk/2009/oct/25/spotter-cards

Irr.org.uk. (2010). 'Court rules against unauthorised police surveillance', *Institute of Race Relations*. Accessed from www.irr.org.uk/news/court-rules-against-unauthorised-police-surveillance/

Kenber, B. (2013). 'Blacklist of "troublemakers" compiled with the help of construction unions', *The Times*. Accessed from www.thetimes.co.uk/article/blacklist-of-troublemakers-compiled-with-the-help-of-construction-unions-fs98ptcz7wx

Legislation.gov.uk. (2000). Regulation of Investigatory Powers Act 2000. Accessed from www.legislation.gov.uk/ukpga/2000/23/contents

Lewis, P. (2018). 'Harass a hoodie: How Essex police take surveillance to the streets', *Guardian*. Accessed from www.theguardian.com/uk/2008/may/30/ukcrime.youthjustice

—— and Evans, R. (2013a). 'Police spies stole identities of dead children', *Guardian*. Accessed from theguardian.com/uk/2013/feb/03/police-spies-identities-dead-children

—— and Evans, R. (2013b). 'Trauma of spy's girlfriend: "Like being raped by the state"', *Guardian*. Accessed from www.theguardian.com/uk/2013/jun/24/undercover-police-spy-girlfriend-child

National Union of Journalists (2009). 'Kent police apologise over Climate Camp stop and search', Accessed from www.nuj.org.uk/news/kent-police-apologise-over-climate-camp-stop-and-search/

—— (2014). 'NUJ members under police surveillance mount collective legal challenge', Accessed from www.nuj.org.uk/news/nuj-members-under-police-surveillance-mount-collective-legal/

NetPol. (2013). 'Police liaison officers – Intelligence gathering, self-policing and the dangers of talking to the police', Accessed from https://netpol.org/2013/03/13/police-liaison-officers-intelligence-gathering-self-policing-

and-the-dangers-of-talking-to-the-police/

—— (2014a). 'Police liaison officers'. Accessed from https://netpol.org/police-liaison-officers/

—— (2014b). 'Review reveals police liaison officers played "pivotal role" in Balcombe protest intelligence gathering'. Accessed from https://netpol.org/2014/06/17/police-liaison-intelligence-balcombe/

—— (2014c). 'So who exactly is now classified as a "Domestic Extremist"?'. Accessed from https://netpol.org/2014/04/22/new-definition-of-domestic-extremism/

—— (2016). 'Is dialogue with police liaison officers really "voluntary"?'. Accessed from https://netpol.org/2016/09/06/liaison-voluntary-dialogue/

Npcc.police.uk. (n.d.). 'About NDEDIU'. Accessed from www.npcc.police.uk/NationalPolicing/NDEDIU/AboutNDEDIU.aspx

Police Spies Out of Lives (n.d.). 'Briefing on "Neither confirm or deny" – A police tactic for secrecy', *Police Spies Out of Lives.* Accessed from https://policespiesoutoflives.org.uk/briefing-ncnd/

Psi.org.uk. (1996). Accessed from www.psi.org.uk/publications/archivepdfs/Role%20pol/INDPOL-0.P.pdf

Redpepper.org.uk. (2008). 'FIT for purpose?', *Red Pepper.* Accessed from www.redpepper.org.uk/fit-for-purpose/

Smith, D. and Chamberlain, P. (2015). 'On the blacklist: How did the UK's top building firms get secret information on their workers?', *Guardian.* Accessed from www.theguardian.com/uk-news/2015/feb/27/on-the-blacklist-building-firms-secret-information-on-workers

Statewatch.org. (2009). 'Strategic review: Operation Oasis'. Accessed from www.statewatch.org/news/2009/jul/uk-kingsnorth%20report-kent-police.pdf

Swain, V. (2013). 'Surveillance and the Right to Protest', *Open Security.* Accessed from www.opendemocracy.net/opensecurity/val-swain/disruption-policing-surveillance-and-right-to-protest

Twitter.com. (2017). 'Netpol'. Accessed from https://twitter.com/policemonitor/status/933677820861140992

Ucpi.org.uk. (2018). 'Undercover policing inquiry'. Accessed from www.ucpi.org.uk/wp-content/uploads/2018/03/20180319-TC-Documents_Final_Version.pdf

10

Spies wide shut

Responses and resistance to the national security state in Aotearoa New Zealand[1]

Valerie Morse

Resistance to state surveillance has long been a feature of life in Aotearoa New Zealand. Yet, perhaps paradoxically, the extent of state surveillance has only ever increased. What are the drivers behind this, and does that mean that resistance to state surveillance is futile? If not, then what are some methods for successful resistance?

Aotearoa New Zealand is a small, Western, liberal, unicameral parliamentary democracy dominated politically, socially and economically by a history of British colonialism and subsequent post-Second World War US influence. Following the arrival of European whalers, traders and missionaries in the late 1700s and early 1800s, representatives of the British Crown signed the Treaty of Waitangi in 1840 with approximately 500 leaders of Māori *iwi*.[2] The Treaty (or more properly, the Māori version, *Te Tiriti o Waitangi*) established a settler-colonial government. The Treaty has always been deeply contentious – both with Māori and Pākehā (European settlers) – and its continuous violations by the Crown have been the source of wars and conflict for nearly 180 years.

This colonial context is central to understanding state surveillance in Aotearoa New Zealand, because the settler-colonial state suffers from both an ongoing crisis of legitimacy and the continual rapacious demands of global capital. The context is thus both very local and specific, and very global and ubiquitous. Both drivers require constant attention and vigilance through an ever-expanding surveillance apparatus.

Dwyer and Dwyer (2005) conceptualise a modern 'national security state' as:

> a type of capitalist imperialism called 'militarism' that is premised both on the ideology that peace and security can only be achieved through the threat and use of greater force and on the presumption of a constant threat against which we must be ever vigilant to preserve the ideal state. This vigilance typically calls for the adoption of anti-democratic steps such as the suspension of basic rights and the resort to secrecy to preserve the democratic state. This is also why the National Security State requires the allocation of large amounts of the nation's resources to weapons and why we find ourselves in a state of perpetual war.
>
> (Dwyer & Dwyer, 2005, p. 165)

An essential component of this national security state is, along with a state of perpetual war, ever-expanding surveillance.

Critically, however, the component parts of this state are neither modern nor recent phenomena, but rather inherent and ever-present in the colonial settler project. That this national security state is viewed as a relatively new formation (in the US in particular, but equally in Canada, Australia and Aotearoa New Zealand) against the backdrop of the genocide of Indigenous Peoples should be clear evidence of the intense campaign of organised forgetting that surrounds and permeates life under neoliberal capitalism in the twenty-first century. It is part of the essential operations of power to engender a collective amnesia – an erasure – about the exercise of violence and dispossession by those with power against those without.

By contrast, our struggles for collective liberation and freedom can be greatly enhanced and informed by what has come before. Instead of re-inventing and relearning strategies and tactics of resistance with each new emergence and configuration of state surveillance, we must embed that history in our social movements. As Milan Kundera wrote in *The Unbearable Lightness of Being*, 'the struggle of man against power is the struggle of memory against forgetting.' Remembering is our greatest tool of resistance. There are others.

THE UNSTABLE STATE: WHY NEW ZEALAND NEEDS EVER MORE SURVEILLANCE

The foundation of the modern New Zealand state created a deeply irresoluble tension guaranteeing as it does *tino rangatiratanga* (absolute authority/sovereignty) for Māori while simultaneously creating a colonial Westminster system. It created a state wherein the legitimacy of rule is an unresolved issue. This crisis of legitimacy is a fundamental driver of ever-expanding surveillance, because those with power fear a loss of control over the stolen resources on which that power is founded. Māori have consistently reminded state institutions that they have overstepped the bounds of the Treaty/*Te Tiriti*, and that particular policies, processes and programmes that the state wants to enact are violations of *rangatiratanga*. It seems abundantly clear that it is not possible for the existing state to operate in a way that is coextensive with *rangatiratanga*. While there is a serious proposal for reform of the existing structure to enlarge the operating sphere of *rangatiratanga*, there is little by way of evidence that a modern, neoliberal state could coexist with another competing structure.

For example, in 2014, the Waitangi Tribunal, the government body charged with investigating violations of the Treaty/*Te Tiriti* reported back to the government that northern *iwi*, representing the largest population of Māori yet to receive any compensation for violations of the Treaty/*Te Tiriti*, had never ceded sovereignty. The government immediately dismissed this finding. Throughout the country's history, the emergence of specific struggles around resources and land has meant that decisions regarding who rules has most often been achieved through violence, or the threat thereof, almost always by the Crown. In contrast to the mythology of amicable race relations, state institutions of surveillance, coercion and dispossession were central to the birth of the new nation-state.

At the time the Treaty/*Te Tiriti* was signed, a new form of policing was deployed that included, among other things, a new methodology of surveillance. Historian Richard Hill notes that

> an essential element of New Zealand policing from 1840 lay in the method of surveillance which was employed. Hitherto, policing … had largely involved *reactive* responses to events after they had disturbed the social and economic order … there emerged in gradual fashion from

> the mid eighteenth century a *proactive* system of patrols, both mounted and foot. Herein lay the germ of the *preventative* policing which was to culminate in the establishment of the 'new police' in London in 1829 – and which was followed by imitations throughout the English-speaking world, including Sydney in 1833 and in New Zealand urban areas from the point of British acquisition in 1840. Regular patrolling was partly for purposes of intimidation, to symbolise and if necessary actualise the all-pervading presence and power of the state, and partly for reasons of surveillance. Patrolling policemen came to learn all facets of their district and its inhabitants, and the possession of such knowledge by the state was the prerequisite for 'corrective' action when 'order and regularity' was threatened by individuals or crowds.
>
> (Hill, 1986, p. 95; original emphasis)

Surveillance was and continues to be conducted for social control of Māori, and used to gather knowledge and information about how communities function and who holds power within them, so that the state and capital can access to their resources. It was and is used to ensure that Māori behave in a way that is acceptable to the powerful. For Māori, that has proven particularly problematic as their very existence is a reminder of the ongoing illegitimacy of white settler rule, and thus unacceptable.

A striking episode of this sort of Crown behaviour – and its devastating effects for Māori – was the case of the Reverend Carl Volkner, a missionary among Whakatohea, an *iwi* in the Bay of Plenty, from 1861 to 1865. This was in the midst of the New Zealand Wars fought by the settler government against Māori who resisted land sales. Whakatohea had not been involved in the war, yet Volkner spied upon his congregation and reported back to the governor on the *iwi*'s loyalty and sympathies. After returning home from Auckland, he was hung and decapitated by the *iwi* for his treachery. Shortly afterwards, other *iwi* unrelated to the incident were held responsible for Volkner's murder and massive swathes of land were confiscated. From the Tūhoe people adjacent to Whakatohea, a million acres was taken as punishment (Stokes, 1990).

DISCIPLINING SUBJECTS

The crisis of legitimacy that is elemental to the foundations of the New Zealand state is complemented by the requirements of global capital for limitless expansion of both resources and markets in creating the conditions for a drive to surveillance. Capital needs surveillance in order to maximise profits: to mitigate risk, to discipline labour, to obtain information and to ensure stable markets.

As a result, along with Māori, other 'dangerous classes' within Aotearoa New Zealand have long been the sustained targets of surveillance such as trade unionists and other radical anti-capitalist organisers.

A New Zealand watersiders union leader declared in 1890 that 'We have no flag, we have no country', foreshadowing the internationalist and militant position of the International Workers of the World (IWW). By 1912, the IWW influence was deeply embedded within the largest workers' organisation in the country, the Federation of Labour, with the IWW's constitution preamble stating that '[t]he working class and the employing class have nothing in common' (Derby, 2009, p. 3).

As a result of the challenge of labour to capital, both organisations and individuals were frequent targets of state surveillance. The period of intense class war in the years prior to World War 1 (WW1), and the anti-war agitation throughout the war by anarchists, communists and pacifists meant radicals were 'monitored, scrutinised and silenced' (Davidson, 2011, p. 43).

Moreover, the end of WW1 did not end surveillance: 'the state also kept tabs on the second wave of syndicalist organisations, such as the Alliance of Labour and the One Big Union Council' throughout the interwar years (Davidson, 2016, p. 25).

Until the 1950s, political surveillance (more rightly understood as politico-economic surveillance) was largely conducted by the NZ Police's Special Branch. Certainly other types of surveillance existed – like health inspectors – and these can be considered political insofar as colonisation is a deeply political project, and the intention of such surveillance was to impose assimilationist policies and hegemonic ideals. Police, however, were responsible for targeting individuals and groups based on the political ideas that they espoused or the implicit threat to industry they were believed to pose. This agency collected detailed, individual files of hundreds of people including members of the Christian Pacifist Society and the NZ Communist Party.[3]

Like its Western friends, the New Zealand state became a post-war Cold Warrior, and joined the 'Five Eyes' intelligence alliance. It soon established its own secret intelligence agency, the New Zealand Security Intelligence Service (SIS):

> NZSIS was established in 1956 as the New Zealand Security Service. Until then, apart from a brief period during the Second World War, national security had been handled by the Police. Between 1956 and 1969, the NZSIS existed without a legislative base. Legislation in 1969 (the NZSIS Act): gave the NZSIS a new name (the New Zealand Security Intelligence Service), recognised its existence in statute, and defined its role: to protect New Zealand from threats of espionage, sabotage and subversion.
>
> (SIS, 2017)

Activists involved in revolutionary political parties and trade unions were acutely aware of the SIS's role in monitoring their organising, undermining their political activities and disrupting the personal lives of individual members (Hunt, 2007, p. 122). In 2009, the SIS file on sitting Green Party Member of Parliament Keith Locke was released showing that he had been surveilled from age 11. His parents had been well-known Communist Party members, and he was a lifelong activist. Along with the intense personal scrutiny, the SIS visited his workplace to warn his boss about his political activities (Taylor & Milne, 2012).

By the early 1970s, and partly as a result of the faltering post-war economy, Māori along with many others began 'to review the validity, the justice of the present system and question it' (Hill, 2009, p. 149). Indeed, 'even Māori who had been drawn into the "equality" myth could see that their people constituted, in general, a subset of the New Zealand working class and suffered disproportionately within the capitalist political economy' (Hill, 2009, p. 150). A rejuvenated Māori political consciousness emerged in organisations such as *Ngā Tamatoa*, a pan-Māori youth organisation struggling for 'Māori control of Māori things' and taking inspiration from a diversity of models including Black power and the American Indian Movement (Hill, 2009, p. 150)

Concurrently, feminist, peace, anti-racist and environmental movements came to the fore of New Zealand life, and provided significant challenges to the prevailing economic, social and political order. By the mid-1970s, a formidable and sustained peace movement was organising across issues of nuclear disarmament, anti-apartheid and decolonisation in the Pacific. When Prime Minister Rob Muldoon, a combative right-wing politician, introduced an amendment to the SIS legislation in 1977 allowing domestic wiretapping, there were large-scale protests. Even a member of Muldoon's own National Party commented that 'New Zealand was well on the way to becoming a police state' (Bodman, 2011,

p. 17) as a result of the bill, which passed into law. Subsequently, during the 1981 South African Springbok rugby tour, Muldoon publicly released an SIS dossier of so-called 'subversives' involved in the anti-apartheid movement (Hunt, 2007, p. 262) – confirming the views of many that the agency was nothing more than a political police force. The SIS was successfully sued for publicising inaccurate information in the dossier (Hager, 2011).

One of the most striking episodes of resistance to the growing authoritarianism and state surveillance that characterised New Zealand society at the time was the 1982 bombing of a new police computer system that centralised transport and justice records by a young anarchist named Neil Roberts. As historian Ryan Bodman argues, this was not the aberrant act of a lone, disaffected young man (as Roberts was subsequently portrayed), but rather part of much broader and stronger currents within New Zealand society:

> During the late 1970s and early 1980s deep concerns permeated society as a socially repressive and authoritarian government raised anxiety amongst many. Specific groups in society, including Pacific Islanders and women who worked outside of the home, were scapegoated by the government for the nation's faltering economic fortunes and were persecuted as a result. The growing power the SIS Amendment Act offered both the Prime Minister and the SIS raised concerns within society and resulted in a massive opposition movement. Meanwhile the police operation during the Springbok tour brought a level of state violence they had never observed to the attention of many New Zealanders.
>
> (Bodman, 2011, pp. 24–25)

NEOLIBERALISM AND BIG DATA

The self-imposed structural adjustment and the implementation of drastic neoliberal policies starting from 1984 created massive social disruption, high levels of unemployment, and a breakdown of the New Zealand state's social safety net. These changes did not and do not go unchallenged, and the same opponents of state and capital's drive for profitability and market efficiency continued to be portrayed as 'the enemies within' and targets of state surveillance.

These economic drivers, coupled with significant technological advancements in computing, meant that some state surveillance began to shift. Academic Jane Kelsey (1993, p. 317) notes,

> The liberal reformers were full of talk about getting the state out of people's lives and maximizing individual freedom. But the links between the liberal programme and state power were much more subtle. The price for retaining some social assistance at the time of retrenchment and targeting was an increase in data-matching, information-sharing and the surveillance of people's everyday lives.
>
> (Kelsey, 1993, p. 317)

Indeed, the neoliberal era can be characterised by extreme attacks on the poor and a punitive and surveillance-heavy environment for anyone seeking social assistance. According to neoliberal ideologies, anyone who had not enthusiastically embraced their personal freedom to be rich had only themselves to blame. This had specific manifestations in proposals for a range of tracking and data-gathering programmes such as individual 'smart' identity cards. Under the 1990 conservative government, a proposal for a nationwide 'Kiwi Card' met stiff resistance within Parliament and from civil libertarians (Wilson, 1991) who noted the government's rationale for the card – catching welfare cheats – did not withstand scrutiny, and that it created more problems than it solved.[4]

More pointedly, these nascent programs would grow in the coming decades into government-wide and transnational data-sharing agreements covering everything from taxes, travel, finances, immigration status, political affiliations, criminal background, educational achievement and entitlements.

One aspect of the neoliberal project is the deregulation of the economy and trade liberalisation. The New Zealand state has been (and continues to be) a vocal advocate of such an approach, and opponents of 'free trade' have found themselves targeted by state, and more recently, corporate surveillance. Again, Māori were at the forefront of this opposition and the inevitable surveillance that accompanied it. Māori academic and activist Maria Bargh (2007, p. 15) writes, 'The threat that neoliberal practices pose for indigenous ways of life, most importantly by extending the market mechanism to all areas of life previously governed in other ways, is the reason for much of Māori resistance.' Unions and so-called 'anti-globalisation' activists were similarly subjected to harassment and surveillance. In one high-profile case, in July 1996, two SIS agents were caught fleeing after breaking into the house of GATT Watchdog organiser Aziz Choudry, while he was involved with organising a conference opposing the Asia-Pacific Economic Cooperation (APEC) forum. More recently, Jane Kelsey, University of Auckland academic and a leading critic of New Zealand's involvement with the Trans Pacific Partnership, a proposed free trade and investment agreement, was 'detained by Australian immigration at Sydney airport ... and told she ... could not enter visa-free like most New Zealanders because she was not an "appropriate person" under Australia's 1994 immigration laws' (Australian Visa Bureau, 2010) despite having travelled back and forth to Australia repeatedly over the previous two years. Dr Kelsey's SIS file purportedly goes back thirty years, and the agency has steadfastly refused to release any of it even in redacted form. She concludes:

> It is apparent from other files that the SIS has an ongoing interest in my critique of globalisation. Various files contain documents that relate to different aspects of neo-liberal economic negotiations, organisations and meetings ... The only potential justification under the post-1999 SIS legislation is 'to identify foreign capabilities, intentions, or activities within or relating to New Zealand that impact on New Zealand's international wellbeing or economic wellbeing'. If my participation in international networks of academic, trade unionists and other activists is enough to satisfy this definition, how many other people are also being monitored for their purely lawful activities that advance economic and social justice through international networks?
>
> (Kelsey, 2009)

While those opposing neoliberalism did not necessarily conceptualise their resistance as 'threats to national security', political elites and the institutions of state surveillance most certainly did (and indeed, still do): 'The rhetoric of protecting national security was a feature of colonisation and more recently neo-liberal practices', writes Bargh (2008, p. 160). During this time, significant effort was expended to incorporate Māori into the structures of neoliberalism, as Bargh argues:

> in the early to late 1980s the more subtle political language of empowerment of individuals through the marketplace was used to incorporate many Māori organisations within a corporate agenda. This resulted in many Māori organisations undertaking duties previously carried out by the state, namely service provision. This limited form of empowerment channelled Māori energy into the market mechanism rather than addressing the more fundamental issue of Māori sovereignty.
>
> (Bargh, 2008, p. 160)

Meanwhile, those that could not be co-opted would continue to be targeted.

In line with the neoliberal ethos, privatised surveillance of activities detrimental to state and corporate power has also blossomed in Aotearoa New Zealand. In 2007, paid informants who had infiltrated the animal rights, anti-war and environmental movement were uncovered. The company responsible for the surveillance – Thompson & Clark (the names of the two ex-police company directors) – paid young university students to join grass-roots campaigns and provide detailed information on the groups, which was then sold to state agencies and other corporations in a monthly newsletter entitled *National Extremism*. An attempt to hold them to account through a formal state tribunal produced a preposterous outcome: the activists' campaigns were each fined NZ$1,000 for daring to question the company's right to surveil (Goldman, 2008). In another instance, an activist involved in union, animal rights, environmental and social justice campaigns – and running what was at the time the country's largest activist email network – was exposed as being a decade-long police informer receiving a weekly paycheck (@ndy, 2008). He was long suspected, and had even been evicted from some activist groups (Horton, 2009). But that information was unknown to most until he was publicly exposed by his then girlfriend, an animal rights activist and computer expert who read his email reports to police while fixing his computer. In 2018, Thompson & Clark were again exposed, this time for spying on victims of the Christchurch earthquakes who sought compensation from their insurer. The spies compared quake victims to 'anarchists', and told the state-owned company they worked for that the victims represented an ongoing threat (Gower, 2018). Details are now emerging of at least three other government agencies currently using the firm for surveillance of activists (Mountier, 2018).

Alongside the privatisation, corporatisation and deregulation of Aotearoa New Zealand, the uptake of computerisation and digitisation has greatly facilitated state surveillance. The ongoing crises of capitalism and the accompanying endless wars of dispossession/terror have meant that state and corporate power are at the ready to quash emergent dissent. The scope of the enemy within has grown, as inequality rises to epidemic proportions enveloping ever more into the fold of the 'dangerous class' of the poor, and further criminalising those already occupying that space. In this way, the rise of mass surveillance and global information gathering, rather than being seen simply as the application or by-product of technology, is a deeply ideological project. As we become more visible to the state and corporate power through the use of digital devices and platforms, state and corporate power becomes more opaque. As an example, the New Zealand government has a decade-long strategy to move towards provision of online government services; the result of which is the disappearance in communities of the face of the state in the local post office, welfare and housing offices while providing mountains of easily digestible (and shareable) data about every person in the country for the state.

Meanwhile, New Zealand intelligence agencies have responded with clever propaganda and sophisticated public relations to the widespread public disquiet about their roles and powers following Edward Snowden's disclosure of NSA documents, a disclosure that implicated New Zealand's sister agencies – the SIS and Government Communications Security Bureau (GCSB) – and the 2011 Kim Dotcom episode (see below). Instead of retreating behind the cloak of secrecy, both the SIS and the GCSB have implemented a new, ostensibly more 'transparent' and 'accountable' image, seeking to build public trust. Closely following the passage of a highly contentious new spying law, media outlets paraded the two new women leaders of these agencies and proclaimed a 'revolution' inside the halls of spy power.[5] However, their targets have not changed: Māori and radical activists, Muslims and other non-white migrant communities are included in their list of suspect groups. Playing on racist tropes and terrorism fearmongering, coupled with claiming supremacy of the new 'cybersecurity' domain for the benefit of the average computer user, these agencies have sought to manufacture consent for their existence. In documents obtained under New Zealand's Official Information Act, it is clear that the GCSB saw the opportunity to speak at the annual 'Kiwicon' computer hacker conference as an opportunity to build trust within the cyber community.[6] Other quasi-public events such as the 'Privacy and Technology Forum' organised by the Privacy Commissioner allowed the GCSB's director to reposition the agency's major spy program – Project Cortex – as a benign computer security programme, which, according to the agency, provides 'advanced cyber threat detection and disruption … capability to protect nationally significant information and networks against online attacks' (Jagose, 2015).

THE PAST IS PROLOGUE

History is a useful tool in order to see state patterns and practices for those who wish to resist and/or deconstruct them. Yet meaningfully disrupting those patterns and practices, deployed as they are by the powerful against the powerless, is difficult. It is a struggle where there are seldom clear-cut victories and what first appear as progressive 'wins' ultimately operate as further methods of oppression.

Time and time again, the legal overreach of the New Zealand state surveillance apparatus has been exposed. There is the 1996 SIS burglary case mentioned above, and the 2003 case of Algerian politician Ahmed Zaoui, who fled to Aotearoa New Zealand seeking refuge only to be held in solitary confinement for two years based on a bogus 'intelligence' dossier provided by biased French security agents; both of these cases were contested in the courts. There was also the 2007 terrorism raids, dubbed 'Operation 8', in which Māori, anarchists and other activists were rounded up by police to 'test-drive' the nation's primary terrorism law. Nobody was prosecuted under terrorism legislation due in part to its hastily crafted post-9/11 domestic provisions. The entire basis of the case was illegally obtained police surveillance footage that ultimately resulted in the dismissal of charges against all but four of the original twenty defendants. In 2011, Kim Dotcom, Internet entrepreneur and founder of the file-hosting site megaupload.com, was arrested in spectacular style by the NZ Police, acting on an FBI request, including a helicopter raid on his north Auckland mansion. Soon after came revelations of illegal surveillance conducted by the GCSB. The Dotcom case appeared at first to be a major blow to the intelligence community, and resulted in a subsequent revelation that an additional 88 people were subject to illegal state surveillance by the GCSB, the context of which we will never know. The end result was the passage of significantly broader surveillance powers for the intelligence agencies.

The result of the agencies' 'overreach' has been an extension of their legal powers to surveil (this includes not only the police, SIS and GCSB, but also a host of other agencies). It is such a frequent methodology of state power expansion – a kind of testing of the limits – that it might be considered a primary way in which agencies successfully acquire long-sought-after power. Yet within this model exists a deep fracture: gaining power through this methodology (and I am not suggesting it is a deliberate strategy so much as a set of organisational settings) requires exposure, and that exposure means risk. In essence, these agencies (police intelligence, security intelligence, etc.) continually push the legal boundaries on particular technologies of surveillance. In rare circumstances, these cases come to public awareness, and there is always the possibility that these agencies will not persuade the courts and Parliament to award the powers sought. Or, as in the case with Operation 8, they lose the court case but win wider powers to surveil.

Demands for so-called 'democratic accountability' for illegal activity in such cases is typically defused by resorting to fearmongering and institutional acquiescence to more 'oversight'. After the Dotcom saga, oversight was indeed expanded. Yet the limited scope of such oversight means that the fundamental premise on which these agencies are founded goes unquestioned. Similarly, the overseers are to all intents and purposes 'part of the club',[7] and vested in the existing political and economic organisation of New Zealand. Meaningful reform is oxymoronic and thus cannot be a goal for those who seek greater space for freedom and collective liberation. Nevertheless, as with many struggles, legislative and organisational reform may be the outcome of more expansive struggles, and reform in this context must be seen as a kind of victory. In the 2013 eruption of opposition, reform was not seen as an acceptable remedy, and as a result, the aforementioned public relations campaign – a real 'hearts and minds' job – was unleashed on the New Zealand public disseminated through stories in weekly magazines,[8] public radio and quasi-public meetings.[9]

Furthermore, an official 'review' of the intelligence agencies was undertaken ostensibly seeking wide public input, yet with terms of reference that predetermined a narrow range of possible outcomes. There was to be no fundamental rethinking of the foundations of the intelligence services. A 'Stop the Spies' campaign including grass-roots group OASIS (Organising Against State Intelligence Services), the New Zealand Council for Civil Liberties, the Anti-Bases Campaign, the Dunedin Free University and the What IF? Campaign began organising in opposition to this official 2015 review.[10] The campaign conducted a 'People's Review of the Intelligence Agencies' hosting public meetings around the country and gathering submissions. A full report was published and thoroughly ignored by mainstream media. The campaign sought to discredit the official exercise as a 'rubberstamp for the Five

Eyes', and a 'whitewash', describing the official review submission form as 'paternalistic' with 'leading questions', and discouraging people from participating (OASIS, 2015).

Further action by the Stop the Spies campaign illustrated that by the end of 2015, the mass opposition to the intelligence agencies that had characterised 2013 and 2014 had largely disappeared from the landscape, with few seeing avenues for action beyond parliamentary change that was clearly not forthcoming. Meanwhile, the media became openly hostile to the remaining resistance, having been successfully captured by agency spin.[11]

There are really two key insights to take away from a reading of Aotearoa New Zealand's history of surveillance and the resistance to it. The first is that the targets of state surveillance are almost invariably those who challenge the economic bases of those who hold power. In this land, that especially means Māori. It is also trade unionists, anti-capitalists, environmentalists, peace and social justice activists, anti-racists, feminists and animal rights activists. These struggles must be understood as economic struggles in order to make sense of the persistence and virulence of state surveillance: against the capitalist order, white supremacy and patriarchy. Specific clauses upholding the existing economic order are included in all major relevant surveillance legislation. In the Intelligence and Security Act (Parliament, 2017),[12] 'the economic well-being of New Zealand' is part of both the SIS and GCSB's roles, while under the Terrorism Suppression Act, anything that causes 'destruction of, or serious damage to, property of great value or importance, or major economic loss' (Parliament, 2002)[13] can lead to a prosecution. The second insight is that while surveillance has only ever increased in Aotearoa New Zealand, the 'excesses' of state intelligence agencies do not go unnoticed nor are they entirely forgotten by the people. There is a collective social discomfort with state surveillance that has arisen in part because of the exposure of the many illegalities these agencies have engaged in. While this does little to build an active sustained movement against surveillance, it does go some way to enhancing public scepticism of these agencies' claims. Such was the case during the 2007 terror raids. Commentators from across the political spectrum were utterly incredulous and remained largely unconvinced of the state's case throughout the punishing five-year-long ordeal. Thus, while there were a couple of short prison sentences that resulted from these raids (and the punishments should not be understated) the primary protagonist, Tame Iti, emerged a folk hero, a cultural icon and leading artist, and perhaps more importantly, the claims of 'terrorism' became a joke. However, by contrast, there was scant public understanding of the particular historical and colonial context in which these raids, and the extensive surveillance that formed the basis of them, should have been placed.

In terms of methodologies of resistance to surveillance, then, an intersectional approach to political struggle where there is substantial awareness and understanding of the ways in which the aspirations of the powerless converge and are complementary makes sense. Our social movements are stronger and more resistant to the effects of surveillance when they have a thoroughgoing analysis of the operations of power, and specific strategies to address it. This means carefully crafting the framing and language that we use in order not to further contribute to mechanisms and agencies of oppression. As an example, among social justice campaigners in Aotearoa New Zealand concerned about the creep of the intelligence agencies into domestic matters, there has been a call for such matters to be exclusively dealt with by police, yet such analysis fails to come to terms with the 180-year history of police surveillance of Māori, and the devastation wrought by that. We need not call for the strengthening of police powers in order to oppose other surveillance agencies. We cannot view the police simplistically as a neutral organisation driven by the quest to solve crimes.

In addition, when our day-to-day campaign work is carefully organised to prefigure the dismantling of hierarchies of power and control (and create decentralised and egalitarian structures instead), we are more resilient and capable of defending our communities from the effects of surveillance and infiltration. Power should not rest in the hands of a few self-ordained activist leaders.

By the same token, the struggle against state surveillance and related practices of social control must be integral to all of our struggles – Indigenous, union, environmental, social justice, or anyone else seeking liberatory social change. Working to dismantle state surveillance must be embedded within our other struggles, not addressed in isolation within a liberal framework of privacy rights.

Similarly the depth of our collective history of resistance, and our analysis of surveillance, must be more widely disseminated. This education is one of our key activist tasks, but it is a significant challenge.

Progressive social change is less organisationally grounded than at any time in the past 150 years: membership of all types of community organisations is in decline in New Zealand society. Unions and long-term grass-roots organisations are thin on the ground and poorly resourced. The stories of social struggle are often difficult to fully document, let alone the political surveillance that accompanies them. The knowledge about surveillance and tactics of resistance of a generation of activists from the vibrant days of the 1970s, 1980s and even 1990s has not been adequately captured, in part because it often exists at the margins, without the kind of documentary evidence that survives over time. By extension, the wealth of learning and analysis does not carry over but must be re-invented and relearned anew.

Yet it is by arming ourselves with such knowledge that we can more fully understand the manifestations and ramifications of particular projects of social control and surveillance, and in the process, craft appropriate and effective strategies of resistance.

NOTES

1 Aotearoa is the Māori word for New Zealand. The term 'Aotearoa New Zealand' is used to refer to the country; 'New Zealand' refers to the government or other institutions.

2 *Iwi* is an 'extended kinship group, tribe, nation, people, nationality, race – often refers to a large group of people descended from a common ancestor and associated with a distinct territory': *Maori Dictionary.* https://maoridictionary.co.nz

3 See Archives New Zealand online list of holdings. Accessed from www.archway.archives.govt.nz/ViewFullSeriesHistory.do

4 See Privacy Commissioner Bruce Slane's analysis of the introduction of photo drivers' licences in 1998: Land Transport Bill: Photo ID Driver Licences. Accessed from www.privacy.org.nz/news-and-publications/reports-to-parliament-and-government/land-transport-bill-photo-id-driver-licences/

5 See Rod Vaughan, 'Secrets and spies', *New Zealand Listener*, 6 August 2015. Accessed from www.noted.co.nz/archive/listener-nz-2015/secrets-spies/ and Claire Trevett, 'SIS boss Rebecca Kitteridge: Out of the shadows', *New Zealand Herald*, 19 May 2016. Accessed from www.nzherald.co.nz/nz/news/article.cfm?c_id=1&objectid=11641373

6 Full text of the documents released under the Official Information Act. Accessed from https://fyi.org.nz/request/3490/response/11922/attach/html/3/2016%2003%2022%20OIA%20Request%20Valerie%20Morse%20Response.pdf.html

7 In 2015, the then Prime Minister John Key responded to BBC interviewer Lucy Hockings that New Zealand's participation in the war in Iraq was the 'price of the club' – the club being the Five Eyes intelligence alliance. See Television New Zealand, 'John Key: The price of being part of Five Eyes is joining ISIS fight'. Accessed from www.tvnz.co.nz/one-news/new-zealand/john-key-the-price-of-being-part-five-eyes-is-joining-isis-fight-6221595

8 See the 2015 personal profile of SIS director Rebecca Kitteridge in the *New Zealand Listener*. Accessed from www.noted.co.nz/archive/listener-nz-2015/secrets-spies/

9 See the 2015 speech by then GCSB director Una Jagose to Kiwicon. Accessed from www.gcsb.govt.nz/news/speech-to-the-kiwicon-9/

10 Ministry of Justice, *Independent Review of Intelligence and Security* (2016). Accessed from https://consultations.justice.govt.nz/independent/iris/

11 See Jane Patterson, 'GCSB speech hijacked by protesters', *Radio New Zealand* (2015). Accessed from www.radionz.co.nz/news/political/283946/gcsb-speech-hijacked-by-protesters

12 (2017). Intelligence and Security Act. Clause 9(c).

13 Terrorism Suppression Act. Clause 5(3) (c).

REFERENCES

All URLs accessed in August 2018, unless otherwise noted.

@ndy (2008) 'Rob Gilchrist: Police Informant', *Slackbastard.* Accessed from http://slackbastard.anarchobase.com/?p=1551

Australian Visa Bureau (2010) 'NZ professor told she would need Australian Visa', 16 November. Accessed from www.visabureau.com/australia/news/16-11-2010/nz-professor-told-she-would-need-australian-visa.aspx

Bargh, Maria (2007). *Resistance: An indigenous response to neoliberalism.* Wellington: Huia.

—— (2008) 'Wars of Terra'. In D. K. Keenan (ed.), *Terror in our Midst* (pp. 151–164). Wellington: Huia.

Bodman, Ryan (2011). 'Neil Roberts and the "Maintenance of Silence"', *Imminent Rebellion*, 11: 15–26. Wellington: Rebel Press.

Davidson, Jared (2011). *Remains to be Seen.* Wellington: Rebel Press.

—— (2016) *Fighting War.* Wellington: Rebel Press.

Derby, Mark (2009). *A Country Considered to be Free: Towards a transnational study of New Zealand links with the Wobblies.* Accessed from https://libcom.org/files/A%20Country%20Considered%20to%20Be%20Free.pdf

Dwyer, Anabel L. & Dwyer, David J. (2005). 'Courts and Universities as Institutions in the National Security State'. In Marcus G. Raskin & A. Carl LeVan (eds), *In Democracy's Shadow: The secret world of national security.* New York: Nation Books.

Goldman, Asher (2008). 'Private Investigators In Court Over Spy Scandal', *Scoop*. Accessed from www.scoop.co.nz/stories/HL0802/S00232.htm

Gower, Patrick (2018). 'Insurance Spying Scheme Labelled Quake Claimants "Anarchists"', *TV3 News*, 8 March 2018. Accessed from www.newshub.co.nz/home/new-zealand/2018/03/insurance-spying-scheme-labelled-quake-claimants-anarchists.html

Hager, Nicky (2011). 'A Short History of the New Zealand Security Intelligence Service', *OASIS from Surveillance*. Accessed from http://oasisfromsurveillance.blogspot.co.nz/p/surveillance-in-nz_17.html

Hill, Richard S. (1986). *Policing the Colonial Frontier: The theory and practice of coercive social and racial control in New Zealand 1767–1867*. Volume 1, Part 1. Wellington: Department of Internal Affairs.

—— (2009). *Maori and the State: Crown relations in New Zealand/Aotearoa 1950–2000*. Wellington: Victoria University Press.

Horton, Murray (2009). 'Spies Among Us', *Peace Researcher*, 39. Accessed from www.converge.org.nz/abc/pr/pr-backissues/pr38.pdf

Hunt, Graeme (2007). *Spies and Revolutionaries*. Auckland: Reed.

Jagose, Una (2015). 'Speech to the Technology and Privacy Forum'. Accessed from www.gcsb.govt.nz/news/speech-to-the-technology-and-privacy-forum/

Kelsey, Jane (1993). *Rolling Back the State: Privatisation of power in Aotearoa New Zealand*. Wellington: Bridget Williams Books.

—— (2009). 'Banging My Head Against SIS Wall of Silence', *Foreign Control Watchdog*, 122. Accessed from www.converge.org.nz/watchdog/22/07.htm

Mountier, Frances (2018). 'Why Have Thompson & Clark Been Allowed to Keep Spying on Us, in Your Name?', *The Spinoff*, 27 April. Accessed from https://thespinoff.co.nz/politics/27-04-2018/why-have-thompson-clark-been-allowed-to-keep-spying-on-us-in-your-name/

OASIS (Organising Against State Intelligence Services) (2015). 'Widespread Lack of Trust in Security Intelligence Review'. Accessed from http://oasisfromsurveillance.blogspot.co.nz/2015/08/widespread-trust-in-security.html

Parliament, New Zealand (2002). Terrorism Suppression Act. Clause 5(3)(c). Accessed from http://legislation.govt.nz/act/public/2002/0034/latest/096be8ed816cbe3c.pdf

—— (2017). Intelligence and Security Act. Clause 9(c). Accessed from http://legislation.govt.nz/act/public/2017/0010/latest/096be8ed81692f26.pdf

SIS (Security Intelligence Service, New Zealand) (2017). *NZSIS History*. Accessed from http://security.govt.nz/about-us/nzsis-history/ (accessed 9 May 2018).

Stokes, Evelyn (1990). 'Völkner, Carl Sylvius', *Dictionary of New Zealand Biography, Te Ara – the Encyclopedia of New Zealand*. Accessed from https://teara.govt.nz/en/biographies/1v5/volkner-carl-sylvius (accessed 4 May 2018).

Taylor, Cliff and Milne, Jonathan (2009). 'Green MP: SIS has been spying on me', *New Zealand Herald*, 7 February. Accessed from www.nzherald.co.nz/nz/news/article.cfm?c_id=1&objectid=10555609

Wilson, Barry (1991).'Where will the Kiwi Card Lead?', *Dominion*, 8 August.

PART III

11

Undercover research
Academics, activists and others investigate political policing[1]

Eveline Lubbers

REFLECTIONS ON RESEARCH INTO CORPORATE AND POLICE SPYING

My research into corporate and police spying emerged from my experiences as an activist in the Netherlands. Experiences show that undercover policing and the criminalisation of dissent is a fundamental aspect of state power in liberal democracies as it is elsewhere. As an activist, I have always tried to find ways to improve security while avoiding unnecessary paranoia.

My roots are in Amsterdam's squatter movement in the 1980s, and I am one of the founders of Buro Jansen & Janssen, an organisation set up to monitor the police and intelligence services. Named after the bumbling detectives in the Tintin comics (Thomson & Thompson in the English translation), the buro supported people and groups that had involuntary involvements with police, intelligence agencies and their corporate counterparts, from confrontations with riot police and getting arrested, to surveillance and being approached to become an informer.

Our main goal was to fight paranoia and fears of conspiracy amongst social movements, by presenting facts gathered by our own research. Buro Jansen & Janssen was rooted in the same network of movements it sought to support, which gained us the trust that was a pre-condition for groups to share their experiences with us. The first aim was to support the campaigners who were targeted, advising them on how to deal with their encounters with the state, at both personal and group levels. We assisted with research and the process of addressing issues of betrayal and distrust within the groups involved. From the late 1980s onwards, the buro published investigations on how the secret service tried to infiltrate the activist movement, and how they blackmailed asylum seekers to work for them as informers.

Since then, I see my role as an active one, chasing evidence where most of it is secret, bringing together the work of investigative reporters, whistleblowers, and people spied upon. Why? To empower activists, defend the right to protest and to fight for transparency and an end to the secrecy enabling political policing, to stand up for the right to protest, and to stand up for a vibrant democracy, or what's left of it. In the end, this is about challenging the capitalist free market economy.

'GARBOLOGY'

The first time I encountered corporate spying was in 1994, when I was involved in exposing a spy named Paul Oosterbeek. Although several people did not really trust him, plans to screen Oosterbeek's background took years to materialise. Only when campaigners from various groups compared their experiences was it discovered that he used a very similar cover story to hide his true identity, a story which he customised at will. Furthermore, at the church-based NGOs he worked for, he would hint at his presumed radical background to explain his aloofness, and when trying to become part of more radical circles would point at his engagement with more moderate groups to explain gaps in his political history. He had created quite a network of information sources, and had worked for several activist organisations and NGOs.

Calling himself Marcel Paul Knotter, Oosterbeek posed as a volunteer and managed to stay undiscovered for over seven years. He promoted his computer skills – rare in the late 1980s and early 1990s – offering to install software and to handle the input of contact details. Meanwhile, he collected discarded paperwork, pretending to sell it for recycling and donate the proceeds to a charity project of choice. At the moment of his exposure, around thirty organisations, ranging from small activist groups to big church-affiliated research foundations such as Pax Christi, knew Oosterbeek as their 'waste-paper man'.

We had discovered a new, and cleaner, form of garbology – detective slang for a particularly dirty kind of research. Activists and advocacy groups in the Netherlands knew their waste paper was being gathered, but not what it was being 'recycled' into: intelligence files for companies they were criticising. Little did they know how interesting their paperwork could be for those companies, to the tabloids and occasionally even to the police, the public prosecutor and the secret service.

The waste-paper example demonstrates how inside information can give companies a strategic advantage. Used at the right moment, it can be an effective weapon – for instance in negotiations with NGOs. But companies do not necessarily acknowledge that they have obtained information on their critics. Using it to anticipate future actions can be advantageous enough – taking away the surprise factor of a specific action or campaign, potentially reducing media coverage.

IMPACT OF EXPOSING A SPY

The case also taught us some other lessons. The impact of our discoveries varied widely amongst the many groups targeted – and this was bound to happen in many cases to follow. For several groups, it was difficult to accept what had happened. Some people could not believe that the nice person they chatted with when he collected their waste paper had actually driven his haul straight to the intelligence consultancy he worked for – even though we followed him going there.

The reluctance to face facts also impacted the decisions about what to do next. For Jansen & Janssen, as well as in my current work, the investigation's final phase is publishing the findings. The aim of exposure is threefold. The first is to raise security awareness amongst campaigners. Sharing the findings with other groups issues a warning about the specific individual and informs a wider audience about the risks of infiltration. The second aim is to hold responsible parties to account. Seeking publicity is essential in challenging questionable exercises of power, and is a way to generate pressure. A public outcry could encourage politicians to address responsible authorities, and maybe start some kind of official review. And thirdly, exposure is another option for acquiring more information.

'Rattling the tree' might evoke memories and reach people beyond the focus of the original investigation. Likewise, official investigations might bring more evidence.

However, exposure as the next step is not self-evident for every group that has been spied upon. While most would, in theory, agree about the importance of making a case, the disclosure of detailed examples of infiltration is not always in the group's best interest.

In general, a group that has experienced infiltration wants to get back to business as usual sooner rather than later. Dealing with surveillance is not part of their core activities and might be regarded as a waste of time. It is also perceived as uncomfortable, even painful, as the events involve profound breaches of trust. Personal feelings of distress and disturbance are matched with fears that the effects of exposure are counter-productive for the group at the organisational level. To have their experiences with spying and infiltration published could position it as careless or sloppy with security; it could keep possible allies or sources from sharing crucial information and have implications for funding their work. For similar reasons, groups often refrain from taking legal actions. In the absence of a legal framework, the options to file a complaint or to report a crime are few as it is. There is a financial risk, and the low chance of success fuels the reluctance to allocate money and energy in moves regarded as counter-productive for the organisation.

Materialising here is a conflict of interest that sometimes hindered cooperation on investigations. The research was usually a joint project – as it should be – between Buro Jansen & Janssen and the groups involved, until we reached a point where goals started to differ. Whilst groups had understandable reasons not to go public, Jansen & Janssen's aim sometimes came to be regarded as yet another disturbance. At the time, we failed to see that exposing the spying was not the self-evident choice for the groups involved as it was for us, and that it was difficult to accept that the interests of a spied-upon group might be different from ours. Instead, the problems that arose were sometimes dealt with as irritations at the personal level, or as political differences.

Too often, difference of opinion is either not taken seriously, or sacrificed for the greater good. Likewise, different interests of preferences for specific strategies can be understood as deviations from the 'right political line'. Working under time pressure and dealing with a lot of stress does not make this any easier. Acknowledging these differences is a prerequisite for building trust, which is crucial in any research, and even more so in research on topics as sensitive as these.

INFILTRATION AS A STRATEGY

These experiences show that infiltration as a strategy to undermine dissent can have damaging effects regardless of the sensitivity of the information gathered. Essentially, the fear of being publicly associated with infiltration is harmful in itself. The focus on the possible damage of exposure sometimes keeps people from making a serious assessment of the actual damage of an information-gathering operation.

Moreover, the perception of publicity as counter-productive may lead to self-censorship. The reluctance to expose detailed findings implies abandoning the opportunity – that is, waiving the rights – to hold corporations accountable for their practices of abusing power. The fact that few political organisations who have been the victim of infiltration are willing to take official action which might disclose the extent of the operation is confirmed by Brodeur's study into the policing of political activities. From 1979 to 1981, he was involved in the Keable inquiry into police wrongdoing in relation to the Quebec sovereignty movement in the early 1970s. He concluded that for political groups, revelations about the extent of infiltration are 'liable to drastically reduce their credibility in the eyes of other movements and their membership' (Brodeur, 1983, p. 510). Ironically, he argues, this turns the victims into partners in secrecy with police, politicians, the courts and the media. The police, well aware of this reluctance to expose experiences, deliberately spread rumours of infiltration to destabilise groups. Brodeur quotes an RCMP document on anti-subversive tactics, in which the police claim to

> have prevented the much-mooted FLQ [*Front de Libération du Quebec*] a simple reversal of our earlier policies ... instead of hoarding our intelligence, we gave it away to individuals identified as particularly susceptible, by our psychologist, among members of emerging cells. The cells in question, exaggerating the extent of our knowledge of them, dispersed as if by magic.
>
> (Ministry of Communication, *The Keable Report*, Quebec (1981), p. 81; cited in Brodeur, 1983, p. 515 fn 13)

Quite similarly, Tim Weiner (2012) explains how the Federal Bureau of Investigation (FBI) Counter Intelligence Program (COINTELPRO, discussed below) conducted extensive operations to undermine the Socialist Workers Party's (SWP) electoral campaigns, and FBI director Edgar Hoover, the programme's architect, sent out 'explicit instructions' to '[i]nstigate conflicts among New Left leaders. Exploit rifts between [Students for a Democratic Society] and its rival factions. Create the false impression that an FBI agent stood behind every mailbox, that informants riddled their ranks. Use disinformation to disrupt them' (Weiner, 2012, p. 274; cited in Woodman, 2016; also see Leonard, 2015; Leonard & Gallagher, 2018). In 1986, after more than a decade of legal procedures, the SWP was awarded $264,000 in damages for harassment and rights violations by the FBI over a period of 18 years. The FBI had subjected the SWP to disruptive activities, surreptitious invasions of premises and the wide use of informants between 1958 and 1976; the operations reached their peak during the Vietnam War and ended in 1976: 'The judge held that there was "no legal authority or justification for such operations," ... and said the evidence had demonstrated that the F.B.I.'s actions had been directed "against entirely lawful and peaceful political activities" of the party' (Blair, 1986; also see US States Supreme Court, 1986).

The issues that arise regarding the exposure of cases of infiltration illustrate the chilling effects of the strategy. The fear of being associated with 'espionage', 'violence', or 'terror' keeps the groups involved from publicly addressing the issue. This dilemma indicates a need for further evidence-based research – more case studies published, more undercover operatives exposed. Substantiation is essential in order to comprehend the meaning and the effects of this aspect of political policing.

CORPORATE STRATEGIES

The exposure of the 'waste-paper man' revealed that there is a market for informal information about activists. While spying and infiltration can have destabilising effects on campaigning groups, spying also involves the gathering of intelligence that precedes the development of corporate counter-strategy.

I started writing about these strategies in the mid-1990s, when groups across the world began to coordinate their campaigns against large transnational corporations. My 2002 book, *Battling Big Business*, was inspired by Naomi Klein's work, *No Logo* (2000), which identifies two important developments that continue to characterise the current time frame. The more companies prioritise brand identity, the more vulnerable they are to attacks on their image. Meanwhile, corporations are becoming less and less restricted by national laws or unilateral treaties. In some cases, they are more powerful than governments, and must be held to account in the same way (Klein, in Lubbers 2002).

The power of spin cannot easily protect big business's growing vulnerability. Embracing mostly voluntary corporate social responsibility (CSR) guidelines is not enough. As long as corporations' actual activities do not change, seemingly altruistic programmes are nothing but public relations (PR) and greenwash. The greening of BP's image over the years did not prevent the Deepwater Horizon disaster from causing unprecedented pollution. Likewise, Shell appears to have ignored lessons from Nigeria in the 1990s (the protest against the sinking of the Brent Spar and the company's involvement in the execution of Ogoni writer and activist Ken Saro Wiwa); they were in court again in 2018 over corruption and pollution in the Niger Delta.

Battling Big Business discussed more overt strategies such as PR, greenwash and sponsorship. It showed that dialogues and partnerships with NGOs are often used to alienate more moderate organisations from their more radical counterparts. The book also explored more covert tactics, such as hiring specialised PR consultants to fight campaigners, corporate lobbying behind the scenes, the use of libel laws to silence critics and think-tanks influencing decision-making processes.

The crucial connection between gathering intelligence on activist groups, and the subsequent development of covert strategy that corporations use to undermine criticism was the point of departure for my research which resulted in *Secret Manoeuvres in the Dark: Corporate and police spying on activists* (2012). The book presents several case studies showing how companies such as Nestlé, McDonald's and Shell use covert methods to avoid accountability.

FIGHTING PARANOIA

Without careful sourcing of information, accounts of surveillance and infiltration risk being dismissed as made-up stories or paranoia.

Hence, the case studies in *Secret Manoeuvres* were uniquely based on previously confidential documented sources. These included notes taken by spies after each undercover operation, surveillance reports, and communications between private intelligence agencies and their clients. Starting from this basic level provided an extraordinary insider view of the methods and routines of private spies. They demonstrate how infiltrators work their way into groups, and how they can use their position once they are trusted. This varies from manipulating friendships and engaging in intimate relationships, to undermining bridge-building between organisations by pushing an agenda perceived as too radical by some coalition partners. The case studies also describe how agents collect information, what details are considered important, and how the results are presented to the client companies.

Further research shows how this intelligence is processed and used in proactive strategies by corporations to act upon perceived threats. The stories include convincing details on why even information not considered to be secret by campaigning groups can be of interest to their opponent.

THE UNDERCOVER RESEARCH GROUP

Most of the case studies in *Secret Manoeuvres* would not have been revealed but for the persistent investigations of activists targeted by corporations or the police, through complicated and drawn-out court cases, and with the help of dedicated investigative journalists and their whistle-blowers. The same goes for the UK undercover policing scandal. It was through the research of friends and comrades who no longer trusted him, and specifically women in relationships with him, that undercover police officer Mark Kennedy was exposed in late 2010. He had lived the life of an activist for over seven years. After his police deployment ended, he returned in a private capacity, trying to sell intelligence to corporate clients. He was a popular, widely trusted member of environmental groups campaigning against climate change, and active in the Dissent Network organising protests against G8 summits across Europe.

Kennedy's exposure brought up the stories of several other women who once had seen the love of their lives suddenly disappearing from the face of the earth. Only when they contacted each other and started sharing experiences, did the scandal begin to unfold. Each of them had unwittingly been deceived into a relationship, targeted by an undercover police officer.

Since Kennedy's exposure, over a dozen similar cases have been uncovered, with still more to come. We now know that since 1968, the British state secretly placed over one hundred long-term undercover officers into scores of political groups to spy on them and subvert their work. Starting with the many groups involved in the Vietnam Solidarity Campaign in 1968, the Special Demonstration Squad (SDS) of the Metropolitan Police infiltrated each group they thought to be a possible enemy of the state, including the peace movement (i.e. the Campaign for Nuclear Disarmament (CND)) and peace camps, the anti-apartheid movement, anti-war, anti-globalisation and animal right groups, family justice campaigns and others.

A number of distasteful police practices have been revealed, including stealing the identities of dead children, and tricking targets into intimate or even sexual relationships with agents – in some cases leading to the birth of children who were subsequently abandoned. Officers also gave witness statements under false names, withheld exculpatory evidence, and actively planned and participated in serious crimes.

Two British secret police units have been systematically infiltrating activists and campaigns, the SDS from 1968 to 2008, and the National Public Order Intelligence Unit (NPOIU) from 1999 to 2011. The apparent lack of supervision and oversight of undercover police operations led to at least a dozen, mostly internal and confidential, official reviews. Moreover, from the very start, the police have done everything in their power to avoid accountability. It took over three years of campaigning and further exposures to convince the government that an independent inquiry into undercover policing was necessary.

None of this would have come to light had it not been for the persistence of those who did the first investigations. The Undercover Research Group (URG) was established to bring together the knowledge of the various people who had been involved before – to learn from it and make it available to others. Research has been crucial in addressing undercover policing and spying on activist groups, and it is always intertwined with campaigning, making voices heard, and finding the truth, essential to hold those responsible to account. We work under the umbrella of the Campaign Opposing Police Surveillance (COPS) and cooperate closely with the women's support group Police Spies Out of Lives, the Blacklist Support group and the Network for Police Monitoring (NetPol).[2]

The importance of research into political policing and spying on activists is best explained by mapping the URG's role in the current undercover policing scandal in the UK. While the emphasis has varied at different moments while the scandal was unfolding, explaining the different aspects recapitulate the essence of research into political policing.

Making information available

Profiling undercover police officers, their supervisors, the units involved and the subsequent careers of those involved in great detail has several aims. A well-referenced resource with an ever-growing amount of information made available benefits those spied upon, the media, as well as people new to the story. Profiles are published on a dedicated platform, part of Powerbase.org, a monitored wiki with factual information (URG, 2014–present). The Undercoverresearch.net blog is used to analyse our findings (URG, 2015 – present). At the same time, the profiles lay the groundwork for further research, the links between police and corporate spying, for instance, mapping the network of former police and intelligence now working in the corporate sector, identifying revolving doors and old boy networks.

Understanding the tradecraft

Analysing our findings and comparing the stories about the various cases of infiltration allowed us to recognise patterns in the undercover work, and identify the spycops' tradecraft. Translating this into *Fifteen Questions* (Salmon & Lubbers, 2015) has proved to be invaluable in assisting groups who want to investigate suspicions of a current or an historical spy in their midst. A booklet called *Was My Friend a Spycop?* (URG, 2017) summarises lessons learned, including the importance of supporting each other, and dealing with inconclusive situations.

Furthermore, identifying the tradecraft also told us something about the scale of things. Recurring patterns indicated that there was a plan behind all of this, that the spycops were taught tactics and strategies, such as feigning to have jobs that would take them away for days at a time – to allow time to visit their family in their other life – or pretending to have psychological problems for which moving abroad seemed the best solution – to prepare their exit from their years as an activist.

Supporting investigations into suspicions

Groups started coming to us with their suspicions. Together, we would start a further investigation to try and find the proof that we are dealing with an undercover officer – or build as close enough a profile. Often it is impossible to get 100 per cent confirmation, as there is no 'smoking gun' and the police would 'neither confirm nor deny' whether we were right. In such cases, we sometimes refrain from publishing the cover name, their photograph, or we might just use their initials.

We have learned to go with the flow, and see who wants to come forward and speak to the press, who would rather stay anonymous, and who needs more time. The fact that most of the undercover officers exposed so far had deceived women into relationships adds an extra dimension to what a group or a network has to deal with. We are very aware of how painful a process this can be for people as they slowly come to terms that an old friend with whom they shared so much of their lives was not who they said they were. It is not our place to judge decisions people make – all we can do is offer our skills and know-how.

Holding those responsible to account

In most countries, there is no specific legal framework addressing infiltration aimed at gathering intelligence (as opposed to gathering evidence which is subsequently tested in court). Thus it is next to impossible to challenge these undercover policing operations as such.

The court route

In the UK undercover policing scandal, lawyers representing those spied upon have identified a number of punishable police practices including the withholding of exculpatory evidence, the tricking of women (and men) into intimate or even sexual relationships with undercover agents, and fathering subsequently unsupported children by undercover officers using false identities (Wistrich, 2013). Hearings in Parliament questioned the more extreme methods employed, such as the use of death certificates of children to provide a false identity for the spies (Home Affairs Committee, 2013). Using parliamentary privilege, Green MP Caroline Lucas has accused one spy of being an agent provocateur, as he was involved in the active planning of and participation in serious crimes, including arson (Lucas, 2012). Consequently, the former officer, Bob Lambert, is now under investigation (Evans, 2017; URG/Powerbase 2012–present). The women who brought the Metropolitan Police to court over the relationships fought for years, but the case ended in a settlement that prevented further disclosure. As part of the agreement, Metropolitan Police assistant commissioner, Martin Hewitt (2015a, 2015b), issued an unprecedented apology to the women (on video, still online at the police website (MPS, 2015)), acknowledging that 'these relationships were a violation of the women's human rights, an abuse of police power and caused significant trauma.'

One of the women is taking the human rights violation to the European Court of Human Rights. The URG works with the lawyers representing victims of spying with assembling evidence, to support witnesses with their statements to the Inquiry, and – depending on the findings – to prepare further legal steps to bring cases to court.

The official inquiry into undercover policing

Three years after Mark Kennedy was exposed, the Home Secretary announced a judge-led public inquiry into undercover policing. We were not the only ones to have doubts about a state-organised Inquiry, but decided to treat it as the best opportunity so far to find out more about undercover spying operations and political policing over the past forty years in the UK. If nothing else, it is a way to keep up pressure and to increase public awareness of the unaccountable, unregulated and unscrupulous activities of Britain's undercover police spies.

Since it began in 2015, at the time of writing the Inquiry has just managed to get through its preliminary phase, the delay mainly caused by the police in their efforts to prevent any accountability and transparency. The first phase was focused on procedures, predominantly applications for anonymity from former undercover officers. Thus it was overly centred on what the police had to say, often in closed sessions. URG research produced the necessary counter-narrative providing those spied upon with the knowledge, guidance and specific detail that empowers them to act. Detailed knowledge was crucial to fight police efforts to undermine the procedures, to correct mistakes made by the Inquiry, to show with concrete examples that their assumptions are nothing but that – assumptions.

The campaign is currently fighting to get a panel appointed of people who can add their real-life experience with institutional sexism and racism, issues that go to the heart of the Inquiry. The Chair has confessed to being 'somewhat naïve and a little old-fashioned' and is consistently ruling in favour of the police, granting them anonymity and secret meetings (see Kaufmann, 2018).

The next battle will be on disclosure, on how much of the files those spied upon will get to see, how much of it will be published eventually, and how. The ideal would be to set up a permanent online archive available for anyone interested. A good example is the archive of the documents released in 2012 after decades of campaigning and investigations into the Hillsborough disaster and police failure that led to the death of 96 men, women and children, all Liverpool supporters crushed in the football stadium in 1989. Phil Scraton (2013), an academic and a major force supporting the Hillsborough families' campaign, contrasts the official discourse with alternative accounts, contemporaneous interviews with bereaved families and survivors – the 'view from below'. The archives are still being 'crowd searched' by a team of victims and researchers, responsible for decisive findings (Hillsborough Independent Panel, 2012–present).

Keeping the issue in the public eye

To maintain the pressure and reach a wider audience, campaigners still need the mainstream media. Investigations into suspicions that result in exposure make for scoops that the media love. But the real value is in going beyond the sensational story. The prerequisite for this is developing a long-term, sustainable relationship based on trust and acknowledgement. Working with dedicated investigative journalists who have the patience and resources for research has its advantages, but can also be difficult.

While trying to build up a relationship, it is easy to forget the difference in position and background. Mainstream media journalists work for large companies, their income is guaranteed, and they can do what they want within certain limits. Usually, however, there is not much time to invest in research, and the target audience must be pleased. The activist researcher works with a small group of comrades, on a shoestring budget and a precarious base, with more time on their hands, generally, and a strong commitment derived from personal involvement and politics.

So while one's aims might overlap at certain moments – to get a story out, expose wrongdoings and disclose what the authorities want to keep under wraps – the differences in position are more fundamental, economically and politically. The media politics come to light in their fear of being accused of bias, or worse, facilitating a soapbox for the spycops campaign for justice.

Apart from the struggle to translate our findings into a story that is attractive enough for mainstream media, providing a 'victim' who wants to speak publicly, locating pictures of undercovers who have disappeared decades ago to circumvent the 'no photo – no story' rule of law for television, dealing with legal departments who ask for endless reassurance, there is a fight to be fought for credits and acknowledgement. The solutions vary from one case to the other. Sometimes we are mentioned and/or linked to a story; sometimes we can negotiate a byline and a symbolic payment. Occasionally, you might be paid a decent fee and travel costs for a few days' research. And sometimes you bite the dust, because it seems more important to get the story out.

We act at the crossroads, able to adapt to roles demanded by the situation. But that could not be done without a sound foundation. The URG has built a reputation of meticulous, very detailed and well-referenced research, and of perseverance where others would stop, and the same goes for the other groups in the spycops campaign. We don't back down, and that pays off in the long run.

WIDER CONTEXT

The exposure of undercover officers and their activities raises many questions, only some of which are being addressed. In the years after the first series of exposures, investigations focused on understanding the units' inner workings, the supervision, hierarchy and careers of former undercovers. The importance of pressing the Inquiry to release these officers' real names is to be able to explore if and how their early career experience with the now-disgraced units has influenced their path since.

The URG also aims to map out the old boy network, to find more examples of the revolving door, such as the case of Gordon Irving, former head of Strathclyde Special Branch, who moved to Scottish Power as their head of security. In that role, he hired private investigation firm Vericola to target environmental activists after environmental protests against coal-powered electricity (URG, 2011a, 2011b; Lewis & Evans, 2011).

This touches upon a fundamental question of why the state would want to counter action on climate and defend vested business interests. What does it mean that the state and large corporations seem to have a shared agenda and operation against what they conceive to be *the enemy*? While many activist groups spied upon in the UK organised against large transnational corporations (TNCs) such as power companies, the involvement of private spies fell outside the remits of the Inquiry.

SECRECY

It is nearly impossible to say how big a phenomenon corporate-government spying is, and why we see so much of it now. Most of it remains in the dark: you don't know what you don't see. But from the case studies that I worked on and the stories that have come to light, we are clearly not looking at isolated cases, but, more likely, the tip of the iceberg.

Secrecy is complicating research. Because I wanted the study to be based on unique source material, the research was almost by definition historical – ongoing operations are hardly ever exposed. Cases of corporate spying are typically covered by a cloak of secrecy. Source material is difficult to access. The passing of time sometimes makes routes of discovery slightly easier, with political and personal sensibilities losing their significance little by little.

However, rather than describing the case studies as historical, I would call them 'a history of the present'. As Garland (2001, p. 2) put it, the research is 'not motivated by a historical concern to understand the past, but by a critical concern to come to terms with the present'. The point is to use history to rethink the present.

Secrecy is the defining character of the intelligence agencies, their activities, and the people working for them – either public or privately employed. Perhaps secrecy should be treated as ordinary rather than exceptional, 'a common, challenging and contentious mode of governing'. In an effort to grasp the meaning of secrecy,[3] Lydia Morgan points to the commodification of secrets, suggesting that the state's secrecy power is situated not in the content, but in the act of making something secret: 'Derrida, observing the intimate connection between controlling information and political power, explained that those who hold the archive, the collated information, hold authority' (Morgan, 2018, p. 61).

Her overview of 'secretive institutions, behaviours and "oversight"' is limited to the Security Service (or MI5), the Secret Intelligence Service (SIS) (or MI6) and GCHQ, and does not include Special Branch and its secret units, the SDS and the NPOIU. As Special Branch operates in line with MI5 – the exact relationship still a question – for the sake of the argument, let's treat Special Branch as an annex of MI5, as Morgan's description fits both:

> As a "self-tasked" organisation, MI5 assesses its own priorities for action, a measure intended to ensure ministerial restraint and protect the service from accusations of political and partisan action. In reality, this advisory role provides a space for MI5 to monopolise its power and the same goes, in extension, for Special Branch.
>
> (Morgan 2018, p. 67)

The Security Service Act 1989 outlined MI5's powers and authority to defend the realm and maintain national security against espionage, terrorism and sabotage. This extensive power also includes safeguarding the UK's economic well-being.

For Morgan, MI5, GCHQ and MI6 typify operational secrecy in the UK. Their concern is to protect modern espionage techniques or 'tradecraft', as the intelligence terminology calls it. She emphasises there is still value in protecting knowledge of techniques used, even if a particular operational result is made public. Its self-tasked mandate is based on its expertise, and MI5 exists by keeping this autonomous advisory role and the accompanying covert action outside the political arena. Special Branch, just like MI5, 'has an interest in maintaining the highest level of operational secrecy achievable because it reduces the scope for scrutiny of its work' (Morgan, 2018, p. 79).

Secrecy's necessity also subtly co-opts debates on the need for governmental transparency and accountability, with even its harshest critics recognising minimal utility in state secrecy. When state secrecy is seen as something to balance against accountability, the focus slips towards how to balance it, overlooking state secrecy's subtler effects and outright neglecting the pre-assigned weight given to secret information. Summarising her analysis, for Morgan, 'the UK has become a fortress state, where state secrecy is the norm and where information is kept from the external actors as well as internal' (2018, p. 76).

The question is, she says, 'who ultimately gets to determine what is in the public interest to keep secret, or even, who gets to determine the public interest: the government or the people?' (Morgan, 2018, p. 83). Unfortunately, Morgan's analysis focuses entirely on state security and fails to take into account the role and the power of other important actors such as large corporations. While clearly very aware of the danger to democracy of such a complex system of secrecy, Morgan does not in so many words challenge the current state of democracy, or the concept itself.

Information pieced together on the UK's undercover policing units over the past fifty years gives the impression of secret and consequently very isolated units. Even within Special Branch, only a limited number of people would know of their existence, and most people would not even have heard about them.

Training was an informal affair where more experienced officers would teach newer ones the ropes. There was a 'Tradecraft Manual' that hardly deserved that name, a binder that held personal experiences, some legal notes on undercover policing and a draft manual pulled together by an officer who was still deployed at the time of writing (Lubbers, 2018).

For years, the SDS chose their own targets, probably steered by the Department of Home Affairs and the MI5. In the mid-2000s, the British police started using the term 'domestic extremism' to distinguish so-called 'single issue' campaigns or political groups with a militant edge from terrorist groups. Animal rights, ecological defence, anti-arms trade, the radical left and the far right have been labelled domestic extremists, and have been targeted by undercover policing units. The UK government has no formal legal definition for domestic extremism (while it has one for terrorism, for instance). In 2014, a revised working definition was finally provided by the Metropolitan Police (MPS 2014): 'Domestic Extremism relates to the activity of groups or individuals who commit or plan serious criminal activity motivated by a political or ideological viewpoint.' The use of the label with or without definition has led to forms of political policing and a way to treat protest as a form of crime.

Likewise, the movement challenging TNCs for their lack of transparency and accountability is countered with responses that rely on secrecy. The case studies in *Secret Manoeuvres* illustrate the unwillingness of corporations to change damaging business policies and expose the lengths companies under attack are prepared to go to evade public protest. While corporate critics become the target of intelligence-gathering operations and covert actions aimed at undermining their work, secrecy enables the avoidance of responsibility and accountability for controversial actions.

Political policing and corporate counter-strategies constitute part of a system of governance that relies on secrecy; and it is this secrecy that is seen as a threat, eroding trust in democracy. However, when secrecy is such an essential part of how the current society is organised, it is impossible to hold the state to account for the secret undercover operations.

SECRECY, POWER AND RESISTANCE

Mapping the close, mostly secret, cooperation between government agencies and corporations aims to provide evidence to initiate and substantiate a much-needed public debate challenging both corporate power and state surveillance.

One way to interpret the excessiveness of political policing and undercover operations is to see them as mission creep. Over the years, research has highlighted how state agencies identify targets by constructing them as such and has shown that such constructions are shaped not only by ethnicity, class, religion, or other characteristics of potential candidates, but also by the organisational structure of policing agencies. Immersed in a world of deception and secrecy, intelligence agencies have been known to develop their own morals, norms and culture.[4] This toxic mix with lack of oversight and no accountability would then lead to *mission creep*.[5]

However, this is only part of the explanation; it is devoid of any responsibility, *blaming the system*, whilst failing to question why the system of political policing was set up and accepted in the first place. In policing political activities, the concept of subversion is suitably amorphous, and often synonymous with left-wing dissent in liberal capitalist states (O'Reilly & Ellison, 2006). The stories in *Secret Manoeuvres* confirm that is the case not only in the public realm, but also in the private, corporate sphere. And as stated earlier, the SDS used the concept of 'domestic extremism' as an undefined label to justify their operations. The result is clear when studying the list of the 59 officers whose cover names have been released by the public Inquiry (as of July 2018). Only two of them were deployed to spy on the extreme right. (There might be a few more, but the Chair has ruled that it is too dangerous to reveal any detail on them; see UCPI, 2018.) Likewise, from files stolen by activists from the FBI office in Media, Pennsylvania in 1971, two hundred infiltrations concerned left-wing groups, and only two focused on right-wing groups (Medsger, 2014, p. 245).

Looking at how protest movements are dealt with, Rune Ellefsen (2012) concluded that this fits with wider patterns in current crime control trends, the Western public order policy. He notes:

> Together with Islamic fundamentalism, drug trafficking, migration and poverty, activists are increasingly being assessed as threats to state security by Western analysts. The goals of order and security seem to come into conflict with social justice goals and citizens' right to privacy, freedom of expression and assembly, in addition to other liberties commonly taken for granted in liberal democracies.
>
> (Ellefsen, 2012, p. 200)

The monitoring and labelling of dissent is seen as a prerequisite for strategies to hinder civil society activities through ridicule, stigma and silencing (Ferree, 2004), as well as criminalising dissent and maintaining power.

Is it sufficient to see undercover operations and political policing as part of the development towards the surveillance state, and has the

UK – like many other Western states – become a fortress state, as Morgan suggests?

It certainly has, but this does not answer the question of what the operations of the secret units tell us about the nature of the state and its relationship to capital. Much of the work on surveillance and repression shows a relative lack of focus on this aspect. An exception is Ellefsen (2016) who, analysing the repression against the Stop Huntingdon Animal Cruelty (SHAC), pointed out how private elites have the ability and resources to use civil law and became the driving force behind criminal justice responses in fighting this anti-vivisection campaign. (The other three techniques included targeted criminalisation, leadership decapitation and extended incapacitation.)

The link between the government defending the interests of the elite and large corporations, including their access to critical resources and labour is crucial. Modern corporations exist to make profit, and to promote and defend their core interests, while modern states seem to be organised to suit the demands of business.

But this is not new. There are quite a few historical examples of corporate strategy and political tactics as well. *Secret Manoeuvres* includes two in the US and the UK dating back to the late nineteenth century.

In those days, agencies like the notorious Pinkerton's provided armed guards and strike-breakers to deal with social unrest in the US. Later, during the Depression and the New Deal reforms in the 1920s and 1930s, employers hired PR professionals to defend the need for violent confrontations and covert operations such as espionage and infiltration.

Special Branch, the Metropolitan Police unit responsible for the last fifty years of undercover policing, was originally set up in 1883 to combat militant Irish Fenians seeking independence from Britain. The then Home Secretary, Sir William Harcourt, envisioned a permanent unit dedicated to preventing politically motivated violence through modern techniques such as undercover infiltration and subversion. Special Branch soon expanded to keep tabs on foreign anarchists, suffragettes and anti-colonial Indians.

During the First World War, the British government and employers' organisations had learned to appreciate the value of propaganda and internal surveillance to monitor and combat labour unrest. This included secret blacklisting of workers.[6] They continued to use such practices in the early 1920s out of fear of the revolutionary spirit that was sweeping across Europe. The Economic League was a long-running project set up by British industrialists to defend corporate interests. This organisation spanned most of the twentieth century and existed until it was officially disbanded in the mid-1990s. Recent discoveries revealed that people involved in the Economic League continued their blacklisting work until early 2009 as The Consulting Association (Smith & Chamberlain, 2015). The Independent Police Complaints Commission acknowledged that 'all special branches were involved in providing information' to a construction agency blacklist (Boffey, 2013). In March 2018, the Metropolitan Police finally confirmed that its officers had passed on information to illegal blacklists (Casciani, 2018). Newly released files at the National Archives revealed that under Thatcher in the 1980s, MI5 secretly blacklisted 'subversive' civil servants. (Cobain, 2018)

Large corporations have long histories of fighting critics with the help of propaganda and active interference. Cooperation with the state in countering people potentially posing a risk to the stability of society or the economy dates back as far as the Industrial Revolution. So, rather than seeing the covert operations only as signs of increasing repression or the mounting surveillance state, it is important to understand the dirty tricks in the context of power in the capitalist state.

'THE WAR AT HOME'

While the URG's work and its detailed analyses of the undercover officers, their units and the hierarchy is crucial in the current fight for justice, there is also a pressing need to go beyond the focus on police and intelligence agencies and their operations, to question the fundamentals of state power.

The Church Committee Report (1976), documenting the FBI's COINTELPRO, noted the dangers of questionable activities justified by dubious intelligence morality. The Commission investigated complaints about spying and countering politically active citizens by the FBI and the US Secret Service, part of a response to the emergence of the new social movements of the 1960s and the 1970s. The exposure of COINTELPRO or 'the war at home' can be attributed to the research of critical investigative journalists.[7] But the true honours go to a small group of anti-Vietnam War activists in the 1970s who broke into an FBI office to take hundreds of files, analyse them and send them to trusted journalists. They never talked about what they had done, until over forty years later, the first journalist to have written about the files managed to find them. Their act of resistance uncovered the FBI's secrets, and the journalist, Betty Medsger, wrote *The Burglary* (2014), about the impact, the fruitless hunt for the burglars and developments since.

The Church Report (1976) extensively documented how the FBI set out to undermine and 'neutralise' groups considered 'enemies of the state'. It shows how US intelligence agencies tended to expand the scope of their activities, and how operations based on 'vague standards' could soon involve 'unsavoury and vicious tactics'. It revealed that '[t]oo many people have been spied upon by too many Government agencies and too much information has been collected' (pp. 4–5). Due to these critical reports, in 1976, the Senate established the Senate Select Committee on Intelligence (SCCI) and in 1977, the House of Representatives set up the House Permanent Select Committee on Intelligence to prevent future abuses.

A milestone and still considered the frame of reference regarding US intelligence oversight (see Schwarz, 2007; Johnson, 2008), the work of the Church Committee gave rise to important reflections on the role of the state in dealing with dissent. Ward Churchill (1992; also see 1988/2002) described the FBI operations as 'counter-insurgency'.

Counter-insurgency is a type of war – 'low-intensity' or 'asymmetrical' combat – and style of warfare that emphasises intelligence networks, psychological operations, media manipulation, security provision and social development that seeks to maintain governmental legitimacy, according to the US Army (FM3-24, 2014).

It has been developed by General Frank Kitson (1971/2010) based on British experiences in suppressing peoples striving for independence under British colonial ruling and perfected during the Troubles in Northern Ireland. Kitson's doctrine sees opposition going through different stages of insurgent activity: the 'preparatory period' and 'non-violence phase', viewed as precursors to an 'insurgency' that challenges the legitimacy and operations of governments and resource-extraction companies. This leads authorities to respond with various pre-emptive and sustained efforts, mixing concession and coercion to defuse social movements and their consequent disruptions of business.

Talking about the drive of the American Indian Movement (AIM) to realise their legal rights to sovereignty and self-determination while their reserved land base contains substantial quantities of critical mineral resources (such as over half of all known 'domestic' US uranium reserves) in the first half of the 1970s, Churchill (1992, p. 83) details how the US government set out to liquidate AIM's political effectiveness in order to maintain and reinforce the federal system of administering Indian Country: 'Loss of internal colonial control over these items would confront U.S. élites with significant strategic and economic problems.' The FBI has since consistently denied that what they were doing amounted to low-intensity warfare, while the operations had all the hallmarks of it.

This did not stop in the 1970s. A recent article series by Brown and colleagues (2017) in *The Intercept* analysing the leaked TigerSwan documents reveals the centrality of counter-insurgency for undermining the Standing Rock anti-pipeline social movement. The documents confirm integrated collaboration between company security, the Bureau of Indian Affairs, and federal, state and local police agencies, revealing a series of tactics used by authorities against Standing Rock. These include aerial surveillance (helicopters, drones), radio eavesdropping, hacking domestic communications (cell phones, Internet, etc.), social media, PR ('social engagement plans'), undercover police and collaborating informants. One protester, Red Fawn Fallis, was sentenced to 57 months in prison in July 2018 after an FBI agent deceived her into a relationship and planted a gun on her (Keeler 2018).

In July 2018, the *National Observer* also revealed how a security consultancy founded by retired police officers in Canada was hired by Kinder Morgan, a company facing protest over their pipeline crossing indigenous land (Sharp & Sunshine Waisman, 2018). So to say there seems to be a continuum would be an understatement.

CORPORATE COUNTER-INSURGENCY

Secret Manoeuvres ended with a plea to look beyond PR and lobbying as essential tools for the modern corporation, affording the means to better anticipate and adapt to societal demands. In particular, I pointed at issue management (IM), a specific form of PR. The literature in business studies on IM emphasises the need for scanning, monitoring and tracking external forces that are a potential threat to the company. The subsequent policy development and the implementation of action, however, are enshrined in an all-encompassing secrecy. The failure to address the issue in business studies is mirrored by the reluctance to discuss covert action in intelligence studies. To recognise IM as the dark side of PR and as a policy of intelligence operations is an attempt to break this silence.

In my book, I left it at pointing out that complying with policies of responsible entrepreneurship can be a double-edged sword. For a corporation, a dialogue with critics can also serve as an intelligence operation or an effort to divide those who want to talk from the more radical groups in a campaign. Andrea Brock and Alexander Dunlap take this further, conceptualising PR and CSR as 'soft' corporate counter-insurgency, as they culminate in a strategy that 'obscures corporate-led environmental degradation, attempts to render resistance illegitimate, and strategically divides communities'.

'Hard' approaches to counter-insurgency are economically and reputationally costly, they argue. This necessitates developing approaches that pre-empt resistance and mitigate conflict to avoid costly disruptions, sabotage and police and/or military expenditures. Reliance on 'soft' approaches includes PR, CSR and greening initiatives that intertwine with 'neoliberal social development' and popular environmental concerns and regulations.

They outline the different techniques used to win hearts and minds in the specific context of a large mining project in Germany:

> This includes securing the support of political leaders, lobbying, involvement in social events, infrastructure projects, astroturf groups and ecological restoration/offsetting work, which combine with overtly repressive techniques by public and private security forces that together attempt to legitimise the mine and stigmatise, intimidate and criminalise activists.
>
> (Brock & Dunlap, 2018, p. 33)

The authors propose to conceptualise these techniques and technologies as 'corporate counterinsurgency',[8] defined as 'firms' efforts to mitigate violence and promote stability through social development and security measures' to 'win hearts and minds' of local populations.

Cases of political policing discussed in this chapter are illustrative of the techniques of domestic counter-insurgency operations to defuse protests and potential insurgencies against critical infrastructure. Brock and Dunlap note a significant overlap here with counter-insurgency logics, especially how protest and dissident groups are discursively separated from 'the population' and labelled as 'the enemy', and how this justifies the use of both coercive and non-coercive methods:

> Recognising techniques and strategies deployed against social movements – militant or otherwise – as counterinsurgency resituates the current state of affairs of 'democratic' politics, while also leading to a practical and analytical reassessment of corporate and governmental activities that aim to socially 'engineer' political terrain to manufacture consent and normalise socially and ecologically destructive activities.
>
> (Brock & Dunlap, 2018, p. 330)

CONCLUSION

Corporate counter-insurgency could serve as a concept in a new approach of political policing that not only covers information gathering, but also relates to the development of covert strategy. The case studies in *Secret Manoeuvres* confirmed that the analysis of intelligence informs how a company deals with critics. This could be implementing a proactive policy to stay ahead of possible problems, or taking preventative action before problems develop – or both. There is a need for research into what these secret policies entail, to allow understanding of the wider context. Why do companies choose to undermine their critics? How are such operations supported by state actors, such as local authorities, the police or (public) intelligence agencies? And if so, what forms do such joint efforts take: as formalised and regularised relationships, or as discrete, ad hoc efforts? What does corporate counter-insurgency look like?

We need to continue building a collection of detailed and evidence-based case studies of corporate and police spying of activists. From there, we can map the network of police units, corporate intelligence and security personnel behind the infiltration operations with a strong critical focus on the state and corporate power. This is about mapping the political economy of these privatised intelligence networks, characterised by secrecy, privileged knowledge and power. Rather than using the more classical network approach of 'who is pulling the strings', we might follow O'Reilly (2010) who states that 'it is more profitable to analyse "the ties that bind" these actors together.'

The concept of corporate counter-insurgency should help to understand how secrecy, power and resistance are linked, while the classic concept of the engineering of consent can be developed by taking into account the various tactics to win people's hearts and minds while trying to separate them from those branded as enemy of the state.

Our research takes the lack of transparency and accountability as a starting point. Given the nature of the institutions we are appealing to uphold our rights, it is unclear what we can expect since our social and political rights do not exist in a vacuum. If the state's prevailing ideology is free market capitalism, these rights are underpinned by economic rights – which uphold, for example, the rights of corporations, and the protection of the system that facilitates that. As Morgan notes, secrecy often prevails over transparency.

That is not to say that we should not hold these state institutions and corporate bullies to account by exposing them. The joint power of research and campaigning can serve – as Phil Scraton (2013) suggests – as 'an alternative method for liberating truth, securing acknowledgement and pursuing justice'.

NOTES

1 Many thanks to Aziz Choudry and Dónal O'Driscoll for their never-ending support and contributions to this chapter.

2 See: http://campaignopposingpolicesurveillance.com/; https://policespiesoutoflives.org.uk/; www.facebook.com/groups/blacklistSG/about/; https://netpol.org/.

3 In short, she proposes a set of three models which illuminate the working and practice of state secrecy: 'Properly understood, state secrecy can be divided into three categories: esoteric, operational and efficient. Esoteric state secrecy restricts access to decision-making and information. It is a facet of power, utilised to control. Operational state secrecy protects techniques, procedures and investigations. It is not as all-encompassing as esoteric state secrecy, but can be cumulative where one demand for secrecy creates another. Finally, efficient state secrecy references the

pragmatic sense in which secret conditions allow faster decision-making and the conceptual limits of transparency in a modern complex state. These categories illuminate how state secrecy's true effects are masked because it is so entrenched' (Morgan, 2018, p. 60).

4 Stanton Tefft, discussing the dynamics of governmental secrecy in his edited volume (1980), demonstrates that intelligence units at both local and national levels operate to predict, control and manipulate their environment. The case studies in *Secret Manoeuvres* show that this also applies to the dynamics of private and corporate secrecy. The internal security required to protect organisations from safety breaches or leaks creates problems such as preventing the flow of vital information (Wilensky, 1967).

5 See: Brodeur et al., 2003; Brodeur, 1983, 2007; Cunningham, 2004; Manning, 2012; Monaghan & Walby, 2012; Monahan & Palmer, 2009.

6 By the time the First World War was over, many of the key components of Britain's contemporary security apparatus were in place: MI5 – in collaboration with the expanded Special Branch – had responsibility for domestic (and, at the time, imperial) affairs, and MI6 functioned as the overseas intelligence agency for non-British domains (Woodman, 2018).

7 See: Boykoff, 2007; Churchill, 2003; Churchill & Vander Wall, 1998, 2002; Cunningham and Noakes, 2008); Donner, 1990; Gelbspan, 1991; Glick, 1999; Leonard and Gallagher, 2015.

8 The definition follows the RAND Corporation's National Security Division (Rosenau et al., 2009, p. 1).

REFERENCES

All URLs accessed August 2018.

Blair, W. G. (1986, 26 August). 'Court Finds F.B.I. Harassed Socialist Group Unlawfully', *New York Times.* Accessed from www.nytimes.com/1986/08/26/nyregion/court-finds-fbi-harassed-socialist-group-unlawfully.html

Boffey, D. (2013, 12 October). 'Police Colluded in Secret Plan to Blacklist 3,200 Workers', *Guardian.* Accessed from www.theguardian.com/business/2013/oct/12/police-blacklist-construction-workers-watchdog

Boykoff, J. (2007). 'Limiting Dissent: The mechanisms of state repression in the USA', *Social Movement Studies*, 6(3): 281–310.

Brock, A. & Dunlap, A. (2018). 'Normalising Corporate Counterinsurgency: Engineering consent, managing resistance and greening destruction around the Hambach coal mine and beyond', *Political Geography*, 62: 33–47. Accessed from www.sciencedirect.com/science/article/pii/S0962629817300835

Brodeur, J. P. (1983). 'High Policing and Low Policing: Remarks about the policing of political activities', *Social Problems*, 30(5): 507–520.

—— (2007). 'High and Low Policing in Post-9/11 Times', *Policing*, 1: 25–37.

——, Gill, P., & Tollborg, D. (2003). *Democracy, Law, and Security: Internal security services in contemporary Europe.* Burlington, VT: Ashgate

Brown, A., Parrish, W., & Speri, A. (2017). 'Leaked Documents Reveal Counterterrorism Tactics Used at Standing Rock to "Defeat Pipeline Insurgencies"', *The Intercept* [Article series contains four parts]. Accessed from https://theintercept.com/2017/05/27/leaked-documents-reveal-security-firms-counterterrorism-tactics-at-standing-rock-to-defeat-pipeline-insurgencies/. N.B. The series meanwhile contains of 13 parts written by the same authors (2018) see https://theintercept.com/series/oil-and-water/

Casciani, D. (2018, 23 March). 'Metropolitan Police Admits Role in Blacklisting Construction Workers', *BBC News Online.* Accessed from www.bbc.com/news/uk-43507728

Church Committee (Select Committee to Study Governmental Operations with Respect to Intelligence Activities) (1976) *Intelligence Activities and the Rights of Americans.* United States Senate. Final Report, Book II. Accessed from www.intelligence.senate.gov/pdfs94th/94755_II.pdf

Churchill, W. (1992) 'Death Squads in the United States: Confessions of a government terrorist', *Yale Journal of Law and Liberation,* 3(1): Article 6. Accessed from http://digitalcommons.law.yale.edu/cgi/viewcontent.cgi?article=1026&context=yjll

—— (2003). 'Agents of Repression: Withstanding the test of time' (Introduction to the new edition of Churchill and Vander Wall (2002)), *Social Justice,* 30(2) (92): 44–50. Accessed from www.socialjusticejournal.org/product/war-dissent-and-justice-a-dialogue-with-scholars-activists-and-former-u-s-political-prisoners-vol-30-2-2003/

—— & Vander Wall, J. (1988 and 2002). *Agents of Repression: The FBI's secret wars against the Black Panther Party and the American Indian Movement.* Boston, MA: South End Press.

Cobain, I. (2018, 24 July). '"Subversive" Civil Servants Secretly Blacklisted Under Thatcher', *Guardian.* Accessed from www.theguardian.com/uk-news/2018/jul/24/subversive-civil-servants-secretly-blacklisted-under-thatcher

Cunningham, D. (2004). *There's Something Happening Here: The New Left, the Klan, and FBI counterintelligence.* Berkeley and Los Angeles, CA: University of California Press.

—— & Noakes, J. (2008). '"What if she's from the FBI?" The effects of covert forms of social control on social movements'., In M. Deflem & J. T. Ulmer (eds), *Surveillance and Governance: Crime control and beyond* (Sociology of Crime, Law and Deviance, Volume 10) (pp. 175–197). Bingley, UK: Emerald Group Publishing Limited.

Donner, F. (1990). *Protectors of Privilege: Red Squads and police repression in urban America.* Los Angeles, CA: University of California Press.

Ellefsen, R. (2012). 'Green Movements as Threats to Order and Economy? Animal advocates repressed in Austria and beyond'. In R. Ellefsen, R. Sollund & G. Larsen (eds), *Eco-global Crimes: Contemporary problems and future challenges*. Farnham, UK: Ashgate. Accessed from www.academia.edu/3260896/Green_Movements_as_Threats_to_Order_and_Economy_Animal_Activists_Repressed_in_Austria_and_Beyond

Ellefsen, R. (2016). 'Judicial Opportunities and the Death of SHAC: Legal repression along a cycle of contention', *Social Movement Studies*, 15(5): 441–456.

Evans, R. (2017, 16 January). 'Probe into Claim that Police Spy Set Fire to Debenhams Could End by July', *Guardian*. Accessed from www.theguardian.com/uk-news/undercover-with-paul-lewis-and-rob-evans/2017/jan/16/probe-into-claim-that-police-spy-set-fire-to-debenhams-expected-to-end-by-july

Ferree, M. M. (2004). 'Soft Repression: Ridicule, stigma and silencing in gender-based movements', *Research in Social Movements, Conflicts and Change*, 25: 85–101. Accessed from doi:10.1016/S0163-786X(04)25004-2

FM3-24 (2014). 'Insurgencies and countering insurgencies', US Army, May. Accessed from http://fas.org/irp/doddir/army/fm3-24.pdf

Garland, D. (2001). *The Culture of Control*. Oxford: Oxford University Press.

Gelbspan, R. (1991). *Break-ins, Death Threats and the FBI: The covert war against the Central America Movement*. Boston, MA: South End Press.

Glick, B. (1999). *War at Home: Covert action against U.S. activists and what we can do about it*. Boston, MA: South End Press.

Hewitt, M. (2015a, 20 November). 'Apology from Metropolitan Police – in full', *Police Spies Out of Lives*. Accessed from https://policespiesoutoflives.org.uk/text-of-apology-from-met-police/

—— (2015b, 20 November). 'Metropolitan Police Apologises for Undercover Officers' Relationships', video. *Guardian*. Accessed from www.theguardian.com/uk-news/video/2015/nov/20/metropolitan-police-apologises-for-undercover-officers-relationships-video

Hillsborough Independent Panel (2012 – present). The Permanent Archive for the Hillsborough Disaster, Disclosed Material and Report. Accessed from http://hillsborough.independent.gov.uk/report/main-section/part-3/

Home Affairs Committee (2013, 26 February). 'Thirteenth Report. Undercover Policing: Interim Report'. Accessed from www.publications.parliament.uk/pa/cm201213/cmselect/cmhaff/837/83702.htm

Johnson, L. K. (2008). 'The Church Committee Investigation of 1975 and the Evolution of Modern Intelligence Accountability', *Intelligence and National Security*, 23(2): 198–225. Accessed from doi:10.1080/02684520801977337

Kaufmann, P. (2018). Submission speech at the hearing of the Undercover Policing Inquiry, 21 March. Published in full at http://campaignopposingpolicesurveillance.com/2018/03/22/spycops-victims-walk-out-of-public-inquiry/

Keeler, J. (2018, 13 July). '"I Was Born Free" – Red Fawn and state-sponsored sexual assault of native women at Standing Rock', *tiyospayenow blog*. Accessed from https://tiyospayenow.blogspot.com/2018/07/i-was-born-free-red-fawn-and-state.html

Kitson, F. (2010 [1971]). *Low Intensity Operations: Subversion, insurgency, and peace keeping*. London: Bloomsbury House.

Klein, N. (2000). *No Logo*. Toronto: Random House.

Leonard, A., & Gallagher, C. (2015). *Heavy Radicals – The FBI's secret war on America's Maoists: The Revolutionary Union / Revolutionary Communist Party 1968–1980*. London: Zero Books.

—— (2018). *A Threat of the First Magnitude: FBI counterintelligence and infiltration. From the Communist Party to the Revolutionary Union – 1962–1974*. London: Repeater Books, London.

Lewis, P. and Evans, R. (2011, February 14). 'Green Groups Targeted Polluters as Corporate Agents Hid in Their Ranks', *Guardian*. Accessed from www.guardian.co.uk/environment/2011/feb/14/environmental-activists-protest-energy-companies

Lubbers, E. (2002). *Battling Big Business: Countering greenwash, infiltration and other forms of corporate bullying*. Devon, UK: Greenbooks.

—— (2012). *Secret Manoeuvres in the Dark: Corporate and police spying on activists*. London: Pluto Books.

—— (2018). SDS Tradecraft Manual, SpecialBranchFiles.uk Project, 23 March. Accessed from http://specialbranchfiles.uk/sds-tradecraft-manual/ and Metropolitan Police Service, Trade Craft – Binder 2, archived at DocumentCloud.org. Accessed from www.documentcloud.org/documents/4418656-SDS-Tradecraft-Manual

Lucas, C. (2012). Commons Debate, Daily Hansard, Westminster Hall, 13 June. Starting at Column 96WH. Accessed from www.publications.parliament.uk/pa/cm201213/cmhansrd/cm120613/halltext/120613h0001.htm

Manning, P. (2012). 'Drama, the Police and the Sacred in Policing' in T. Newburn & J. Peay (eds), *Policing: Politics, culture, and control* (pp. 173–194). Oxford: Hart.

Medsger, B. (2014). *The Burglary: The story of J. Edgar Hoover's secret FBI*. New York: Vintage.

Monaghan, J. & Walby, K. (2012) 'Making up "Terror Identities": Security intelligence, Canada's Integrated Threat Assessment Centre and social movement suppression', *Policing and Society*, 22(2): 133–151.

Monahan, T. & Palmer, N. (2009). 'The Emerging Politics of DHS Fusion Centers', *Security Dialogue*, 40(6): 617–636.

Morgan, L. (2018). '(Re)conceptualising State Secrecy', *NILQ*, 69(1): 59–84. Accessed from https://nilq.qub.ac.uk/index.php/nilq/article/view/78

MPS (Metropolitan Police Service) (2014). Response to FOIA request made by Kevin Blowe (No: 2014030001361_11 April).

—— (2015, 20 November). 'MPS Apology: Long Term Sexual Relationships', video. Accessed from http://news.met.police.uk/videos/mps-apology-long-term-sexual-relationships-21074

O'Reilly, C. (2010) 'The Transnational Security Consultancy Industry: A case of state-corporate symbiosis', *Theoretical Criminology*, 14(2): 183–210. Accessed from doi:10.1177/1362480609355702

O'Reilly, C. & Ellison, G. (2006). 'Eye Spy Private High: Re-conceptualising high policing theory', *British Journal for Criminology*, 46(4): 641–660.

Rosenau, W., Chalk, P., McPherson, R., Parker, M., & Long, A. (2009). *Corporations and Counterinsurgency.* Santa Monica CA: RAND. Accessed from www.rand.org/pubs/occasional_papers/OP259.html

Salmon, P. & Lubbers, E. (2015, 2 November) *The Fifteen Questions We Work With.* Undercover Research Group. Accessed from http://undercoverresearch.net/1260-2/

Schwarz Jr, F. (2007). 'The Church Committee and a New Era of Intelligence Oversight', *Intelligence and National Security*, 22(2): 270–297. Accessed from doi:10.1080/02684520701303881

Scraton, P. (2013). 'The Legacy of Hillsborough: Liberating truth, challenging power', *Race and Class*, 55(2): 1–27. Accessed from doi:10.1177/0306396813499488

Sharp, A. & Sunshine Waisman, D. (2018, 13 July). 'Spies', *National Observer.* Accessed from www.nationalobserver.com/2018/07/13/kinder-morgan-company-used-private-investigators-monitor-pipeline-protesters-heres-how-it

Smith, D., & Chamberlain, P. (2015) *Blacklisted: The secret war between big business and union activists.* London: New Internationalist.

Tefft, S. (ed.) (1980). *Secrecy, a Cross-Cultural Perspective.* New York and London: Human Sciences Press.

UCPI (2018, 25 July). Update note July 2018, Undercover Policing Inquiry website. Accessed from www.ucpi.org.uk/wp-content/uploads/2018/07/20180725-seventh_update_note_July_2018.pdf

Undercover Research Group (2011a). Profile of Gordon Irving, URG portal. *Powerbase.* Accessed from http://powerbase.info/index.php/Gordon_Irving

—— (2011b). Profile of Vericola. *Powerbase.* Accessed from http://powerbase.info/index.php/Vericola

—— (2012 – present). Profile of Bob Lambert. *Powerbase.* Accessed from http://powerbase.info/index.php/Bob_Lambert

—— (2014 – present) Undercover Research Portal. *Powerbase.* Accessed from http://powerbase.info/index.php/UndercoverResearch_Portal

—— (2015 – present). Undercover Research Group. Accessed from http://undercoverresearch.net/

—— (2017, 6 July). 'Was My Friend a Spycop?', *Undercover Research Group.* Accessed from http://undercoverresearch.net/2017/07/06/friend-spycop-publication-now/

United States Supreme Court (1986). Munro v. Socialist Workers Party, No. 85-656. Accessed from https://caselaw.findlaw.com/us-supreme-court/479/189.html

Weiner, T. (2012). *Enemies: A history of the FBI.* New York: Random House.

Wilensky, H. L. (1967). *Organisational Intelligence.* New York: Basic Books.

Wistrich, H. (2013, 23 January). 'Explaining the Judgment Over Secret Tribunal', *Police Spies Out of Lives* [Support group for women's legal action against undercover policing]. Accessed from http://policespiesoutoflives.org.uk/explaining-the-judgment-by-harriet-wistrich/

Woodman, C. (2016). 'How Do We Best Explain Domestic Western Intelligence Operations Aimed at Internal Dissent?' (Degree essay, unpublished).

—— (2018, 23 April). 'The Infiltrator and the Movement: Infiltration into left-wing groups is just the sharp edge of an entire armoury of political policing', *Jacobin*. Accessed from https://jacobinmag.com/2018/04/uk-infiltration-secret-police-mi5-special-branch-undercover

Notes on contributors

Nafeez Ahmed is an award-winning investigative journalist, bestselling author and international security scholar. A former *Guardian* environment blogger, he is currently editor-in-chief of INSURGE intelligence, a crowdfunded investigative journalism project. He is also 'System Shift' columnist at VICE's science and technology magazine, *Motherboard*, and a columnist covering regional geopolitics at *Middle East Eye*. In 2016, he published an investigation into the global far right, *Return of the Reich: Mapping the global resurgence of far-right power*, commissioned by the British hate crime watchdog, Tell MAMA UK. The investigation demonstrated a wide-range of neo-Nazi connections between the Donald Trump campaign, far-right movements in Europe and the UK's Conservative government. Ahmed's latest book is *Failing States, Collapsing Systems: BioPhysical triggers of political violence* (Springer, 2017).

Emily Apple is a writer and activist from the UK. She is an editor and writer at *The Canary* and writing her first book, *Dear Martin: Letters to a corporate spy*. As an activist, she has been involved in a variety of social justice campaigns, and has co-founded numerous organisations including the Network for Police Monitoring and Counselling for Social Change. She has been spied upon by police and corporate spies, and is a core participant in the Undercover Policing Inquiry – the public inquiry into police spying on protest groups in England and Wales.

David Austin is the author of *Fear of a Black Nation: Race, sex, and security in Sixties Montreal* (Between The Lines, 2013, winner of the 2014 Casa de las Americas Prize), and *Dread, Poetry and Freedom: Linton Kwesi Johnston and the unfinished revolution* (Pluto/Between The Lines, 2018); he is the editor of *You Don't Play with Revolution: The Montreal lectures of C.L.R.* James (AK Press, 2010), and *Moving Against the System: The 1968 Congress of Black Writers and the making of global consciousness* (Pluto/Between The Lines, 2018).

Bob Boughton is Associate Professor of Adult Education at the University of New England in Australia, where his research focuses on mass literacy campaigns, popular education and social movement learning. He has been an activist in the Timor solidarity movement in Australia since 1975, and was a member of the Communist Party of Australia from 1975 until its dissolution in 1991. In 2015, he received the Order of Timor-Leste for his contribution to the country's independence struggle.

Aziz Choudry is Associate Professor in the Department of Integrated Studies in Education at McGill University, Montreal, where he holds a Canada Research Chair in Social Movement Learning and Knowledge Production, and is Visiting Professor at the Centre for Education Rights and Transformation at the University of Johannesburg. He has been involved in a range of social, political and environmental justice movements and organisations since the 1980s. He is the author of *Learning Activism: The intellectual life of contemporary social movements* (University of Toronto Press, 2015), co-author of *Fight Back: Workplace justice for immigrants* (Fernwood, 2009), and co-editor of *Learning from the Ground Up: Global perspectives on social movements and knowledge production* (Palgrave Macmillan, 2010), *Organize! Building from the local for global justice,* (PM Press/Between the Lines, 2012), and *NGOization: Complicity, contradictions and prospects* (Zed Books, 2013), *Just Work? Migrant workers' struggles today* (Pluto, 2016), *Unfree Labour? Struggles of migrant and immigrant workers in Canada* (PM Press, 2016) and *Reflections on Knowledge, Learning, and Social Movements: History's schools* (Routledge, 2018).

Radha D'Souza is Reader in Law at the School of Law, University of Westminster, London. She is the author of *Interstate Disputes Over Krishna Waters: Law, science and imperialism* (Orient Longman India, 2006), *What's Wrong With Rights? Social movements, law and liberal imaginations* (Pluto, 2018) and numerous articles and book chapters. Her research interests include global and social justice, social movements, law and development, colonialism and imperialism, social theory, socio-legal studies in the 'Third World' and water conflicts. She teaches law and development and has previously taught in sociology, development studies, human geography, as well as public law and legal theory. Radha is a social justice activist and practiced as barrister at the

High Court of Mumbai in India. Her articles have been published in *Law, Social Justice & Global Development Journal* (*LDG*), *Social & Legal Studies, Natural Resources Journal, Journal of Critical Realism, Political Geography, Geoforum, Philosophy East and West, McGill Journal of Education, Economic and Political Weekly, Polylog: Journal of Intercultural Philosophy* and *Osgoode Hall Law Journal*, among others.

Jane Duncan is a Professor in the Department of Journalism, Film and Television at the University of Johannesburg. Before that, she held a Chair in Media and the Information Society at Rhodes University and was the Executive Director of the Freedom of Expression Institute. She has also worked in the community arts sector, including at the Afrika Cultural Centre and the Funda Centre. She has three postgraduate degrees, and has written widely on freedom of expression, the right to privacy, social movements and the right to protest, and media policy. She is author of *The Rise of the Securocrats: The case of South Africa* (Jacana, 2014), and *Stopping the Spies: Constructing and resisting the surveillance state in South Africa* (Wits University Press, 2018).

Gary Kinsman is a long-time queer liberation, anti-poverty, Palestine solidarity and anti-capitalist activist on Indigenous land. He is currently involved in the AIDS Activist History Project and is the author of *The Regulation of Desire: Homo and hetero sexualities* (Black Rose, 1996), co-author (with Patrizia Gentile) of *The Canadian War on Queers: National security as sexual regulation* (UBC Press, 2009) and co-editor of *Whose National Security? Canadian state surveillance and the creation of enemies* (Between The Lines, 2000), *Sociology for Changing the World* (Fernwood, 2006) and *We Still Demand! Redefining resistance in sex and gender struggles* (UBC Press, 2017). He currently shares his time between Toronto and Sudbury, where he is Professor Emeritus at Laurentian University. His website is http://radicalnoise.ca/

Eveline Lubbers is the author of *Secret Manoeuvres in the Dark: Corporate and police spying on activists* (Pluto, 2012) and *Battling Big Business: Countering greenwash, front groups and other forms of corporate deception* (Green Books, 2012).
Web: http://undercoverResearch.net Twitter: @UndercoverNet
Web: http://SecretManoeuvres.org Twitter: @evelinelubbers

Sunaina Maira is Professor of Asian American Studies at University of California, Davis (https://asa.ucdavis.edu/people/faculty/sunaina-maira). She is the author of *Missing: Youth, citizenship, and empire After 9/11* (Duke University Press, 2009) and *Jil [Generation] Oslo: Palestinian hip hop, youth culture, and the youth movement* (Tadween, 2013). She co-edited *Youthscapes: The popular, the national, the global* (University of Pennsylvania Press, 2004) and *The Imperial University: Academic repression and scholarly dissent* (University of Minnesota Press, 2014). Her recent books include *Boycott! The academy and justice for Palestine* (University of California Press, 2017) and *The 9/11 Generation: Youth, rights, and solidarity in the War on Terror* (NYU Press, 2016), a study of South Asian, Arab, and Afghan American youth and political movements focused on civil and human rights that addresses issues of sovereignty and surveillance in the War on Terror. Maira has been involved with various community organisations and anti-war and global justice groups in the Bay Area and nationally in the US.

Valerie Morse is a Wellington, Aotearoa New Zealand-based anarchist and activist. She works in grass-roots groups addressing war and militarism, the growth of state and corporate data sharing and surveillance, and climate change. Valerie holds Master's degrees in International Relations, and Library and Information Studies, both from Victoria University in Wellington. The New Zealand state tried to charge her as a terrorist in 2007, but fortunately didn't have the evidence. She is the author of two books: *Against Freedom: The war on terrorism in everyday New Zealand life* (2007), and *The Day the Raids Came: Stories of survival and resistance to the state terror raids* (2010), both available for free download from Rebel Press (NZ).

Index